SUPERPOWER COMPETITION AND SECURITY IN THE THIRD WORLD

SUPERPOWER COMPETITION AND SECURITY IN THE THIRD WORLD

Edited by

Robert S. Litwak
Samuel F. Wells, Jr.

A WILSON CENTER BOOK

BALLINGER PUBLISHING COMPANY
Cambridge, Massachusetts
A Subsidiary of Harper & Row, Publishers, Inc.

International Standard Book Number: 0-88730-253-X (CL)
0-88730-286-6 (PB)

Library of Congress Catalog Card Number: 87-24187

Printed in the United States of America

Library of Congress Cataloging-in-Publication Data

Superpower competition and security in the Third World / edited by
  Robert S. Litwak, Samuel F. Wells, Jr.
      p. cm.
    Rev. papers originally presented at a series of seminars on "The Third
  World and international security: competing East-West perspectives and
  policies" sponsored by the Wilson Center's International Security Studies
  Program in 1985.
    "A Wilson Center book."
    Includes index.
    ISBN 0-88730-253-X
    ISBN 0-88730-286-6 (pbk.)
    1. United States—Foreign relations—Soviet Union.
    2. Soviet Union—Foreign relations—United States.
    3. Developing countries—National security.   I. Litwak, Robert.
  II. Wells, Samuel F.   III. Woodrow Wilson International Center
  for Scholars. International Security Studies Program.
  JX1428.S65S86 1987
  327.73047—dc19   87-24187
                                                                         CIP

CONTENTS

PREFACE

Recent years have witnessed a proliferation of volumes in the field of "regional security" studies. These contributions to the literature can loosely be divided into two categories, reflecting the relative orientations of their authors. Some are written by regional specialists and highlight the primacy of indigenous factors in determining local outcomes. Others are written by those whose interest is the foreign policies of the great powers and who tend to regard regional security questions as a function of the global East-West competition.

In practice, these two groups of policy analysts have tended to talk past each other. The contending reactions to the 1979 Iranian Revolution provide an illustrative example of the problem. No one would question that the immediate causes of the revolution were rooted in that society's domestic structure; yet, at the same time, the overthrow of the shah, and the subsequent reorientation of Iranian foreign policy away from the United States, had enormous East-West implications. The issue is not one of a simple either-or choice. Rather, the challenge is that of bringing together these contending regionalist and geopolitical perspectives on regional security within a unified framework of analysis. This volume represents an effort to meet that challenge.

During 1985, the Wilson Center's International Security Studies Program sponsored a series of seminars on "The Third World and International Security: Competing East-West Perspectives and Policies." The meetings were divided into two parts and reflect the structure of this book. In Part I, noted specialists on the foreign policies of the Western powers and the Soviet bloc have attempted to delineate how these states define their interests and conduct their policies in the Third World. Part II of this volume features specific case studies that are of interest because they focus on regions in which outside powers have declared interest and might be drawn into local conflicts. Participants in these Wilson Center meetings included a broad mix of Third World regional experts, as well as specialists on Soviet, American, and European policies. The prepared papers have been revised in light of the expert commentaries and updated to take account of subsequent developments.

This project was financed by the Robert Wood Johnson, Jr. Charitable Trust, which has provided generous support to the International Security Studies Program's Core Seminar series over the years. We are grateful to the directors of the trust, and especially to Seymour Klein, for their assistance, counsel, and continuing interest in the activities of the Wilson Center.

Within our program staff, we wish to express our gratitude to Helen Loerke and Monica Marsolais for their expert editorial work and preparation of this manuscript for publication, and to Torii Ann Bottomley and Andrea Hamilton, who served as manuscript coordinators and supervised the book throughout the editing and production processes. At Ballinger, special thanks are due to Barbara Roth for her careful coordination of the editorial process.

The editors believe that this volume makes a valuable contribution to the literature on regional security issues. Needless to say, we are responsible for any of the book's shortcomings.

Robert S. Litwak
Samuel F. Wells, Jr.

INTRODUCTION

Robert S. Litwak
Samuel F. Wells, Jr.

During the postwar era, the Third World has been a principal arena of East-West rivalry. From Southeast Asia to the Middle East to Southern Africa to Central America, the superpowers have found themselves on opposing sides of regional conflicts, locked in a global competition for influence. Through a subtle and complex feedback process, this struggle between East and West on the periphery (so-called gray areas) has had an important effect on the central U.S.-Soviet strategic relationship. Regional conflicts in the Horn of Africa and Afghanistan, for example, were largely responsible for derailing the detente process in the late 1970s—thus prompting Zbigniew Brzezinski to lament that "SALT lies buried in the sands of the Ogaden." East-West competition in the Third World is more, however, than just a complicating factor in the Soviet-American relationship. There is also the very real danger that the superpowers might be drawn into these conflicts in support of local clients through inadvertent escalation or policy miscalculation. This fear led many informed observers to invoke the 1914 analogy following the Soviet invasion of Afghanistan and the American response in the form of the Carter Doctrine. These superpower moves in and around the Persian Gulf served to underscore that the Third World is not only a major arena for superpower competition, but may also constitute an important stake in that global rivalry.

As a prelude to the discussion which follows in succeeding chapters, it would be useful to explore in further detail the process by which the Third World became transformed into a central arena of East-West competition. In exploring this historical evolution, three factors stand out in importance. The first is the stabilization for interbloc relations in Europe. During the period from the enunciation of the Truman Doctrine through the 1962 Berlin crisis, the geographic focal point of the cold war was Europe—and, in particular, Germany. The ceasefire lines of May 1945 demarcated the de facto divide between East and West. The creation of contending alliances—NATO and the Warsaw Pact—gave this tacit political arrangement a military reality. Under these circumstances, any East-West dispute raised the spectre of generating a European crisis. Thus, the Korean War was initially perceived as a Soviet feint to draw American attention and resources away from Europe; likewise, many Western policymakers believed that Khrushchev would respond to the U.S. naval blockade of Cuba in October 1962 by again limiting outside access to West Berlin.

Historians of the cold war have noted the irony that by militarizing the cold war in Europe—a process symbolized by opposing alliance structures—the architects of postwar policy created a key prerequisite for a political settlement. Since the 1962 Berlin crisis there have been no major East-West crises in Europe. Political problems have tended to be of an intra-alliance nature (as in Czechoslovakia in August 1968). The set of tacit understandings governing European security have now been codified through such instruments as the 1972 Quadripartite Treaty on Berlin and the 1975 Helsinki Accords. In so doing, Europe, despite the phenomenal concentration of military resources on both sides, has been politically insulated from crisis. With this stability at the center (Europe) came new pressures on the periphery (the Third World). As the gray area not covered by alliance commitments and nuclear weapons, the Third World became the zone where East-West competition could be waged with minimal apparent danger of uncontrolled escalation.

Within the Atlantic Alliance, the contending perspectives and (to a certain extent) interests of the United States and its West European allies have led to repeated differences over Third World issues. During the early 1970s, for example, Nixon and Kissinger pursued a "linkage" strategy that sought to relate perceived Soviet adventurism on the periphery to the development of relations at the center. The Europeans bristled at an approach which appeared to hold the tangible benefits of European detente hostage to Third World instability. Similar misgivings were evidenced when the Carter administration sought to impose stiff economic sanctions against the Soviet Union in the wake of the December 1979 invasion of Afghanistan.

The second factor contributing to the transformation of the Third World into an arena of East-West competition has been the development of Soviet military capabilities—particularly power projection forces. In contrast to the United States, which emerged from World War II as an established global power, the Soviet Union, although considered a "superpower," lacked the naval and airlift capabilities to provide it a truly global reach until the late 1960s. During the 1960–61 Congo crisis, for example, the Soviet Union was unable to offer effective materiel support to its regional client. The period following the Cuban missile crisis witnessed a sustained buildup of Soviet conventional, as well as strategic nuclear, forces. With the expansion of Soviet projection capabilities, Moscow was able to mount impressive military airlift operations to Egypt and Syria in 1973, Angola in 1975–76, and Ethiopia in 1977–78.

While the development of power projection capabilities has facilitated superpower interventions, the third factor affecting East-West competition in the Third World is the turbulent nature of the target environment itself. Endemic political instability—a product of the modernization process—promotes regional conflicts, which, in turn, provide ample opportunities for Soviet and American activism. Despite the tremendous diversity in the Third World, the countries of Asia, Africa, and Latin America—as a class of states—share broadly similar political characteristics. The problem of weak institutionalization is pervasive; many regimes in these regions face crises of domestic legitimacy. One observer has labeled the present period the age of "post-decolonization." In many parts of the Third World, the existing state structures are a legacy of colonialism. Often, these state boundaries do not conform with the geographical bounds of various national groupings. Thus, the postwar period has witnessed numerous clashes arising from contending notions of "nation" and "state" in the Third World. In some cases, the conflict has been within a given state structure, as in the Congo (1960–61) and Biafra/Nigeria (1967–68). At other times, the dispute has spilled across international frontiers, as in Ethiopia/Somalia (1977–78). As witnessed during the postwar period, these types of regional conflict create the preconditions for outside power intervention and involvement.

Given the political volatility of the Third World, it is not surprising that the superpowers have found it difficult to forge durable influence relationships with the states in these regions. Both have suffered political turnabouts in the wake of regime changes (e.g., U.S.-Iranian relations after the 1979 revolution) or foreign policy realignments by existing regimes (e.g., Sadat's policy toward the Soviet Union after 1972). Although Washington and Moscow proclaim their sensitivities to the nuances of regional politics, both have tended to view Third World developments as a function of East-West competition.

As discussed by Shahram Chubin in Chapter One, the dichotomy between contending geopolitical and regionalist approaches has been the hallmark of the U.S. foreign policy debate on the Third World during the post-Vietnam period. Thus, while advocates of the regionalist school point to indigenous factors (i.e., local socio-economic circumstances) as the underlying cause of the Central American crisis, adherents of the geopolitical approach emphasize the role of Cuba and the USSR. American policy seems to oscillate between these poles. President Jimmy Carter was strongly criticized for pursuing a world order agenda (e.g., human rights) and downgrading the importance of Soviet-American rivalry in international politics. By contrast, President Ronald Reagan, who assumed office in the aftermath of unprecedented Soviet activism in the Third World (capped off by the 1979 invasion of Afghanistan), has made the global containment of the Soviet Union the centerpiece of his foreign policy. A natural offshoot of this strategy has been the Reagan Doctrine—an undisguised plan to roll back Soviet power in the Third World through the support of insurgency movements in Nicaragua, Angola, Kampuchea, and Afghanistan, among others.

Neil MacFarlane observes in Chapter Two that the presence of an American administration both militantly anti-Soviet and committed to real increases in defense spending has coincided with a reevaluation in Moscow of Soviet policies toward the Third World. General Secretary Mikhail Gorbachev came to power in March 1985 at the end of a thirty-year cycle of activism in the Third World that began under Khrushchev. This historical record, especially the Brezhnev legacy, is at the heart of continuing discussions within the Soviet foreign policy elite. From the Soviet perspective, the balance sheet after thirty years of activism is clearly positive. Yet the gains accrued by the USSR are not as unambiguous as Western observers declared them to be—or as Soviet policymakers perhaps hoped. Moreover, Soviet gains have often proved transient and carried considerable politico-economic costs, thus raising the question of just how much success the USSR can actually afford. Soviet commentaries also reflect a recognition that their policies along the Afro-Asian periphery (e.g., Angola, Ethiopia, etc.) were a major factor underlying the demise of detente. To place the current Soviet "debate" about the Third World in its proper context, one must clearly differentiate between declaratory policy and actual behavior. Official pronouncements by the Soviet leadership and theoretical writings from the relevant foreign policy institutes continue to express reservations about heightened Soviet involvement in the Third World. Although these themes are present in current Soviet discussions, they have not as yet been translated into a less activist pattern of foreign policy behavior.

Despite the unsatisfactory experience with detente in the 1970s, the Soviet and American leaderships continue to acknowledge their shared interest in resolving regional conflicts to avoid the danger of superpower entanglement and inadvertent escalation. In September 1984, Secretary of State George P. Shultz and former Soviet Foreign Minister Andrei Gromyko agreed to a series of informal discussions on regional problems with the potential for widening into major conflicts. Since that time, bilateral meetings at the Assistant Secretary/Deputy Foreign Minister level have focused on the Middle East, Afghanistan, Southern Africa, and the Far East. In addition to these recent publicized meetings, there have been persistent unconfirmed reports of information exchanges between the two sides vis-à-vis the Iran-Iraq war. More prominently, regional questions were a major agenda item at the Reagan-Gorbachev meeting in Geneva in November 1985. These issues were also addressed in one of the working groups of senior officials of the Reykjavik meeting between Reagan and Gorbachev in October 1986.

Such periodic consultations, while unlikely on their own to yield solutions to regional issues, provide a channel for communication and thereby reduce the risk of unstructured superpower competition in the Third World. As is evident, contending Soviet and American conceptions of regional stability militate against a formalized "code of conduct" governing superpower rivalry in the developing world. The prognosis is the continued pursuit of unilateral advantage by both sides in Third World regions to the extent that their resources and local circumstances permit. Within this context, the rules of engagement are likely to remain tacit at best.

This collection of essays by leading specialists from academia and government is divided into two parts. The first section explores how the foreign policies of the Western powers and the Soviet bloc have evolved during the postwar period. The second section focuses on specific regional cases in which these outside powers have declared interest and might be drawn into local conflicts. In pursuing this approach, the purpose is to integrate the perspectives and concerns of the regionalist and geopolitical approaches in order to provide a basis for more informed debate and policy choices.

1 UNITED STATES

Shahram Chubin

THE CONTENT AND BACKGROUND OF U.S. FOREIGN POLICY

U.S. policy toward the Third World has been characterized by an ambivalence and inconsistency that cannot be attributed solely to a lack of clarity in American goals or even to the changing nature of its interests. The area encompassed by the term Third World is immensely varied, and policy toward it is bound to reflect this. Furthermore, the importance of particular regions within the Third World is bound to fluctuate over time, depending only partially on conditions within the regions themselves. Changing priorities within the United States always preclude any great stability in policy toward an area as variegated as this—particularly since there is little national consensus on its importance. In addition, the Third World is in flux, precluding the possibility and perhaps the desirability of a stable policy by outside powers.

There are, to be sure, continuities and recurrent themes in U.S. policy toward the Third World. For forty years the United States has been challenged by the need to define its interests in the Third World in a manner consistent with its own values and its concept of a desirable international order. This has entailed a tension at times between an emphasis on the short term and tactical versus the longer run and architectural. It has called for a reconciliation of the necessary with the desirable, of U.S. exceptionalism with mundane reality. The need to integrate short-term needs with a larger vision of world order is not unique to U.S. policy in the Third World, but it is in its most stark form in that context because it is the most permissive environment—where the margin for choice as to emphasis in policy is greatest—and because it serves, often subliminally, as a reminder to the United States of its clear and pristine hopes in the dawn of its own great Revolution.

Many historical themes thus recur in the U.S. attitude toward the Third World: the alternation between ideals and self-interest, the former arguing for sympathy and solidarity between the first new nation and the others, the latter for a more hardheaded attitude between a crusading universalism and somber withdrawal and selectivity. In the Third World, the burdens of world power are particularly onerous: how to compete with the USSR without becoming tainted; how to use power selectively to contain the USSR but not to encourage repression or inhibit change in societies; how to deal fairly and honestly with the world's weak and poor from a position of power and status.

The need to reconcile short-term needs with a larger vision of a desirable international system has been derailed by the pervasive confusion about U.S. interests in the Third World. The U.S. encounter with the Third World substantially began in the cold war period. Global competition made the region important; it appeared to become both the arena for rivalry and a stake in the competition. As an arena, it was the safest area for East-West rivalry—a truly "gray area" left uncovered by nuclear weapons, pacts, or commitments—and in some senses a safety-valve for competition that had been repressed elsewhere by nuclear weapons. As a stake, the importance of the Third World is somewhat more controversial. There is little debate that in a global competition between two blocs representing two different systems, the Third World becomes important. But this type of bipolar world does not correspond to reality anymore, and the "hearts and minds" of third areas are seldom a high priority in anyone's foreign policy today.

U.S. interests in its international milieu are often articulated but rarely specifically defined. John Foster Dulles observed that the United States could not "survive with its institutions intact in a predominately hostile world." Jeane Kirkpatrick reminded the Republican Party Convention in the summer of 1984 that "the U.S. cannot remain an open, democratic society if we are left alone— a garrison state in a hostile world." Quite apart from specific dependencies, the quality of life would be impaired: "We need friends and allies with whom to share the pleasures and protection of our civilization." Of course the relationship between U.S. national security and any specific faraway nation may be tenuous at best, but this perspective has the virtue of not confusing U.S. world interests with the sum of its individual material interests. Diplomacy is not accounting, and in this respect the Third World "matters" more than quantitative trade indices or the percentage of new materials imported in a given quarter.

The indeterminacy and confusion underlying U.S. policies in the Third World reflect a similar uncertainty about U.S. interests as well as an inability or unwillingness to integrate the short- and longer-run interests into a stable framework for policy. The problem is not simply one of policy failure but rather reflects conceptual and analytical differences that pervade the field. There are two principal competing paradigms that highlight different and valuable dimensions of international security providing partial insights into possible policies. The first looks at U.S. interests in the Third World as a subset of U.S.-Soviet policy. It assumes the centrality of the East-West struggle and views the Third World as a problem or an opportunity rather than as a different class of actor. In this conception immediate security issues dominate the agenda with specific emphasis on allies, access, basing rights, raw materials, security, and so forth.

The second view, often an alternative but ideally a complement, sees the Third World not through the prism of East-West relations but historically. It sees the "revolt against the West" and the establishment of *world* politics, as opposed to a European order, as a truly salient feature of today's international relations. It emphasizes the broader structure of world order, global issues, interdependence, international regimes for food, population control, like sharing of the global "commons," and nuclear nonproliferation equality. Broadly speaking, the two approaches correspond to a "globalist" and "regionalist" dichotomy that has been discussed elsewhere.[1]

The prescriptions that flow from these two images of world politics are very different. The first emphasizes strategic interdependence, access and mobility, the importance of allies, and the indivisibility of both the threat and credibility. The relationship between the center and the periphery is fluid: "If you don't pay attention to the periphery . . . the periphery changes. And the first thing you know the periphery is the center. . . . What happens in one place cannot but affect what happens in another."[2]

The second school is more sensitive to the diversity of regional circumstance and finds in diversity and local nationalisms strong barriers against communism and natural allies for the West. Its definition of security is broader, encompassing more than military policy and alliances and emphasizing economic and technical assistance. More certain of indigenous resilience, this perspective is less fearful of Soviet "advances," which it sees as inherently self-limiting. It values regional organizations and a more decentralized international system. Finally, this approach not only argues for accommodating to change but sometimes urges the need for it. John Kennedy, in saying that the United States should be "marching at the head of this world wide revolution," only articulated a strain that persists in U.S. political culture—most recently in the incarnation of Jimmy Carter, who wanted "to be on the right side of change."

A major problem with the two images has been their integration. While drawing the line against aggression, often in universalistic terms ("a threat to freedom anywhere is a threat to freedom everywhere"), the geopolitical school tends to emphasize the perception of power and image of credibility in an undifferentiated way, blurring the interests being defended. "It was too easy," John Kennedy said in June 1961, "to dismiss as Communist-inspired every anti-government or anti-American riot, every overthrow of a corrupt regime, or every mass protest against misery and despair."[3] At the same time, there clearly were and are cases where Soviet activities exacerbate local problems or where events, though local in origin, have profound East-West consequences. Nevertheless, systematic Soviet opportunism comes into play when there is sporadic instability in the Third World, making it harder to argue the case for causation rather than reaction. George Liska observed in 1970, "As it became harder to identify a centrally directed threat, critics of U.S. policy began to argue that it was being invented."[4]

The difficulty of disentangling regional cause from geopolitical effect is not simply a result of alternative images of international security or analytical deficiencies. It is also due to different conceptions of U.S. interests and divergences on quite basic values.

Sometimes it is due to a reluctance to see the United States assume large military commitments—whether due to the risks of entanglement, the domestic opportunity costs of the expenditure, or the "irrelevance" of the Third World. Sometimes it is due to a rather narrow equation of interests with "strategic interests"—further narrowed to real estate or specific resources.

The definition of interests in the Third World has proved difficult. In the early postwar period, a case for forward deployment of forces could be made on the need for bases in some countries on the Soviet periphery, on the necessity for U.S. "leadership," and on the universal struggle for freedom. While the United States is now vulnerable to missiles, less confident of its global mission, more sensitive to the necessary choices between idealism and realpolitik, and more conscious of the costs of a global military competition, it is also more economically interdependent now than in the past. As risks and costs have increased, the moral issue has blurred, and restoration of a bipartisan consensus to replace or refine containment proves elusive.

Containment originally envisioned forward defense against Soviet aggression or Soviet-assisted subversion. Massive retaliation was substituted for it after Korea but lacked credibility in deterring small wars and salami tactics, while the pacts sponsored at the time proved regionally divisive. Attempts to meet the threat on the ground by expanded conventional forces (2½ wars) proved expensive and risked entanglement. The Kennedy administration emphasized counterinsurgency against subversion and political reform as a preventive measure. In June 1969 Nixon and Kissinger devised a doctrine that would enable a reduction of U.S. commitments while encouraging regional self-defense efforts through arms transfers, while at the same time maintaining the American nuclear shield. Carter sought to demilitarize relations with the Third World but ended with a renewed emphasis on U.S. conventional forces deployable to the periphery, and a reliance on regional structures as supplementary measures. As John Lewis Gaddis has observed, recurrent issues in U.S. policy toward the Third World have been whether to seek a perimeter or stronghold defense and whether to deter aggression with symmetrical or asymmetrical responses. In relation to the first set of issues, Gaddis has shown the tendency for specific, concrete interests in a global contest to become generalized by the phenomena of credibility and perceptions. Gaddis observes that while symmetrical responses protect against incremental threats and allow for more levels of response to indirect challenges, they also entail surrendering the initiative to the adversary, who chooses the nature and location of the competition, and furthermore require long-term commitment of resources that are unlikely to be forthcoming. Asymmetry avoids these problems by recognizing the limits of resources, stressing the necessity for choice and a variety of means, and retaining the initiative. However, it provides little psychological reassurance, and in crises it tends to react with crash programs.

Having mentioned the indeterminacy of U.S. interests in the Third World, the lack of consensus characterizing U.S. policy, and the costs and dangers of involvement, and on the other hand, having noted continuities and dualism in U.S. policies and the perceived costs of abstention in terms of general interests as well as for deterrence, we conclude that there has been a reluctance and inability to defend U.S. interests concretely. To be sure there are certain recurrent motifs: Israel, access to oil, denial of Soviet predominance, and so forth. But neither the depth—"vital"—nor the scope or extensiveness of these interests has been rigorously defined. This is partly due to the interrelationship among interests, to the need for flexibility, and to the contingent nature of interests. Perhaps at most there can be reference to priority areas that are more concrete and somewhat less controversial. But one suspects that an unwillingness to discuss interests in balance-of-power terms is the principal reason why leaders have leaned on specific tangible issues like oil or general milieu interests like freedom.

A similar cloudiness has been present in defining threats. This is due to the interaction of indigenous and external factors that blur the distinction between cause and consequence and render the attainment of a consensus on appropriate responses—or instruments—more arduous and precarious. "The U.S. can win wars," observed Henry Cabot Lodge in 1959, "but the question is can we win revolutions."[5] It is also attributable to the difficulty of defining threats independent from interests; not all interests are principally threatened by the USSR, and those matters that are do not thereby necessarily constitute U.S. interests.

Except for broad rhetorical genuflections in favor of freedom, peace, and justice, little has been vouchsafed of U.S. goals and objectives in the Third World. This has made the reconciliation of short-term necessities and longer-term aims impossible. The tendency to focus on the immediate or on the vague and hortatory makes the building of a stable consensus difficult. It tends to distort the discussion by overemphasis on the USSR and on U.S. reactions, and it continues to provide no framework for reconciling ends and means. If the United States is to be engaged in a protracted competition with the USSR, which a democracy is by nature ill equipped to manage,[6] greater attention to the education of the citizenry will be necessary. In short, the criteria for U.S. involvement in the Third World need to be rooted in a set of objectives that do not depend on daily events and that correspond to U.S. interests as a superpower, not merely as an importer of raw materials or a purveyor of an ideology.

THE REGIONAL ENVIRONMENT

Despite criticisms that the United States has "backed the wrong regional horses" and admonitions that it should be more "sensitive to regional concerns,"[7] there has been a strong inclination to be responsive to the needs of these countries. The Kennedy administration epitomized this with its interest in preempting revolutionary change through nation-building and in its emphasis on the necessity for reform. The Alliance for Progress and the Peace Corps reflected this interest. Robert McNamara, while eschewing the role of gendarme for the United States, observed that "the irreducible fact remains that our security is directly related to the security of the newly developing world." He went on to argue that while the United States wanted to help these countries achieve security, "we do not always grasp the meaning of security in this context." McNamara noted that there was a direct link between economic conditions and security and also between "the incidence of violence and the economic status of the countries." He predicted that violence would increase and that the United States must act on the assumption that "security is development and without development there can be no security." He concluded that "given the certain connection between economic stagnation and the incidence of violence, the years that lie ahead for the nations in the southern half of the globe look ominous. This would be true even if no threat of communist subversion existed, as it clearly does."[8]

The Kennedy administration sought to practice geopolitics through "good regionalism" and aligned itself with local nationalism. In the Middle East it treated Abdul Nasir's incursion into Yemen with kid gloves in the hope that its tolerance would suggest to progressive forces sympathy and understanding for change rather than a reflexive support for the status quo. The Carter administration did likewise.

Nor has perspective been a problem. Even the most recalcitrant cold warriors have been aware of the poor fit between superpowers' needs and those of the developing countries. The problem, John Foster Dulles observed, has been that "while we think first of the danger that stems from international communism, many of *them* think first of encroachment from the West, for that is the rule they have actually known at first hand."[9]

The difficulty of formulating a policy or set of policies toward the Third World has not stemmed from a one-dimensional, cold war emphasis or from a lack of sympathy or insensitivity to the perspective of these states. Rather it originates in the very different conditions of these countries and their consequent needs and priorities, which the United States, or indeed any other power, is only marginally able to affect or influence. It is to this regional environment, which conditions U.S. policy, that we now turn.

The states of the Third World (a term betraying its East-West origins) have certain characteristics in common that sharply differentiate them from the advanced countries and that affect their societies' perceptions and scope for action. Generally these states are new, not sanctioned historically, and fragile. They are unstable politically and unlegitimized by popular vote. In most, insecurity is the prevalent domestic condition. Economic development has tended to be unbalanced both regionally and sectorially. Moreover, economic development has not tended to increase the prospects for political stability, nor has it led to political development. In most cases violence in these countries has been associated with intrastate conflict in defining borders and the scope of government authority. Locally, there are few regional balances of power tempered through war that may encourage peaceful relations; rather the environment is permissive for the use of force among these states. Finally, these states generally view the West with respect and resentment; the colonial past and the intrusiveness of Western culture do not increase these states' inclinations to seek formal alignment with the West. At the same time, Western technology and ideas threaten their societies and encourage them to embrace tradition defensively. The large and growing cultural gap between this category of states and the West will continue to challenge both.

How do these observations affect the conditions for U.S. policy? First, they make alliance or even partnership difficult and where it is possible, transient. Second, external security concerns, where they exist, relate to regional concerns of direct moment to them. Third, the East-West competition is marginal to the concerns of most of these states, although they may not be unwilling to manipulate it to achieve their own aims, to diversify their options, and to increase their regional importance.

In some cases the regional environment is very complex indeed. The Middle East subsystem, for example, has long been penetrated by European global politics. So pervasive is this penetration that one cannot study the politics of the region without reference to the intrusive powers and their interests and influence. Leon Carl Brown has argued that the Middle East "has been so continuously interlocked politically with the Western power system as to be virtually an appendage of it." The intricate blending of regional and great power rivalries, the premium on agility and on hedging bets, and the tendency toward homeostasis in the system give politics in the Middle East an essential stability. At the same time, the tendency to see events dichotomously, whether globally and regionally or in reactionary and progressive terms, oversimplifies a reality that is more rewardingly seen as an unbroken continuum.[10]

The complex and variegated politics of such regions impose a heavy price on states that seek to organize or even influence them. The regional environment is kaleidoscopic, characterized by multiple issues and alignments. The "outside power" is provided with few clear choices. There is no "dominant conflict" around which a security consensus can be mobilized that is also acceptable to the United States.[11] Regions are seldom homogeneous. Fragmentation and differentiation both in terms of economic conditions and security interest characterize most regions. The East-West competition is imposed on a pattern of complex interactions that have deeper roots in most regions. There are no unambiguous guidelines in terms of policy. Orchestrating regional approaches requires a simplification of issues around one core theme and will seldom prove effective. Regional norms against alignment can be used by excluded states to spoil such schemes. A differentiated approach to a region will require more subtlety in reconciling different emphases and treading carefully over the interconnections of issues and links between subregions.

If the nature of Third World states and their regional environments condition and even determine the degree of success a power like the United States can have in achieving its interests, it is also the case that U.S. policy is limited by its own conceptual, administrative, and political inadequacies.

These liabilities range from a legalistic-moralistic tradition in foreign policy, an emphasis on means rather than ends, to overconcentration on the immediate and topical, with a tendency to slight history. A national temperament that values pragmatism and encourages optimism often results in framing issues in overly simplistic ways: an exaggeration of the Soviet component of a threat, for example, or a similar hyperbole on the "success" of foreign aid. This type of exaggeration may be necessary to generate support—whether for the defense budget or a policy— but it tends to set up its own antithesis and disappointment follows, a reaction sets in, and the national mood swings in the other direction.

Likewise, an earlier crusading zeal about the relevance of the American experience to the Third World appears to have been replaced by what is either greater realism or possibly simple disillusionment with the results to date. In truth there are few commendable models—politically or economically—in the Third World. The durability of influence in these countries is dubious, and reversibility appears more prevalent. The costs of such involvements appear to some to be dubious (whether in relation to political identification with unsavory regimes or financially), and the value is difficult to discern where success is difficult to define. This has led to a demythologization of the Third World and fewer illusions about the scope for U.S. actions. One consequence is to see resources committed to these areas as competing with domestic needs rather than as complements to national security policy and part of, say, the defense budget.

Interest groups in the United States tend to cluster around quite specific regional issues. It is difficult to generate a powerful constituency in support of broader and vaguer U.S. interests in the

Third World. These issues, argued elsewhere,[12] constitute actual or potential security interests that need to be tackled in conjunction with specific regional issues. In summary they are:

1. nuclear proliferation;

2. growing inequality affecting the quality of international life, ghettoization, debt repudiation, radicalization, and loss of control; and

3. population pressure leading to migration to advanced Western countries.

Unfortunately none of these issues has the sense of urgency or gravity that a "Soviet threat" imparts to more concrete cases. In the absence of bipartisan support, forthright leadership, and a concern for security issues *broadly construed*, U.S. involvement in the Third World will remain episodic, fitful, and oscillating between activism (overextension) and withdrawal (retrenchment), and thus be conducive neither to influence nor security.

Political constraints on U.S. policies in the Third World only underscore the fact that after all is said and done—after the best analysis, the maximum input from regional experts, the acceptance of the constraints arising from regional conditions—knowledge remains no substitute for choice. As Leonard Binder has reminded us, policy goals are a result of a political process, not of regional expertise.[13] In the final analysis, fluidity or inconsistency may be dictated by regional dynamics and the ebb and flow of events that evade control. Even the best-conceived and -formulated policy will not escape the necessity for decisions that rest on moral choices and policy commitment. There will thus always be intrinsic limits to the capacity of the United States to influence events abroad—particularly, as has been shown, where the objectives and their environment are so different from those of the United States. Recognition of these limits should encourage a greater sense of realism as to what can be achieved and a greater determination to use the margin that exists for a sustained commitment to the Third World. Here, as in the competition with the USSR, there is unlikely to be a "final stabilization."

THE FIRST REAGAN ADMINISTRATION

Whatever the specific interests of the United States in the Third World, it was turmoil in these areas, aggravated and exploited by the USSR, that finally buried detente. Henry Kissinger had sought to combine a policy of sanctions and inducements to encourage the USSR to restrain any proclivity to gain unilateral advantages in these areas vis-à-vis the West. He had argued that detente could not survive "irresponsible" behavior and that there was an inherent linkage between Soviet policy and the possibilities of growth in U.S.-Soviet relations in other areas. Kissinger subsequently argued that Congress had not given him the means to fashion his policy successfully and that the breakdown of executive authority during Watergate both weakened U.S. leadership drastically and allowed Soviet exploitation to follow.

The Carter administration came to office on a wave of self-generated optimism and confidence, determined to put East-West relations into a much broader perspective of international history. Despite growing Soviet activism in Third World areas, Carter was unwilling to draw any drastic conclusions. By June 1978, after muffled criticism at Wake Forest in March, Carter observed:

> To the Soviet Union, detente seems to mean a continuing aggressive struggle for political advantage and increased influence in a variety of ways. The Soviet Union apparently sees military power and military acceptance as the best means of expanding their influence abroad. Obviously, areas of instability in the world provide a tempting target for this effort. And all too often they seem ready to exploit any such opportunity.[14]

Carter argued that to be stable, detente "must be broadly defined and truly reciprocal. . . . A competition without restraint and without shared rules will escalate into grave tension and our relationship as a whole with the Soviet Union will suffer."

Perhaps the initial concept of detente was flawed. Certainly agreements on certain principles of conduct toward third areas in May 1972 and June 1973 gave a false sense of formality and assurance. Also the concept of linkage was ambiguous: It could as easily jeopardize U.S. interests in arms control by "linking instabilities" and making them hostage to other developments as it could encourage Soviet restraint in third areas. Furthermore, linkage was, as its critics argued, an expression of weakness, an acknowledgment that the United States lacked the means and will to "meet the threat" symmetrically, on its own terms. The Carter administration appeared less concerned with Soviet activism than with avoiding contamination by taking the "wrong" side in regional disputes. Furthermore, it was reluctant to resort to measures— such as the postponement of arms control agreements—that would "punish" the USSR but would also be hard on U.S. interests.

Ultimately the period 1972–79 divulged a number of lessons that still persist and that influence the Reagan administration's outlook on the relationship between the Third World and U.S.-Soviet relations. For brevity they may be put starkly:

1. Soviet activism in third areas was correlated in time with a confidence that there would be a shift in the balance of forces in their favor.

2. Whatever the cooperative dimensions in superpower relations, however much U.S.-Soviet interests may overlap in certain areas, it is a mistake to assume that the USSR will change its nature and forgo the emphasis on competition and advantage in the safest and most exploitable areas of the world.

3. Soviet attitudes in these areas will be animated by a zero-sum approach, an opposition to Western interests and positions for its own sake. Competition in the Third World will thus be more significant than the intrinsic importance of specific issues; it will be an indicator, a mirror, and a barometer of the competition and, most important, the yardstick by which credibility and commitment, which affect perceptions of power and leadership qualities, will be judged by ally and adversary alike.

4. The nature of the Soviet system precludes maturation into responsibility and restraint. Its comparative advantages in military power, security assistance, propaganda, and so forth dispose it toward encouraging instability and conflict rather than peace and order where it is ill equipped to compete with the West. Consequently, it is the task of Western power to hold the ring until the Soviet system changes. (Ironically this is reminiscent of Kennan c. 1947.)

5. The uncertain but potentially important connections between the core and the periphery (which reflect the superpower competition in microcosm) are bound to inculcate a degree of

caution in superpower activities there. Better a competition that carries risks and will encourage caution than a false sense of harmony that will lull the United States and encourage unilateral advances by the USSR.

Secretary of State George P. Shultz has observed that the United States should not be mesmerized by its interest in arms control and thus ignore Soviet activities elsewhere:

> Important as it is, arms control has not been and cannot be the dominant subject of our dialog with the Soviets. We must also address the threat to peace posed by the Soviet exploitation of regional instability and conflict. Indeed, these issues, arms control and political instability, are closely related. The increased stability that we try to build into the superpower relationship through arms control can be undone by irresponsible Soviet policies elsewhere.[15]

The change in emphasis from the preceding administration was clear: There is less reluctance to make Soviet activities in third areas a test of its overall intentions.

It may seem striking, therefore, that this administration has not sought to delineate very precisely what its interests in these third areas are. It would seem that, with the exceptions of oil in the Persian Gulf and the combination of historical interaction and geographic proximity in Central America, these are not overwhelming. Certainly few would demur from Robert Osgood's observation that, with the exception of Southwest Asia, developments in the Third World do not intrinsically affect U.S. security—unless U.S. policy mistakes and excesses make them critical to U.S. interests.[16] Nor would the proposition put forward by two critics of the Reagan defense policy, that nuclear weapons have reduced the strategic importance of countries in the Third World, elicit much controversy.

> The notion that events in Southeast Asia, Southern Africa or other jungle areas could tip the world balance of power is even more doubtful in a world of second-strike capabilities. Nuclear weapons make conquest much harder, and vastly enhance the self-defense capabilities of the superpowers. This should allow the superpowers to take a more relaxed attitude toward events in third areas . . . since it now requires much more cataclysmic events to shake their

defensive capabilities. Whatever had been the strategic importance of the third world in a nonnuclear world, nuclear weapons have vastly reduced it.[17]

Nevertheless, there persists a sense in which perceptions of power, resolve, and credibility make competition in the Third World indivisible from competition in the core area. Outcomes on the periphery affect perceptions in the central area for both adversaries and allies. They become both test cases and substitutes for crises over more concrete stakes in the center that are too dangerous to allow. Of course this view provides few guidelines for distinguishing between the vital and the marginal, and it potentially elevates every local disturbance into a test of superpower strength. The alternative of selective containment based on the principle of balance of power, or the defense of areas truly vital to Western security, would draw the line much more restrictively and would also have the great advantage of defining interests in such a way as to make more feasible the acquisition of capabilities to defend them.

The Reagan administration has not sought to define its interests more selectively but has preferred to expand its power and leave the definition of its wider interests vague. At the same time, it has encouraged and pressured its allies to do more "out-of-area" to narrow the gap between security commitments and the means of meeting them. The administration came to office with the firm intention of refurbishing American military power, reviving its alliance relationship, and restoring a sense of national purpose and confidence. There was little guilt about an emphasis on the centrality of military power and on the priority attached to looking at issues in East-West security terms. This meant that the Third World was seen in this context, and ties with those states were based on resisting the USSR. Allies who were prepared to follow the U.S. lead were to be rewarded and opponents punished; there was to be a policy of reciprocity in this area as in others.

Instead of looking at the Third World in North-South terms or as a homogeneous group, the Reagan administration saw a variety of states with diverse needs and priorities that had to be dealt with separately from issue to issue. World order goals ranging from nuclear nonproliferation to economic redistribution would have to take second place to pressing security issues, particularly the threat of Soviet or Soviet-assisted aggression. This meant greater emphasis on arms sales and less on the public discussion of the domestic politics of allies. The administration specifically emphasized the threat to the Third World posed by Soviet proxies such as Cuba, Libya, and Nicaragua and saw these states as destabilizing agents acting, in effect, to extend Soviet influence. Their policies, which were parallel to those of the USSR, were seen to be dangerous because they could not be directly attributed to Moscow; because they tended to draw the Soviets into situations they might not otherwise be in; and because these states were generally held to a less stringent standard of accountability, giving them leeway to become independently dangerous factors and thus fostering regional instability. The Reagan administration appeared to be prepared to use these states as symbolic tests of will, as places to draw the line against East bloc nibbling.

The Republicans came to office with considerable assets. There existed a national consensus in favor of a military buildup and strong support for a more assertive, less acquiescent approach to world affairs. Physical posture was to replace moral posturing: Standing tall took the place of feeling good. The country and the alliance craved more decisive leadership. The new government was convinced primarily of the errors of its predecessor; it was determined to undo them and to reverse course. After five years the continuities of policy in practice are perhaps more revealing than the divergences in rhetoric sometimes suggest.[18]

In the first two years, great emphasis was put on economic and domestic issues and on alliance relationships. The military buildup was initiated, or rather continued. The two areas of primary regional concern—the Gulf and Central America—did not allow any respite. Efforts to improve the military balance in the former—whether through arms sales to Saudi Arabia, a defense package for Pakistan, or access to facilities—were given priority. In Central America and the Caribbean, despite rhetoric about "going to the source," the administration was as divided in its councils as its critics were, and it pursued a policy of seeking a stable center in El Salvador and combining pressure on and opportunity for Nicaragua to desist from destabilizing its neighbors. In neither respect was policy a radical departure from that of the preceding government.

With the exceptions of the use of force in the Gulf of Sidra in 1981 and 1986, and in Grenada in 1983, and the interception of an Egyptian airliner carrying PLO terrorists in 1985 (all limited and discrete operations), Washington proved cautious in the exercise of military power and conscious of its practical limits—even in areas where, as in Central America and the Gulf, it had proclaimed its vital interests potentially at risk. Ideological in its foreign policy, it proved nimble in extricating itself from open-ended engagements (such as in Lebanon) that might undermine it and adept at *not* pushing an issue to the bitter end when its allies disagreed with it (sanctions against the East bloc, assistance out of area, etc.).

It showed itself prepared to contemplate positive inducements as much as military sanctions (witness the Caribbean Basin Initiative and the aid package envisioned in the Kissinger Bipartisan Commission). Further testimony to its pragmatism is the willingness to sponsor an initiative (such as the September 1982 Reagan peace plan in the Middle East) and to drop it when overtaken by events. Much the same is evident in the celebrated "strategic consensus," which ran afoul of regional sensibilities and priorities as had its predecessor, the Eisenhower Doctrine.

In many respects, the Reagan administration's focus on the East-West dimension of security threats to the Third World was a shift in emphasis, rather than policy, toward these states. In practice, regional instabilities and Soviet opportunities, domestic vulnerabilities, and regional conflicts tend to interact in ways that are difficult to disentangle. If the Carter administration focused on the regional sources of these disorders—such as South Africa's racist policies—its successor emphasized the Soviet or Cuban role in aggravating what would otherwise be a more limited problem. Here and in the Middle East, Reagan, like his predecessor, was aware that a precondition for effective containment was active involvement in the resolution of regional disputes. Rather than isolate and pressure regional states, he preferred, through "constructive engagement" and strategic cooperation, to elicit their trust to exercise influence.

The Reagan administration's foreign policy was in tune with national sentiment, which was tired of introverted preachiness and keen to seize the initiative but also reluctant to embark on crusades or increase the risks of war. Even in this most sensitive area of the Third World, Reagan was careful not to test the national consensus too hard. In the Gulf he started to deemphasize the military instrument and talk of other measures to deal with oil interruptions. In Central America, as one European commentator put it, "Only a small liberal core appeared to have any serious doubts about the inherent right of the U.S. to maintain its paramountcy in the hemisphere, if subversion and military force were necessary."[19] Nevertheless, this was not severely tested by Reagan's policies, which appeared only marginally different from those advocated by Walter Mondale.

In the first four years, the Reagan administration put primary emphasis on "restoring" the military balance as an essential backdrop to and precondition for any intensive policies on the Third World or discussions with the USSR. To some it appeared that this was intended as a substitute for strategy and policy. To many it was evident that the integration of power and purpose was still a long way off. There was no greater clarity than before about the irreducible core of interests that were in fact vital to the United States, beyond the traditional North Atlantic allies, to the democracies (including Israel, Australasia, and Japan), and possibly also to the Gulf, Central America, and South Korea. What were the conditions under which threats to other countries important to the United States would elicit a U.S. response? In 1983 AWACS aircraft had been dispatched to reassure Egypt and Sudan after Libya sent troops into northern Chad. What were the criteria for U.S. involvement in such circumstances? The source of the unrest? The source of the threat? The credibility of the United States as an ally? The intrinsic importance of Chad itself? Or the international norm at risk (intervention in a civil war)? While, as John Gaddis has added, there has been a tendency at times to define interests as a function of the Soviet threat (rather than independently), this relinquishes the initiative to the adversary and is a recipe for unlimited expense and entanglement. These and related questions persist.

PROBLEMS AND PROSPECTS

The past five years have shown that increased tensions between the superpowers may make East-West competition in third areas more, rather than less, restrained. This is not to deny that these areas will remain the litmus test of each other's intentions and provide temptations for involvement, but rather to emphasize changes in at least two dimensions—the superpowers and the regional context. Each superpower is currently preoccupied with its domestic needs, its principal allies, and its immediate periphery. Third areas do not loom as high priorities for them, particularly given both the costs of involvement and the relative paucity of results. Few areas are likely to have the same combination of saliency and immediacy, of vulnerability and urgency, as did the Persian Gulf earlier. From the U.S. view, other candidates like Central America have the advantage of proximity, which makes any serious Soviet involvement highly unlikely. Besides the Middle East and Korea, where military balances must be kept, the major political issue—South Africa—is important more for the possible domestic impact that prolonged racial violence in that region may have on the United States than for any strategic importance it might possess.

Regional environments, too, have changed. Whatever centrality the East-West competition had in the lives of these countries has long been replaced by more local concerns. Alignment appears less and less relevant to their needs unless it is a tactical means to increase foreign assistance. Many states are better armed and more likely to use these arms against their neighbors, thus making their regions more turbulent and complex environments for outside powers but providing the latter with opportunities for alignment, arms transfers, and exacerbation of local disorder.

It appears unlikely that tensions between U.S. commitments to Europe and the periphery will be as stark as they may have appeared in the aftermath of Soviet activism in the Third World and at the height of Western oil vulnerability. Pressures on allies to do more will diminish. Nevertheless, the conjunction of Soviet activism stemming from military confidence and local opportunity will continue to raise the prospect of simultaneous crises that will test Western, and especially U.S., military capabilities. Perceptions of the military and strategic balance will remain important both in influencing Soviet actions and in affecting allies' responses.

In this connection, it seems reasonable to anticipate no major changes in Soviet policy toward the Third World. Whether due to an expanded definition of security, a newfound pessimism about the Third World, or a confidence born of global military power,

Moscow appears to equate its status with involvement in third areas. Given their comparative advantage in the military security area, it appears unwise to assume a Soviet willingness to stabilize regions and to forgo the spoiler role unless and until accorded some diplomatic reward.

To transform the USSR into a status quo power, or a "responsible" power, in relation to third areas would appear to be a vain hope. Both the nature of the Soviet Union and the Soviet-American rivalry militate against such a possibility. Peaceful competition in these areas is bound to favor the West. Competition in gray areas is bound to be seen as zero-sum, whatever the objective parallelism of interest. The May 1972 agreement, which pledged the two sides not to seek unilateral advantages at the expense of the other directly or indirectly, in retrospect appears fatally flawed. It was too general—focusing on "principles" rather than areas where each might have acknowledged interests.

If competition is inevitable and agreement on general rules of restraint unlikely, should the United States be simply content with the inherent caution and limited detente that stems from the existence, in Raymond Aron's phrase, of two enemy brothers? Restraints, after all, will come from a military balance and the credible threat of retaliation, not from vague agreements on general principles. Nor need the lack of a structured relationship imply the absence of regulation, for deterrence will continue to operate and retaliation to inhibit certain acts; Soviet risk-taking in Nicaragua, for example, could see increased U.S. activism in Afghanistan or elsewhere as a response.

But this cannot be a complete answer. The lack of control of the superpowers over their clients, the inherent ambiguities of commitment, and the difficulties of ascertaining and computing the respective balance of interests in areas of overlapping concern must argue for improved dialogue to avoid miscalculations. In areas like the Persian Gulf, where there has been a war since 1980 and where the superpowers do not have a history of interaction, such an informal dialogue has been taking place. In the Arab-Israeli conflict, where the superpowers have interacted continuously over the past two decades, the dialogue is a continuing process, although punctuated by regional conflict. In that area, the Soviet Union, with its weaker regional clients (or friends, if you will), has been obliged to intervene periodically to prevent the complete humiliation of its allies and to do so in a manner that threatens—but only threatens—a confrontation. Such defensive interventions to stabilize its friends have appeared to demonstrate a high Soviet propensity for risk-taking. In fact, such appearances, which have a ritualistic element and are understood as the minimum possible Soviet response under the prevailing conditions, are belied by the strict delimitation of the Soviet commitment.

More recently there have been signs that Moscow may be prepared to play its rather weak regional hand and seek entry into an international conference for a Middle East settlement. The Soviets' interest in an institutionalized role in the Middle East is longstanding and understandable. However, the USSR's ability to "deliver" its friends and retain influence in the region after a settlement (given the likely terms of a settlement) is open to doubt.

Assuming that the Soviets indeed seek such a conference, not only to become co-chairmen when it convenes but to become co-guarantors when it is finished (i.e., assuming serious, goal-oriented aims), it remains open to doubt whether they will be able to retain much regional influence in a post-settlement Middle East. Put differently, it is difficult to envisage a settlement in the near future that would allow the USSR to retain, much less gain, regional influence. The USSR's regional policies are focused on Washington, and the gain in prestige in the attainment of the right to an equal say in world affairs may be considered as outweighing the regional objectives of its divided and lackluster Arab protégés.

More generally there is the question of the price the Soviets are likely to demand for good behavior for "inclusion" in decisions affecting international security. There is also the question of timing: It is one thing to include the USSR in a peace settlement after substantial agreement by regional parties and quite another to involve it from the outset. In the latter case, Soviet leverage must be very strong to deliver (or sacrifice) local clients, and U.S.-Soviet relations must be such as to encourage such global deal-making.

The question whether arms control agreements should be linked to East-West competition in third areas, whether agreements in the mutual interest should be made hostage to areas where competition exists, is in practice the same question posed in relation to U.S.-Soviet relations in the Third World. Should the superpowers deny their undeniable common interest in reducing the prospect of confrontation in these areas because of the existence of competition in other parts? The answer remains the same: The alternative is not unregulated competition, and the possibility of agreement turns on very specific circumstances. Theoretically, the scope for superpower agreement in third areas includes

1. regulating competition through agreement on principles or on rules of engagement (formally or tacitly),

2. agreeing on an area of acknowledged predominance (or exclusivity) for one (a "free hand"), and

3. adopting joint approaches that are active. The range of approaches could include accepting each other's separate presence, coordinating a joint presence (perhaps as guarantors of some agreement), and partitioning the area or governing it jointly. A passive joint approach would be a "hands-off" agreement—a formal decoupling measure.

One can imagine tacit decoupling measures and informal dialogue, as in the Iran-Iraq War, more easily than joint management. In areas where interests are clear and historically sanctioned, possibly with a learning process associated with international crises (as in the Arab-Israel case), a measure of restraint has been virtually institutionalized. In grayer areas there may be less historical connection, no obvious interest, and no crisis interaction to instill caution and predictability on the other side.

It may be possible over time to create new islands of detente in the Third World that testify to a common interest, while leaving other areas unregulated. If so, as in Europe, the stakes will have to be comparable for either side, and even then it will not escape buffeting from crises in areas further afield. A major difference in any case is the greater instability of domestic politics in these regions, which might at any time upset superpower agreements or change the incentives for their maintenance.

For the foreseeable future, tacit rather than formal arrangements seem more likely. Mutual suspicions will encourage the superpowers to look at each other's behavior for signs of responsible conduct as a condition for agreements rather than as products.

If the United States is to remain globally engaged, it will have to have some criteria for so remaining, separate from the specter of a Soviet threat. To restore a stable bipartisan consensus that can be sustained for a long period, interests will have to be defined in a manner consistent with American values and in step with her capabilities. This entails the integration of tactical needs with an overarching conception of a desirable world order, of narrow security imperatives with longer, world-order needs. In short, it raises anew the need to reconcile the tendency toward universalistic formulae with the need for ad hoc responses, general and diffuse milieu goals with specific concrete interests. If global policy is to have coherence, it must have common elements, even if it is applied differently from region to region.

A narrow fixation on security issues defined exclusively in terms of the Soviet threat will provide neither the basis for a national consensus nor a yardstick for the judicious and economic use of power. Such a policy will provide few guidelines for how to deal with areas *before* they become crisis points or how to deal with states that are important without being allies or adversaries. It will have little to say about how to help the weak and very poor states or the new struggling democracies (in Latin America and elsewhere) requiring encouragement. Furthermore, it will tend to encourage emphasis on the short term, on the military (and possibly covert) elements in the competition, without emphasizing the strong and visible political limits to the exercise of military power.[20] Above all, it will have nothing to say about the ultimate objectives of containing the Soviet Union and shoring up allies. What is containment buying time for? If it is for diversity, justice, and equal opportunity, some elements of these will need to be evident in policy. The most important challenge for the United States in relation to the Third World is to achieve a greater sense of perspective about its interests, threats to them, and capabilities for meeting them. While interests cannot be defined in the abstract and must depend on particular scenarios (the conjunction of other events, timing, the identity and degree of other powers involved, etc.), they can be differentiated into categories. It is evident that the number of Third World countries of direct and vital importance to U.S. security is rather limited. U.S. interests in most countries are "less than vital." Interests may be a function of location, resources, value to allies, similar values and institutions, and historical relationship:

Central America	= U.S. physical security
The Persian Gulf	= oil; largely for the allies
South Korea	= the balance of power in Northeast Asia; Japan's interest
Israel	= historical commitment; democracy

The number of places where a threat to a Third World state would constitute a threat to the balance of power or to U.S. physical security is also limited, although measures that impair U.S. access and mobility, damage U.S. credibility, or weaken its allies could potentially affect that balance. Generally, leaving aside the question of allies' interests, I would suggest the following broad indicators to gauge interest:

1. Geographic/historical relationship of intensity and importance of Central America

2. Specific importance of region or country to U.S. interests

    A. Concretely in terms of resources or location (e.g., Saudi Arabia)

    B. Similarity of values as demonstrated by acts over time (e.g., Israel)

3. Degree of Soviet involvement

    A. Longevity or novelty of involvement

    B. Direct or indirect involvement

    C. Scale of involvement: small or massive

    D. Effect of involvement: marginal or decisive

U.S. interests will be engaged according to the *nature* and *degree* of Soviet (and outside power) involvement. These can vary from *direct* involvement in a vital area, to *indirect* assistance in a less than vital area, to combinations of these. Similarly the degree of involvement and the *effect* of involvement will need to be considered.

U.S. sensitivity to Soviet or other threats will vary greatly from region to region: greater sensitivity to Soviet acts in Central America and the Persian Gulf and lesser sensitivity to Soviet acts in Africa. The tolerance for the establishment of Marxist-Leninist states will also vary: Ethiopia or South Yemen does not compare with the Caribbean. The location of the state and the degree of alignment with the Soviet Union will be considered jointly.

Attempts to establish very tight or very loose guidelines run the risk of irrelevance. Soviet involvement can vary in other ways besides scale, novelty, and decisiveness; the *form* of involvement itself may be the salient point, whether in direct military involvement, arms supplies, or subversion through third parties.

If U.S. and Western interests are not confined to a few critical strong points but indeed relatively broad and subject to many threats and pressures, while U.S. military capabilities are constrained (among other ways, politically), there is a need to acknowledge both the limits to U.S. commitments and the availability of nonmilitary instruments that can be used. In connection with the latter, many questions remain unanswered, including the role of economic assistance, the potential contribution of allies, the function of regional security institutions, and the assistance that defusing regional conflicts might make in policies designed to stabilize areas and contain the spread of radical influence.

Even in areas where military means are a primary instrument, the presence of the United States need not be formal or intrusive to be effective. In some areas the existence of direct interests need not mean direct involvement (as in the Persian Gulf); in others it may (as in Korea). In both of these areas, admittedly the military factor will rank high. In Southern Africa and Latin America, disconnected and virtually autonomous, the relationship with any strategic balance will appear tenuous. Attempts to change the situation radically will require a degree of effort that will be virtually self-limiting. Here economic assistance will assume greater importance.

In the future, the United States will have to find a means of restoring support for containment that is affordable and effective. A policy of maximal containment that seeks to defend the perimeter symmetrically (i.e., meets the threat on its own terms) will not be sustainable economically or politically; an asymmetric maximal containment policy will not be sustainable politically. A species of selective or modest containment appears more feasible. This could vary with an emphasis on strong-point defense (i.e., key areas) while choosing symmetrical *and* nonsymmetrical means as a response. Rapid deployment forces, regional allies, regional multilateral institutions, allied assistance, economic assistance, and diplomatic initiatives along with exploitation of Soviet vulnerabilities, the weakening of Soviet proxies, and a willingness to talk with Moscow should go together.

There are no simple formulae in furthering Western interests in the Third World. Threats will not be exclusively of Soviet making and will not all call for military responses. The American tendency to see issues in dichotomous terms and to deal with them now in one way, now in another, according to political cycles operating in Washington (rather than the "real" world), only serves to deny the United States the advantages of a wider range of instruments and to perpetuate a reputation for immaturity, emotionalism, and unreliability.

NOTES

1.   Shahram Chubin, "The U.S. and the Third World," in *Third World Conflict and International Security*, Adelphi Paper no. 167 (London: International Institute for Strategic Studies, 1981).
2.   Dean Rusk, in John Lewis Gaddis, *Strategies of Containment* (New York: Oxford University Press, 1982), p. 202.
3.   Ibid., p. 209.
4.   George Liska, "The Third World," in Robert Osgood and Robert Tucker, eds., *America and the World: From the Truman Doctrine to Vietnam* (Baltimore, Md.: Johns Hopkins University Press, 1970), pp. 38–82.
5.   Gaddis, *Strategies of Containment*, p. 176.
6.   De Tocqueville noted that protracted war is a threat to democratic states' values.
7.   Mohammad Ayoob, "The Role of the Third World in the East-West Relationship," Adelphi Paper no. 190 (London: International Institute for Strategic Studies, 1984).
8.   Robert McNamara, *The Essence of Security* (New York: Harper and Row, 1968), pp. 140–50.
9.   Gaddis, *Strategies of Containment*, p. 179.
10. Leon Carl Brown, *The International and Regional Politics of the Middle East* (Princeton, N.J.: Princeton University Press, 1984), pp. 4, 77, 235, 247–48, 270.

11. In the Middle East there are Arab-Israeli, Arab-Arab, and Arab-Iranian conflicts. In addition there are the Islam-Israel and Islam-USSR issues as well as the East-West issue.

12. The direct link between these issues and U.S. security interests is difficult to make in a few lines. For a fuller discussion, see my paper, "The Nature of Security Problems of Developing Countries," presented to IISS Conference on Regional Security, London, November 1983. Published as an *Occasional Paper* by the Graduate Institute for International Studies, Geneva, June 1984.

13. Leonard Binder, "Failure, Defeat, Debacle: U.S. Policy in the Middle East," *World Politics* 36 (April 1984): 437–60.

14. "Speech of the President on Soviet-American Relations at the U.S. Naval Academy," *New York Times*, 8 June 1978, p. A 22.

15. U.S. Congress, Senate Committee on Foreign Relations, "United States-Soviet Relations," 98th Cong., 1st sess., June 15 and 16, 1983, S. Hrg. 98–74, pt. 1, p. 14.

16. Robert Osgood, "The Revitalization of Containment," in *Foreign Affairs: America and the World 1981* 60, no. 3 (January 1982): 497.

17. Barry R. Posen and Stephen Von Evera, "Defense Policy and the Reagan Administration: Departure from Containment," *International Security* 8, no. 1 (Summer 1983): 33.

18. This is also Robert Osgood's view writing after two years; see "The Revitalization of Containment."

19. David Watt, "As a European Saw It," in *Foreign Affairs: America and the World 1983* 62, no. 3 (January 1984): 525.

20. The record of the past few years suggests that military force in the future will be applied selectively, multilaterally, and in discrete doses limited in duration. The constraints on the use of military force particularly in small wars has been well discussed by Eliot Cohen, "Constraints on America's Conduct of Small Wars," *International Security* 9, no. 2 (Fall 1984).

2 WESTERN EUROPE

Christopher Coker

EUROPE AND MILITARY INTERVENTION IN THE THIRD WORLD

Until the OPEC crisis of 1973, it seemed that Europe had dealt itself out of the game of military intervention in the Third World. The pretensions of Britain and France to world power status did not survive into the 1960s. The task of maintaining an extra-European role, formidable enough while they were still colonial powers, was made more demanding by the ever escalating costs of defense at home. In addition they faced two serious challenges—domestic protests in their own societies against military intervention overseas (more muted, to be sure, in France than in Britain) and the increasing reluctance of their former dependencies to accept without question the authority and style of European leadership. Critical of America's attempts to prop up its worldwide imperial system as the United States had once been critical of European colonialism, Europe was prompted to question the American interpretation of Soviet intentions and to look for other explanations of Third World instability, the roots of which many suspected ran much deeper than Soviet subversion.

This divergence became more marked after 1973, when the United States became even more preoccupied by the threat to Western interests beyond NATO's narrow area of operations and even more sensitive to Europe's unwillingness to incur new obligations beyond the European theater, a concern that gave rise to Henry Kissinger's famous remark about interests and responsibilities.[1]

For details on French military capabilities in Africa, I am indebted to David Yost and to John Chipman, who allowed me to see sections of his Adelphi Paper, *French Military Policy in Africa and African Security*.

From the European side this divergence has become even more marked since 1979, when there was a resurgence of American power. It is not as Kissinger maintained ten years ago, that Europe has only regional interests; it has global interests but only limited means to protect them. And the means it has at its disposal have been seriously undermined since 1979 by American military intervention.

There are three critical issues to be considered. First, to what extent Europe really is merely a civilian power, as François Duchêne perceived at the time of its first rift with the United States (1973), and whether the perceived threat of a resurgent America requires Europe itself to develop a military capability. Second, do the Europeans face an even more intractable problem in their own inability to agree on a response? Many of the smaller European powers are still opposed to the deployment of military forces overseas. Agreement that there is a Soviet threat in the Third World has so far stopped short of leading to any constructive suggestions about the contribution Europe might make to American operations, not to mention the contribution that Europe might make on its own account. Finally, Europe's exclusive military relationship with Africa will be discussed, although that relationship is less exclusive than the Europeans like to think and considerably less independent than many American observers imagine.

THE UNITED STATES VERSUS EUROPE: THE UNNOTICED CONFLICT

Ever since Kissinger's acerbic remarks, those whose job it is to follow events in NATO have spoken in terms of a European challenge to the United States. The attraction of using the Third World to redress the balance of power between the Old World and the New has a history, of course, that predates the "Third World" as a political expression. In the late 1940s, Ernest Bevin expressed the hope that "if only we pushed and developed Africa, we could have the United States dependent on us and eating out of our hands in four or five years."[2]

A more skeptical Atlanticist, Charles de Gaulle, dreamed the same dreams in his 1944 Brazzaville Declaration, when he spoke of a France that, through its association with Francophone Africa, might number 100 million people. This potent image has in some sense remained ever since, more so perhaps in the last few years, among those who feel that Europe not only should disassociate itself from Washington in those areas of the developing world where its own interests run counter to those of the United States, but that it should also be prepared to actively oppose the reassertion of American hegemony.

This position was expressed most succinctly by Hedley Bull, who maintained that while it was not in Europe's interest to allow the Soviet Union to establish military supremacy over the world,

> Europe's interests in the struggle are not the same as America's. Western Europe has no particular interest, for example, in the restoration of the kind of U.S. predominance in the world as a whole that existed from the late 1940s to the early 1960s which some elements in American society seek to rebuild for reasons of national pride, or nostalgia, or misplaced ideological zeal.[3]

These remarks draw attention to an unnoticed conflict: not Europe's challenge to America, but America's challenge to Europe.

We may all differ as to why the United States has sought to reassert its power in recent years; why on almost every front it has become more interventionist, not less; and whether the "reassertion of American hegemony" poses any particular threat to European interests. But it is clear why the Europeans are uncomfortable with it. For them, the reassertion of American power is less an affirmation of strength than an indication of weakness, a loss of confidence in the nonmilitary tools of influence, and, worse still, a belief that only by intervening militarily can it maintain a world environment conducive to its own well-being.

The policies of the last few years seem to illustrate all the classic signs of Raymond Aron's description of an imperialist, rather than an imperial, republic, a power that needs to intervene by military force to establish control because it can no longer maintain its influence by nonmilitary means. When Aron wrote *Imperial Republic* ten years ago, he applied the epithet "imperial" to the United States, that of "imperialist" to the Soviet Union.[4] For Europe that distinction has become rather blurred.

It was in response to Soviet imperialism that Washington asked the Europeans to make a more positive contribution in the 1970s;

in response to American imperialism, it is not clear what contribution the Europeans can make at all. In a recent essay, Peter Foot, reviewing Europe's military options, concluded that it still had recourse to a variety of responses in the nonmilitary field, especially that of economic aid,[5] but the setback of European diplomatic efforts in the Middle East and the failure of its initiatives in Southern Africa in the face of a more aggressive and self-assertive South Africa, abetted if not aided by the United States, have merely served to bring home the transparency of economic power. As a political instrument, economic power may still be important, but it is not quite as important as European academics once imagined, and it looks increasingly questionable in a neo-mercantilist age.

More to the point, the limited scope of European economic initiatives in the developing world from Central America to Southern Africa has rendered questionable, if not incredible, the hope voiced by more radical European writers than Hedley Bull that Europe might be able to challenge American policy on behalf of the South. The problem is no longer that diagnosed by Kissinger in his memoirs—that Europe wants the option to conduct a policy separate from the United States and, in the Middle East, objectively in conflict with it.[6] The Middle East is merely one area of the world where American military intervention, direct or by proxy, has undercut Europe's nonmilitary initiatives.

At least Kissinger has been remarkably consistent. In 1981 he complained once again that it was not helpful having two separate policies for the Middle East, that unless they were coordinated they would "run the risk of undercutting each other."[7] The European challenge has remained a powerful and enduring element of Henry Kissinger's thinking. Like the Bourbons, however, he seems to have learned little and forgotten nothing. Ironically, far from undercutting the Camp David process or the Reagan peace plan, the Euro-Arab dialogue has been undercut and effectively nullified by U.S. policy. Only one Arab country in recent years has subscribed to Kissinger's thesis. In 1982 the Jordanian option made little headway, in part, because Hussein attached too much importance to the Euro-Arab dialogue and exaggerated the European Community's influence in Washington.[8]

Because Europe relies on the United States to secure its interests in the Middle East, it has had to tread softly. This was not always the case. In the late 1950s, the United Kingdom remained sufficiently strong in the Gulf to preserve the Al bu Said dynasty in Oman from U.S. attempts to expand Saudi control over the northern part of the country, a forgotten dimension of British policy (1955–59) that reveals much more about Britain's present position in the Middle East than the much discussed campaign in Dhofar in the late 1970s. The British preserved some independence of action even at the very end of their "moment" in the Middle East by maintaining a substantial military presence in the area (80,000 men). Their absence today makes them peculiarly unsuited to resist the reassertion of American hegemony, even though this time it is not Oman but Saudi Arabia that may suffer.[9]

In default of a military presence, the Euro-Arab dialogue never looked very promising. In the words of Henri Simmonet, the Belgian foreign minister, in 1977 it never looked likely to constitute "an adequate forum for negotiations on the problems of the Middle East."[10] Its final demise was brought about by the more assertive policy of Israel, which was partly made possible by the forging of a U.S.-Israeli alliance too powerful for Europe to challenge, even though it produced interests inimical to its own.

The Europeans were horrified by Reagan's offer of a "new strategic relationship" in September 1981, an offer renewed by the president in his discussions with Shamir in November 1983. They were horrified by the thought of Israel being used as a base for American operations in the region, although that idea, too, was never taken up. Like many Americans they began to fear that Israel's military power had reached such a height that the state could no longer be controlled. The Israeli response to the Fahd peace plan in August 1981 along with provocative military flights over Saudi Arabia reminded many Europeans of Israel's earlier threat to bomb the Saudi oil fields if Israel were ever pushed into what Henry Kissinger described in the same period as "emotional and psychic collapse."[11]

Yet the United States wanted a proxy in the area and Israel fitted the bill. The occupation of southern Lebanon may not have been precisely what it wanted at the outset, but Alexander Haig was quick to see the advantages of putting the Soviet Union's two "proxies" in the region, Syria and the Palestine Liberation Organization (PLO), on the defensive. Recognizing that Europe, even if it had wished, could not perform the role ascribed to Israel, the Reagan administration was persuaded to look elsewhere.[12]

The situation in Southern Africa is much the same, if potentially less divisive. The year 1978 saw Israel's first incursion into Lebanon, and it also saw South Africa's first invasion of Angola. Since then Europe has found itself having to define its own interests in the region in a climate that is essentially hostile, if not overtly threatening—a climate that owes much less to the Soviet Union than to the Reagan administration's tacit support and even encouragement of Pretoria. In that respect, it has once again suffered from America's search for proxies. As the administration was told by the House Foreign Affairs subcommittee on Africa in February 1984, it is now implicated, whether rightly or wrongly, in South Africa's regional aggression.[13]

The European Community, by contrast, has been unequivocal in its support of the Southern African Development Coordination Council (SADCC) since its inception in 1979. Maurice Foley, the European Commission's deputy director of development, explained at SADCC 3 that the Community's commitment to the enterprise was "total,"[14] so total in fact, that the commission reportedly urged the council to exclude from its meetings other rival organizations, including the Economic Commission for Africa.

Eager for South Africa to play a major role in the region, the Reagan administration has been much less critical of South Africa's attempts to set back SADCC's progress. Indeed, the United States has gone so far as to warn SADCC's members that if they continue in their criticism of Pretoria, it might have to reevaluate its support.[15]

In contrast, the European Community has gone out of its way to identify the republic as a major threat to its own economic interests. At the SADCC's Blantyre conference (1982), it parted company from the United States by condemning South Africa's destabilization attacks on the grounds that they were a serious threat to its own regional development programs.[16] Later it assured SADCC that it intended to become directly "involved in the development process right up to the frontiers of apartheid."[17]

In the early days the African states were inclined to take the commission's assurances seriously. On a trip to Europe in October 1983, SADCC's chairman expressed the hope that continuing

South African attacks on the region's key economic installations might bring Pretoria into conflict with the Community.[18] A few months earlier at the SADCC summit in Maputo, a number of countries raised the question of European military aid for Mozambique, South Africa's main economic target.[19]

More realistic observers at the conference, however, accurately predicted that Europe would never find the political will to provide a military component to its economic program. Since then, its policy in Southern Africa has been reduced to "common assessments, votes and declarations," not common action, to quote Bonn's ambassador to South Africa.[20]

How reminiscent of the fate of the Euro-Arab dialogue. In the Middle East, Israel's invasion of Lebanon and the destruction of the PLO as a major military unit made Europe's role largely irrelevant without in any way increasing Israel's prospects of security or of salvaging the Camp David process. Similarly, as the European Commission noted after the signing of the Nkomati accords between South Africa and Mozambique in March 1984, South Africa's destabilizing tactics dealt a body blow to the African National Congress without securing its long-term political future.[21]

But they have also dealt the Europeans out of the game. Europe is now stuck with American policies and America's allies. Like the Arabs, the Africans have become tired of its "pious and unfulfilled promises of assistance," to quote Botswana's foreign minister.[22] Such is the apotheosis of a civilian power, the fate of countries that continue to cling to the once fashionable orthodoxy that force no longer has a role in economic security, a proposition elaborated at length in the British Defence White Paper of 1980, which argued that "diplomacy, development and trade policies will usually have a greater contribution to make."[23] Perhaps they might have if the United States, in its obsession with excluding the Soviet Union altogether from the management of regional security, had not abetted its proxies in undercutting Europe's position. To a country less serious than the United States, the outcome might seem ironic.

FUTURE CONDITIONAL: EUROPE AS A MILITARY POWER

In light of these examples of European impotence, writers such as Hedley Bull would have Europe develop a military capability of its own on the understanding that unless its dependence on American military power is reduced, it will have no option but to acquiesce to American military decisions.

In the field of European security, the debate about a more active European role has gone on for many years. Many authorities and not a few governments have argued the case for strengthening European political cooperation (EPC) to allow the European Community to discuss defense issues; others have argued for developing specific European perspectives in NATO thinking. Some have even argued for a more active European role overseas, with Valéry Giscard d'Estaing recently promoting the idea of a European rapid deployment force (ERDF).

Such schemes, however, probably have no future, only a past. Americans looking at the alliance from their side of the Atlantic may well see a Europe unwilling to work with the United States in defense of overseas interests common to all. For years American scholars have traded in potent images of disunity, describing the Atlantic Community as a "troubled partnership," a "fantasy," or an "unhinged alliance."[24] Yet how many Europeans, I wonder, would not find these descriptions equally applicable to Europe as well, to a community whose capacity for conceiving grand designs in recent years has been matched only by its incapacity to carry them through to a successful conclusion. To a European observer, the European movement looks broken-backed.

Events surely provide a challenge to the view that as the European Community requires participation, so greater participation will breed a closer community. Thirty years after the collapse of the European Defense Community, Europe is no nearer coordinating a specifically European defense program. The failure in 1980 to achieve European union, on which such a program seems to depend, was merely one development among many in what Alberto Spinelli calls "the state of profound crisis" through which Europe is passing.[25] At this stage in its evolution, we can see what a network of contradictions the European movement embodies. Rather than talk in general terms about a European security role, it is surely better to concede the malaise while working to allay its symptoms.

Clearly, the smaller European powers would be deeply unhappy with a European role in the sphere of military operations. For a country such as the Netherlands, Europe's civilian status allows it to be more active in the Third World, rather than less, precisely because the South finds it less threatening. For the center-left Den Uyl government (1973–77), Europe had to be "active in the world but not in the sense of playing the big power game."[26]

The Dutch have been consistent in their opposition to any talk of a European security community since the Spierenberg committee report in May 1974, which argued that a common security policy could only follow European union, not precede it. At the height of the rift with Washington in 1973, they insisted on wording the Document for European Identity so that it would not give the impression that Europe could ever be entirely responsible for its own security.[27]

Contrary to American perceptions, countries such as the Netherlands and Denmark have displayed considerable caution in entering into any obligations that would lessen their dependence on the United States. In NATO they have interests, not responsibilities; as members of a European security community, they might have to shoulder their fair share of responsibilities as well. It was not surprising, therefore, that after the publication of the London Report in November 1981, the Danish foreign minister Kjeld Olesen was quick to point out that the words "political security" did not mean that defense matters could be discussed outside Europe.[28]

In that sense, the European challenge to the United States in the 1970s was also a challenge to Europe itself, one that found the Europeans far from united and capable of taking concerted action, but rather deeply divided and uncertain whether to act at all. The country that has suffered most has been France, the last European power with extra-European pretensions. The Americans may complain about European "neutrality," but in 1981 Giscard d'Estaing was equally critical of Danish "neutralism."[29] Out-of-area operations may well have a bone of contention between the United States and Europe in the past, but it was French, not American, operations that came in for special criticism from NATO's Scandinavian members at the NATO Council meetings of 1977 and 1978. The Americans may have complained about Europe's patent inability to act in a crisis, but in the summer of 1974, when France was president of the European Council of Ministers, it was equally critical of its European partners for failing to act in Cyprus.

One could say that the Atlantic and European conflicts have become mirror images of the other, like one of Italo Calvino's self-reflecting "invisible cities." The Europeans, for example, are just as critical of French unilateral actions as they are of American unilateralism, perhaps more so since the French often claim to have acted on Europe's behalf or even at its behest, as they did in Zaire in 1978 (a description as true to events as Lyndon Johnson's insistence that the 1965 Dominican intervention was an Organization of American States operation). On other occasions, of course, they have made no such claims. In November 1981 they repudiated the Euro-Arab dialogue; the following year they launched a joint Franco-Egyptian plan for peace, without in either case consulting their Community partners.[30]

The European, like the Atlantic, problem is unlikely to be resolved. One can only speculate that having become members of a "civilian power," the smaller European states, in continually defining and defending a nonmilitary response to security, have found the doctrine increasingly comfortable and convenient. During the Shaba operation of 1978, even the Belgians who took part wished only to evacuate their own nationals, not to reestablish order. The two operations were distinct from the beginning. The French landed the day before; Brussels was informed only through Kinshasa of the French decision to intervene.[31]

When the French later brought up the idea of European logistic support for an inter-African peacekeeping force to replace their own soldiers, the Belgian and Danish governments blocked the idea. The Danish foreign minister insisted that the proposal was "totally alien to co-operation within the EC" and refused to discuss the matter in EPC, thus effectively applying a veto.[32]

It must not be thought that the smaller countries are any less supportive of Western interests than are the French. Even Scandinavian and Dutch support for national liberation movements in Southern Africa, which so often appears to be out of step with French and American thinking, is intended to underwrite the West's position, certainly not to undermine it. In a statement to Parliament in 1977, the Danish foreign minister described his government's support for the nationalists as part of a "Western crusade."[33] Unfortunately, countries like Denmark no longer believe that crusades should have a military content; instead, they believe that Europe can best defend itself by its example, not its exertions.

No one would say that Europe could not devise an out-of-area role for itself if it wished. The most recent initiative in the security field, the Solemn Declaration on European Union, adopted at the Stuttgart summit in June 1983, was yet another step in reaffirming the EPC's emphasis on common security. But it seems true to say that even France, and certainly Germany, no less than the smaller countries, have found it convenient to bypass European institutions whenever national interests are at stake.

In 1983 the French refused to allow the Western European Union (WEU) assembly to discuss Operation Mantra in Chad on the rather specious grounds that it was not a matter of European interest but of national security. France is not even a member of the one European institution that *has* agreed to coordinate the security policies of its members—the Eurogroup—which reached that decision in 1984, although little, if any, progress seems to have been made since.

The last *institutional* link outside the Community, the Eurogroup, and the WEU is the Franco-German axis on which the Mitterrand government has put particular emphasis in recent years. Unfortunately, there is no prospect, immediate or long term, of the Germans ever agreeing to take part in out-of-area operations. Their constitution, as well as habits of mind, rule out any significant contribution beyond Europe itself. In October 1982 the Bundestag did debate whether or not Europe should provide a military guarantee in the Middle East to reinforce the Venice Declaration, only to conclude that it would be politically unacceptable.[34] Germany did not take part in the Sinai Peacekeeping Force two years later and was noticeably absent from the Gulf patrol as well as from the three-nation naval exercises off the Horn of Africa in the summer of 1978.

The German attitude to EPC really says it all. For Bonn, it provides a "privileged," not an exclusive, instrument of foreign policy. Bonn could hardly treat it otherwise since the German government tends to see EPC as an "alibi" for not having to make a choice between relations with Israel and relations with the Arabs,[35] between a defensive and offensive policy in the Third World, for not confronting the priorities and choices that Britain and France have had to confront since the 1950s. Germany's problems are, in that sense, Europe's writ large: the politics of evasion, of *attentisme*, a passive waiting on events, an unwillingness to confront problems head on. In one of his periodic sideswipes at the alliance, Kissinger described it as "an accidental array of forces in search of a mission." It is not a bad description of Europe itself as it confronts the problems of the Third World and its own role in resolving them.

EUROPE AND U.S. OUT-OF-AREA OPERATIONS

It is hardly necessary to recount all the elements that have produced a consensus within NATO that security in the Middle East needs some form of reinsurance. On the one hand, there is increased alarm at many aspects of Soviet behavior, perhaps most notably the airlift of Cuban troops to the Horn of Africa in 1978, and on the other, there is greater awareness of the West's inadequacies. That consensus found formal expression in two NATO communiqués, the first in May 1980, when America's allies agreed that it should divert forces assigned to Europe to the Persian Gulf instead, and the second in November 1982, when the Europeans offered to provide the Rapid Deployment Force (RDF) with logistical assistance.[36] Having acquiesced in these new priorities, however, the Europeans have been the first to find these obligations troublesome.

The reason is hardly surprising. The RDF represents one component, perhaps the most telling, of a much broader pattern—what Pierre Hassner has described in a different context as "the relativisation of NATO" in American defense planning.[37] If the defense of Europe really is no longer the most immediate priority of the Pentagon, the Europeans can hardly be expected to contribute to NATO's further relativization themselves by transferring military resources to another theater of operations, even one so near home.

Even if they were prepared to participate in out-of-area NATO operations, what could they contribute? The promise of logistic support needs to be looked at very carefully if it is not to become a poisoned chalice. Europe's combined total of oilers, ammunition ships, and transport vessels is only two-thirds that of America's. One authority contends that the most Europe could manage, without detracting from its own military requirements, would be four ships to support each U.S. carrier task force.[38]

Obviously, the position may improve over time. The 1984–88 military program in France makes provision for an expansion of French sea transport capabilities to enable France to transport equipment that cannot easily be lifted by air. But we are talking about a very limited expansion—only three new landing barges, hardly a basis on which to supplement a rapidly expanding American force—but one that could prove politically expensive if the price is European input into when and where the RDF is used.

In that connection Washington would do well to remember that the Europeans have been reluctant to be associated with the RDF because they see it as an American force, not a NATO one. It is because the Middle East is seen as an extension of Europe, as the Americans always maintain, that the Europeans are so sensitive to Arab sensibilities. When allied shipping became the target of Iraqi attack rather late in the Gulf war, the Europeans showed as little enthusiasm as the Saudis for military operations to secure the Straits of Hormuz. Britain and France, after all, had discussed a similar operation to secure the Straits of Aqaba seventeen years earlier, only to reject it. The political costs of acting in 1984 were, if anything, much greater.

Possibly the promissory notes have come up for repayment. In the face of a Soviet threat that taxed Britain and France for much of the postwar period, a Western security system has been revived at last, but the Europeans seem unwilling to pay toward its upkeep. Perhaps this is not a test of their interest in reinsurance but of their unwillingness to be identified with the United States, a country whose political judgment they trust no more than that of Saudi Arabia. Unwilling to pay the costs of the new American base at Ras Banas, as Washington asked,[39] the Europeans would probably be equally unprepared to put their own bases at the RDF's disposal, even in a crisis. After all, their bases were closed during the airlift to Israel in 1973, and it was on the assumption that they might be closed in the future that the KC-10 tanker program was given congressional approval.[40] Portugal, the one country that allowed the U.S. Air Force to use its Lajes base in 1973, closed it in 1980 during the Proud Phantom exercise.[41] In such a politically uncertain world, European logistic support is likely to prove more a liability than an asset.

The question remains: Do the Europeans have many military options themselves? In 1981 Giscard d'Estaing claimed that there were only four European powers interested in playing a role overseas.[42] It is probable that two of these lack, if not the capability, then the political will to do so.

Italy may have expanded its Mediterranean fleet in the last few years, but its decision to take part in the Sinai Peacekeeping Force was undertaken not of its own volition but under American pressure.[43] Its predisposition to be bullied by the United States was the remarkable aspect of the affair, not its willingness to have a military presence in the Middle East for the first time since the eclipse of Mussolini's *mare nostrum.*

The Germans have three air-transportable brigades and a fleet capable of operating beyond the Tropic of Cancer. But when two destroyers visited the Indian Ocean in 1980, they were not allowed to deploy in the Gulf, and the commander of the formation was specifically instructed not to cooperate with other allied forces in the area.[44] This self-denying ordinance seems to represent the bottom line of a policy of showing the flag, which trade may follow or even precede, but not the guns to reinsure it.

We are left, therefore, with only two European powers that have any claim to be taken seriously as out-of-area powers—Britain and France—both of which have still not come to terms with the fact that their geographical pretensions and actual resources are ridiculously at variance.

Britain, West of Suez

Only twenty years ago, a Labour party defense spokesman, Denis Healey, wrote a Fabian Society tract to explain why Britain was a world power first and a European power only secondarily: "Britain is a world power whether we like it or not. History has saddled her with interests and responsibilities in every continent. . . . We should count ourselves fortunate that we have the power to exert some influence in every continent."[45] Within five years the decisions made by Healey as secretary of defense had, in his own words, effectively "set the seal on the transformation of Britain from a world power into a European power."[46] As chancellor of the exchequer five years later, he could not even find the money to maintain specialist forces for NATO's southern flank and, in the final resort, to maintain a naval presence in the Mediterranean. By the time the Labour government left office in 1979, indeed some time before, Britain had ceased to be a European power; instead it had become a power predominantly concerned with the defense of northwestern Europe.

In the United States political observers still seem to be preoccupied with the retreat east of Suez in 1968, which many would like to see reversed, rather than with the much more recent retreat west of Suez between 1974 and 1979, which suggests that both are irreversible.

Britain may still have remained dependent on its non-European trade and lines of maritime communication, but within four years it had withdrawn from the Mediterranean, abandoned the Malta base, reduced its forces in Cyprus, pulled out of the Central Treaty Organization (CENTO), withdrawn its last two frigates from the Caribbean, and pared down the defense of the Falklands to a bare minimum.

This latter decision, of course, precipitated the Argentine invasion and elicited in response the largest British military operation of the postwar period. But the Falklands conflict was unique, its long-term consequences probably limited. In its aftermath the former Chief of Defense Staff Lord Carver remarked that he could think of no other defense commitment for which the task force would have been suitable, not even the defense of Belize.[47]

Is Britain, therefore, to all intents and purposes, "out of the business of military intervention in the Third World?"[48] East of Suez, most likely so. Its last commitment to the Five Power Defence Agreement in the Far East was a small contribution to the Integrated Air defense system. The decision to relinquish even a nominal administrative role in Hong Kong may be taken to mark the formal end of Britain's "moment" in the East.

In the Indian Ocean the joint Anglo-French and Anglo-Dutch exercises of the early 1970s are merely historical memories. The Royal Navy can no longer afford to pre-position equipment in the area, in the absence of which, as the 1978 exercise showed all too clearly, operations of any duration simply cannot be sustained.[49] The Gulf patrol has had to rely on the rotation of a small number of ships, never more than two destroyers or frigates with accompanying supply vessels—a pale reflection of its former presence in the region. The French naval presence, with its backing of an aircraft carrier and adjacent bases, was much stronger. Had it not been for the Falklands War, the Royal Navy would have lost as many as twenty surface escorts, its two aircraft carriers, and the assault ships *Fearless* and *Intrepid*. If the navy has been reprieved, one wonders for how long. It is important to remember that the projected cuts of 1981 were to have been in line with an increase in real defense spending of 3 percent between 1979 and 1984. In other words, the point has long since been reached where rebuilding the navy, much less expanding it, is probably no longer possible. Even maintaining it at its current level of strength is proving prohibitively expensive. By the end of the 1980s, Britain may not be able to afford many more oceangoing surface ships than the present Dutch navy.[50]

The same problem applies to the new RDF, which the government has recently announced for future operations in Africa and the Caribbean. At 10,000 strong it may not appear very expensive, but even a Conservative government is likely to balk at the cost of finding light tanks and air defense systems that do not form part of standard Royal Marine equipment (the unit which will largely comprise the new force), especially if, like the French government, it finds that the costs of transport exceed the book value of the cargo.

The costs of a properly balanced force of very modest pretensions has been conservatively calculated at 700 million pounds, a figure that may seem very reasonable until one recalls that this is precisely how much it costs to maintain the RAF's front-line strike force.[51] At a time when Britain is trying to double its first-line force as well as maintain the Second Tactical Air Force in Europe, the money is unlikely to be forthcoming within the next few years. On the eve of the east-of-Suez decision, Navy Minister Christopher Mayhew observed that there was something rather incongruous about performing a role beyond Europe "with the sound of gunfire drowned by the rattling of collection boxes."[52] The incongruity is no less apparent today than it was fifteen years ago.

France and Eurafrique

The last example, that of France and Eurafrique, is much more interesting because it is taken in the United States either to represent a role unique to France or to illustrate the makings of a *pax Bruxellana*.[53] Some years ago one of the most eloquent apologists of Eurafrique, Leopold Senghor, pointed out to the

Americans that in view of their own role in the Western Hemisphere, they could hardly object to the fact that Africa had become "Europe's Latin America."[54]

To radical and conservative writers alike there is, indeed, something of a colonial relationship between Europe and Africa. The Lome Convention, which associates all Europe's former dependencies with the European Community, is the direct offspring of the Yaounde Convention, which successfully translated a neo-mercantilist colonial order into a more modern neo-colonial system of market provision.[55] Even within Lome the French have carved out a sphere of influence of their own—the eighteen members of the French African Community, a customs union with a shared currency whose exchange rate is pegged to that of the French franc and whose economic programs are dependent on the French economy.

It was Kwame Nkrumah who compared the first Yaounde summit to the Berlin conference of 1884 at which the European powers divided Africa among them. If the development fever of the 1950s, the last flush of European colonialism, stimulated what the *Oxford History of East Africa* calls "the second colonial occupation" of the continent, we are surely witnessing a third inspired by the competition for resources. Although ten years ago the Organization of African Unity (OAU) insisted on the need to extend national control over Africa's mineral wealth, it was during its second development decade that both Mali and Zaire were forced to denationalize their mining industries, under pressure from European companies that seemed to wield much the same influence as the old mining houses of the colonial era.

Even the stakes are the same: The continent's mineral wealth in the north (uranium) and in the south (cobalt and chrome) both fall under the Second Lome Convention's Sysmin agreement, introduced to halt the dangerous decline in mining investment. And when it comes to military intervention, conflicts are still fought out through the agency of foreign expeditionary forces—in Chad (French and Libyans), in Zaire (French and Belgians), and in Angola and Ethiopia (Cubans)—except that there are now far more foreign troops in Africa than there ever were in the days of formal empire. (Despite the 400,000 French forces in Algeria from 1958 to 1962, Algeria was not a dependency but a department of France.)

Even the excuses for intervening are resonant with themes first heard a hundred years ago: the need to protect the lives of foreign nationals (a much greater problem now that there are over 200,000 French citizens working in Africa, three times the number before independence); the need, perhaps, not to open the continent to free trade but to keep it within the capitalist system; the need, of course, to outflank other powers. It could all be part of the liturgy of the *mission civilisatrice*, except that this time it is invoked by African rulers such as Mobutu and Senghor in their own defense.

Any form of colonialism, however, whether quasi, neo, or merely a form of "informal influence," is likely to bring with it formal political responsibilities, and this is just what Europe is beginning to find difficult to discharge, particularly in the field of security. In Africa it has to confront the unpalatable truth that a civilian power cannot translate itself into a military power overnight and may not ever be able to affect the transition completely. In Southern Africa, in the face of a militant *pax Afrikaanse*, Europe can be said to have responsibility without power; in the north it has power but not ultimate responsibility. In that sense, it may be said that Europe's strategic reoccupation of Africa in the late 1970s followed, and did not precede, its economic reoccupation in much the same way that its strategic decoupling in the 1960s followed several years after the formal process of decolonization.

Although it is only the French, of course, who can still be expected to continue a tradition of military intervention, capacities of the French rapid deployment force, its Force d'action rapide, which came into service in August 1983, must not be exaggerated. Its separate units do not train together, and much of their equipment cannot be used with that of the African forces in whose defense they are likely to be used. Although the airlift capability actually increased in 1986, in that many of the Nord 250I/ Nordatlas aircraft were replaced by Transall C-160s with a longer flight range, Operation Mantra in Chad showed how expensive such operations have become. The combination of various commitments in the period from mid-1983 to mid-1984 strained French overseas power projection capabilities to the highest degree since the Algerian war. More to the point, whether in Lebanon or Chad, they brought hardly any political return.

In this connection it should be remembered that African operations are never as simple as they are often made out to be.

In Chad the French have intervened on behalf of several different governments since 1968, all of which have come to terms with the very forces against whom the French were called in. Yesterday's allies become tomorrow's enemies with bewildering frequency, which perhaps would not matter if French forces were suitable for operations other than those that French military writers call "punctual" (i.e., of short duration). Unfortunately, in Africa there are often no clear-cut tasks to be accomplished, with the inevitable result that commitments can become distressingly open ended. At most, France can only prevent other powers such as Libya from moving into political vacuums, but such vacuums, as Gerard Challiand writes, are likely to multiply as the post-colonial and neo-colonial order begins to break down completely in the next phase of Africa's development.[56]

We must also remember that the third "occupation" of Africa has, in one respect, been similar to the first: So far there have been no conflicts between the participants. The French have not yet fought the Libyans, the Cubans, or the East Germans directly. How long will this situation obtain? In Zaire the French insisted on an American assurance that it would intervene if the Cubans crossed the border. The 82nd Airborne Division was kept on twenty-four-hour alert at the height of the conflict.[57]

There are signs, in short, that Europe's commitment to Africa could in certain circumstances become overextended and emerge like the empires that resulted from the first partition of Africa, top heavy with the insurance they were carrying. This time, however, it has been reinsured by the United States, which was only an observer, not a participant, at the 1884 Congress.

At the time of the French intervention in Chad in 1981, some American journalists were heard to remark that "a French accent marked the American approach to Africa," so closely were the two countries interlinked.[58] Instead of being a matter for self-congratulation, the Pentagon should be worried that Africa may already be a wasting asset in European policy and that French military intervention may one day become more of a liability than an asset to the United States.

The Korean War was probably the last time the Europeans were prepared to fight beside the United States under American leadership in a theater of operations outside Europe. Episodes like the Falklands War may not be the last time Washington has to rescue its allies from difficulties of their own making. In these circumstances, might it not be time for the United States to question Churchill's dictum that the only thing worse than fighting with allies is fighting without them?

NOTES

1. In his speech calling for the "Year of Europe," Kissinger stated: "There have been complaints in America that Europe ignores its wider responsibilities in pursuing economic self-interest too one-sidedly and that Europe is not carrying its fair share of the burden of the common defense." Full text of speech cited in *New York Times*, 24 April 1973, p. 14.

2. Cited in R. B. Manderson-Jones, *The Special Relationship: Anglo-American Relations and West European Unity* (New York: Crane Russak and Co., 1971), p. 39.

3. Hedley Bull, "European Self-Reliance and the Reform of NATO," *Atlantic Quarterly* 1, no. 1 (Spring 1983): 26.

4. Raymond Aron, *Imperial Republic: The United States and the World* (Cambridge, Mass.: Winthrop, 1974).

5. Peter Foot, "Western Security and the Third World," in Lawrence Freedman, ed., *The Troubled Alliance: Atlantic Relations in the 1980s* (London: Heinemann, 1983), p. 140.

6. Henry A. Kissinger, *Years of Upheaval* (London: Weidenfeld and Nicolson, 1982), p. 716.

7. Henry A. Kissinger, "Three Issues for Our Survival: The Price Europe Must Pay," *The Times of London*, 30 July 1981, p. 12.

8. Adam Garfinkle, "America and Europe in the Middle East: A New Co-ordination," *Orbis* 25, no. 3 (Fall 1981): 642.

9. Abdul Mansur, "The American Threat to Saudi Arabia," *Survival* 23, no. 1 (January/February 1981).

10. Ode Roeymaker, "La Belgique et les conflicts israelo-arabes," *Studia Diplomatica*, no. 5 (1980): 605.

11. For a discussion of U.S.-Israeli interests that differ from Europe's, see Fred Halliday, "The Reagan Administration and the Middle East," *Atlantic Quarterly* 2, no. 3 (Autumn 1984): 219–34.

12. Theodore Draper, "The Western Misalliance," *Washington Quarterly* 4, no.1 (Winter 1981): 51.

13. *Washington Post*, 17 February 1983. In Southern Africa the situation is even more complex than this. The weakest part of South Africa's strike power is in the air. It has only two light bomber squadrons with

a few ancient Canberra and Buccaneer aircraft, which are vulnerable to the increasingly advanced Soviet-supplied anti-aircraft missiles. The answer seems to lie in close cooperation with Israel. South Africa has already acquired more than twenty Israeli Kfir aircraft and may work with the Israelis on the coproduction of a more advanced fighter, the Lavi, scheduled to be operational in the early 1990s.

14. Cited in Douglas Anglin, "Economic Liberation and Regional Co-operation in Southern Africa," *International Organisation* 37, no. 4 (Autumn 1983): 700.

15. *African Economic Digest*, 27 November 1981.

16. *The Manchester Guardian*, 27 November 1982.

17. *The Manchester Guardian*, 11 October 1982.

18. *The Times of London*, 17 October 1983.

19. Bernard Weimer, "U.S. and the Front Line States of Southern Africa: The Case for Closer Co-operation," *Atlantic Quarterly* 2, no. 1 (Spring 1984).

20. Ekkehard Eichoff, "Aspects of German-South African Relations," *International Affairs Bulletin* 7, no. 1 (1983): 30.

21. *The Manchester Guardian*, 23 February 1984.

22. Cited in Weimer, "U.S. and the Front Line States," p. 74, n. 22.

23. Stanley R. Sloan, *Crisis in the Atlantic Alliance: Origins and Implications*. Prepared for the Committee on Foreign Relations, U.S. Senate; Congressional Research Service, Foreign Affairs and National Defense Division, Library of Congress (Washington, D.C.: Government Printing Office, March 1982), p. 18.

24. For a number of other descriptions see Simon Serfaty, *Fading Partnership: Europe and America after Thirty Years* (New York: Praeger, 1979), p. 104.

25. Alberto Spinelli, "Towards the European Idea," *Sixth Jean Monnet Conference*, June 13, 1983.

26. Cited in Alfred Pijpers, "The Netherlands: How to Keep the Spirit of Fouchet in the Bottle," in Christopher Hill, ed., *National Foreign Policies and European Political Co-operation* (London: George Allen and Unwin, 1983), p. 168.

27. J.J.C. Voorhoeuve, *Peace, Profits and Principles: A Study of Dutch Foreign Policy* (The Hague: Nijhoff, 1979), p. 180.

28. Niels Jørgen Haagerup and Christian Thune, "Denmark: The European Pragmatist," in Hill, *National Foreign Policies*, p. 114.

29. "Who displayed the 'Neutralist theses' at the last European Council," *Le Monde*, 28 February 1981, p. 8.

30. Françoise de la Serre and Phillipe Défarges, "France: A Penchant for Leadership," in Hill, *National Foreign Policies*, p. 68.

31. Jean-Claude Pomonti, "The deployment of parachutists was done to preclude panic among the Europeans," *Le Monde*, 30 May 1978, p. 1.
32. Christian Frank, "Belgium: Committed to Multilateralism," in Hill, *National Foreign Policies*, p. 102.
33. Cited in Mai Palmberg, "Present Imperialist Policies in Southern Africa: The Case for Scandinavian Disassociation," in Douglas Anglin, ed., *Canada, Scandinavia and Southern Africa* (Uppsala: Scandinavian Institute of African Studies, 1978), pp. 144–45.
34. Reinhard Rummel and Wolfgang Wessels, "The Federal Republic of Germany: New Responsibilities, Old Constraints," in Hill, *National Foreign Policies*, p. 47.
35. Ibid., p. 40.
36. John Vinocur, "NATO Backs U.S. Operations in Mideast," *New York Times*, 3 December 1982, p. A 3.
37. Pierre Hassner, "Intra Alliance Diversities: NATO in an Age of Hot Peace," in Kenneth Myers, ed., *NATO: The Next Thirty Years* (Boulder, Colo.: Westview, 1980), p. 384.
38. Dov Zakheim, "Of Allies and Access," *Washington Quarterly* 4, no. 1 (Winter 1981).
39. Halliday, "The Reagan Administration and the Middle East," p. 6.
40. Zakheim, "Of Allies and Access," p. 92.
41. Rowland Evans and Robert Novak, "The Shrinking American Eagle," *Washington Post*, 23 July 1980, p. A 21.
42. *Le Monde*, 29 January 1981.
43. Gianna Bonvicini, "Italy: An Integrationist Perspective," in Hill, *National Foreign Policies*, p. 79.
44. Dieter Braun, *The Indian Ocean: Zone of Conflict or Zone of Peace* (London: Hurst and Co., 1983), p. 108.
45. Denis Healey, *A Labour Britain in the World* (London: Fabian Society, 1964), p. 16.
46. Cited in John Baylis, *Anglo-American Defence Relations: The Special Relationship* (London: Macmillan, 1980), p. 74.
47. Field Marshall Lord Carver, "Feet on the ground in defense planning," *The Times of London*, 23 June 1982, p. 11.
48. Pierre Lellouche and Dominique Moîsi, "French Policy in Africa: A Lonely Battle against Destabilisation," *International Security* 3, no. 4 (1979): 131.
49. Christopher Coker, *The Future of the Atlantic Alliance* (London: Macmillan, 1985), p. 107. *HMS Invincible's* 1983–84 tour of the Far East highlighted the problems of effecting repairs.
50. John Mauer, "The Decline of British Seapower," *Orbis* 27, no. 2 (Summer 1983): 479–95.

51. Keith Hartley, "Can the U.K. Afford a Rapid Deployment Force," *RUSI Journal* (March 1982): 20.

52. Christopher Mayhew, *Britain's Role Tomorrow* (London: Hutchinson, 1967).

53. Johann Galtung, *The European Community: A Superpower in the Making* (London: George Allen and Unwin, 1973), p. 117.

54. Cited in Elenga M'buyinga, *Pan-Africanism or Neo-Colonialism?* (London: Zed Press, 1982).

55. Reginald Green, "The Lome Convention: Updated Dependence or Departure towards Collective Self-Reliance?" *African Review* 6, no. 1 (1976): 43.

56. Gerard Challiand, *The Struggle for Africa: Conflict of the Great Powers* (London: Macmillan, 1980), p. 25.

57. Christopher Coker, NATO, *The Warsaw Pact and Africa 1949–84* (Macmillan, 1985), p. 125.

58. Cited in David Yost, "French Policy in Chad and the Libyan Challenge," *Orbis* 26, no. 4 (Winter 1983): 980.

3 SOVIET UNION

S. Neil MacFarlane

Social progress has never been continuous and rectilinear; at all times it has been contradictory and has been accompanied by ebbs and flows, by development along an ascending line and by retrograde motion.

—P. Fedoseyev

INTRODUCTION

In the mid- and late 1970s, Soviet direct and indirect intervention in Asia and Africa was a matter of growing concern to Western policymakers.[1] Soviet actions in Angola, Ethiopia, and Afghanistan raised fundamental questions about the Soviets' perception of their own security and the nature and extent of their designs in areas often far removed from the borders of the USSR. The Soviets' military activity in the Third World poisoned the atmosphere of detente and, in conjunction with their buildup of strategic nuclear weaponry and of conventional and nuclear capabilities in the European theater, stimulated massive increases in Western, and particularly American, defense spending to redress the nuclear and conventional balances.[2]

The fact that many in the West were surprised or disappointed by Soviet behavior in the Third World during the period of detente suggests some misperception of the nature of Soviet policy in Asia, Africa, and Latin America. It appears that we suffered from a degree of mirror-imaging—a belief that since we accepted (at least from 1975 onward) that the detente relationship precluded unilateralism in the Third World, the Soviets did too.

In reaction to this disappointment, the pendulum of American perceptions of the Soviet Union swung in the opposite direction. One frequently heard the view that the USSR was organically expansionist. As the Soviet Union's capabilities grew, so necessarily did its assertiveness in the international arena. In conjunction with the attainment of strategic parity and the growth of Soviet force projection capabilities (see Table 3–1), the USSR showed itself increasingly willing to deploy military instruments in the Third World and became more aggressive and adventurist. As the inexorable growth in the Soviet military continued, so too did the growth in the seriousness of the Soviet challenge to the West.

Both these positions are to some extent flawed. On the one hand, given certain constants underlying Soviet policy toward the Third World, it is unrealistic to expect that the USSR would give up seeking unilateral gains in the Third World as part of a broad-ranging political understanding with the West. Indeed, there are good reasons to suppose that periods in which East-West relations

Table 3–1. Growth in Soviet Force Projection Capabilities, 1970–84.

	1970–71	1974–75	1980–81	1984–85
Long-range air[a]	5 An-22	30 An-22	60 An-22	55 An-22
			75 IL-76	225 IL-76
Aircraft carriers	0	0 (+2)	2 (+2)	3 (+1)
Helicopter carriers	2	2	2	2
Long-range amphibious	?[b]	?[b]	28[c]	61[d]
Airborne divisions	7[e]	7	8	8[f]

a. Excludes short- and medium-range An-12 and IL-18, which could be used in force projection within moderate distances of the Soviet border.
b. It is not possible, on the basis of 1970-71 and 1974-75 IISS data, to separate out long-range amphibious capabilities.
c. Includes Ivan Rogov, Alligator, and Ropucha, but not Polnochny, classes. It is worth noting that parallel to this expansion in amphibious naval capabilities, there was a rapid growth in Soviet civilian maritime transport with "roll-on and roll-off" capabilities.
d. Same classes as in c.
e. 7,000-7,500 per division.
f. One of which is for training.

Source: International Institute for Strategic Studies, *The Military Balance* (London: IISS, 1970–71, 1974–75, 1980–81, 1984–85).

are good are likely to be ones in which the USSR is particularly assertive in the Third World.

On the other hand, to maintain in a somewhat fatalistic fashion that the Soviet challenge in the Third World is inexorably growing fails to recognize that many of the internal and external factors encouraging Soviet force projection are variable over time and, for that matter, are to some degree responsive to Western policy. Despite the sustained growth in Soviet military capabilities, Soviet policy in the Third World appears to follow an oscillating pattern of assertion and quiescence in response to the changing fortunes of interventionism, to change in Third World politics, in East-West relations, and in the Soviet internal situation.

In defending these propositions, Soviet objectives and interests in the Third World must be addressed, as well as capabilities possessed and constraints faced by the Soviet Union in its attempts to use these instruments. Costs and benefits from previous policy in the Third World will not be addressed in a comprehensive fashion, though, as shall be seen, the balance of cost and benefit stemming from activities in the Third World appears to support the contention that Soviet behavior is likely to remain less assertive in the 1980s than it was in the previous decade.

OBJECTIVES AND INTERESTS

Why should it be that the USSR is so interested in establishing military position and political influence in the Third World? This question may be addressed with reference both to the characteristics of the international system and to the nature of the Soviet polity.

With regard to the former, and at the risk of sounding banal, in a system where there is no real mechanism for subordinating the perceived interests of particular states to the common interest of humanity, interstate conflict over scarce goods is an ineradicable element of world politics. So, consequently, is a concern for security, which traditionally involves strengthening oneself and weakening one's adversaries.

Since World War II, only one power has been capable of mounting a serious threat to the USSR. That power is the United States. The fact that we may consider ourselves benign has nothing to do with whether the Soviets consider us so. It is probable that Soviet defense decisionmaking, like our own, responds not to actual but to potential threats and, given the stakes, tends toward worst-case analysis. In posing conventional threats to Soviet security, the United States is dependent on positions along the periphery of the USSR and on maritime lines of communication that pass through waters washing much of the Third World. Moreover, the United States and its alliance system are to some degree dependent on resources originating in regions such as the Middle East and Southern Africa.

For these reasons, and independent of any considerations peculiar to the Soviet system, it would be surprising if the Soviet Union did not compete for influence and position in the Third World to the extent that its capabilities enable it to do so. Given the character of the international system and the particular configuration of that system in the aftermath of World War II, a concern to maintain Soviet security gives the USSR an interest in establishing itself and disestablishing the United States in these areas. This is particularly relevant to areas of the Third World on the immediate periphery of the Soviet Union, but it also applies to regions lying along important sea lanes.

This analysis is, however, insufficient. It fails to take into account a complex of factors peculiar to the USSR that, on the one hand, favor a maximalist conception of national security and, on the other, supplement the security motive with considerations of ideological commitment, national aspiration, and regime legitimation, which render the incentive to expand and to challenge Western positions all the more compelling.

With regard to the former, one might argue that Soviet perceptions of insecurity feed upon a specific geographical condition—Russia's lack of defensible frontiers—the historical expression of which has been a long experience of invasion. Zbigniew Brzezinski recently argued that to attribute Soviet "insecurity" to a history of invasion is a "journalistic cliché," because "Russia historically was not so much a victim of frequent aggression but rather the persistent aggressor herself. . . . Any list of aggressions committed in the last two centuries against Russia would be dwarfed by a parallel list of Russian expansionist moves against her neighbors."[3] This may be true in quantitative terms, but it seems somewhat irrelevant, if not a non sequitur. A people's experience of invasion by others, rather than their invasions of others, influences their perception of threat. The argument that the experience of World War II, for example, did not affect popular and elite perceptions of external threat suggests nothing more than a lack of familiarity with Soviet political culture or, for that matter, with human nature. In this respect, it is not surprising that Russia's people and its leaders evince a considerably greater sense of imminent threat than do, for example, America's people and its elite. One result of this perception has been a sustained outward expansion from the Russian heartland in all directions.

It is worth stressing that the notion that historical experience stimulates Soviet expansionism does not in any sense legitimate or justify such action. From the point of view of those suffering the effects of this expansionism, it matters little what its roots are. The purpose here, however, is not to judge the legitimacy of Soviet actions but to understand them.

This historical influence is reinforced by a world view that sees conflict as an ineradicable element of relations between socialist and capitalist states. In this context, socialist states can never be completely secure until capitalism has been eliminated. With such a conception of security, it is not surprising that what in the Soviet frame of reference are probably seen as defensive actions (including not only territorial acquisition but the military buildup) appear aggressive and threatening to those on the other end of the stick.

But beyond these considerations, which are essentially defensive in origin if not in expression, there is a consciously expansive dimension as well. Many commentators have noted the messianic strain in traditional Russian attitudes toward other peoples, which in early years was linked to the defense of orthodoxy against Turk and Catholic, and which in the nineteenth century took on the secular form of Pan-Slavism with respect to oppressed kindred peoples in eastern, central, and southern Europe. Russian expansionism in the same century, at the expense of predominantly Turkic peoples in the Caucasus and central Asia, combined religious (the conversion of the infidel) and secular (the Russian "civilizing mission") considerations as both motive and justification for czarist imperialism.[4]

The twentieth-century variant of this Russian messianism is Marxist-Leninist universalism. Though one might argue about its relevance to policy, there is little question in my mind that the

Soviet Communist Party (CPSU) leadership has shared and still shares a fundamental commitment not only to the survival of socialism in the face of the capitalist threat, but to the replacement of the world capitalist system with international communism. This ideological imperative is, however, important perhaps not so much in that Soviet foreign policy is directly motivated by a commitment on the part of the party leadership to save the rest of us from ourselves, but because the current regime to some extent draws its legitimacy from a claim to be pursuing these objectives and to being on the leading edge of a global revolutionary process that will establish the socialist millennium.

The question of legitimacy is at least three-pronged.[5] It concerns relations between the leader or leading coalition and other members of the Soviet oligarchy, between the party and revolutionary forces elsewhere, and between the party elite and the broader mass of the population.[6] In the first instance, in conditions of latent or active competition for power within the oligarchy, retrogression or lack of progress in the world revolutionary process may be used as ammunition by challengers to undermine the authority of the leader. In this sense considerations of leadership politics favor expansion. The strength of this factor is, however, not constant, since it depends on the strength of the leader's internal position and on the policies being pursued toward the capitalist states. It is likely to be strongest during periods when the leadership is pursuing cooperative relations with capitalist states, since such policies render it particularly vulnerable to charges of opportunism. In other words, and as noted earlier, detente, far from discouraging Soviet activism in the Third World, may actually stimulate it, as the leaders seek to preserve their authority through a forward posture in these areas.[7] However, those who make this point tend to ignore its converse, which applies to the present situation. Periods of tension in East-West relations are ones in which the pressure upon the leadership to prove its continuing revolutionary commitment is lower.

This intraparty effect is closely paralleled by an interparty one. The legitimacy of the Soviet claim to leadership over what remains of the world communist movement and, more broadly, over what Soviet commentators refer to as the "world revolutionary movement" is predicated to some extent on active support of revolutionary causes in the Third World. The lack of such support invites criticism from those seeking to challenge this claim to leadership. More positively, support for Third World revolutionary movements and regimes may serve as a basis for continuing influence or, more modestly, good relations with groups seeking to assert their independence from Soviet tutelage.

Again, these effects are variable over time. The manipulation of Third World issues as part of a struggle for leadership of the world communist movement was particularly significant in the early and mid-1960s and, after a hiatus during the Cultural Revolution, in the early and mid-1970s, when Chinese questioning of the USSR's revolutionary credentials pressured the Soviets into more substantial support of Third World radical regimes than they might otherwise have chosen. In this sense, there is probably some truth to Colin Legum's assertion that "Sino-Soviet rivalry was a major feature of Moscow's approach to the Angolan conflict."[8] By the late 1970s and early 1980s, however, and again largely for internal Chinese reasons (the "four modernizations" campaign, based in large part on the cultivation of a close trading and financial relationship with the Western powers), the Chinese dimension to Soviet activism in the Third World had largely disappeared.

With regard to the Western communist parties, it may be surmised that the pressure on the Soviets to underline their internationalist commitment to the national liberation revolution was particularly intense during the blossoming of Eurocommunism. Along these lines, Joan Barth Urban has argued that:

> The West European CPs [Communist Parties] have always welcomed the extension of Soviet economic and ideological ties to the Third World at the expense of "imperialist hegemony" in this region. Indeed, at the very time when the PCI [Italian Communist Party] was intensifying its overtures to China in 1978, leading Italian spokesmen were also underscoring their party's enduring affinity with the CPSU, precisely because of the Soviet contribution to Third World liberationism.[9]

It is probably true that much of the political capital gained in this context by support for liberation movements in Africa in the mid-1970s was lost in Soviet participation in the suppression of the Eritrean movements, in Soviet support for the Vietnamese invasion of Cambodia, and ultimately in the Soviet invasion of

Afghanistan.[10] But by this time, in view of the NATO rearmament and dual-track decisions of 1978 and 1979, the USSR could limit its losses by depicting itself in international communist circles as being assailed by a new capitalist encirclement led by a warmongering American administration.

The third constituency among whom Soviet activism in the Third World is a source of legitimacy is the Soviet people. In the absence of serious democratization within the USSR, there are several ways in which the Soviet regime can pursue popular legitimacy, a commodity of increasing value since the leadership forswore the use of mass terror as a means of ensuring obedience: They can satisfy the material aspirations of the population and/or justify the failure to meet these aspirations in terms of the need to strive for a generally recognized greater good.[11] Two greater goods are generally appealed to—the ideological commitment to a worldwide transition to socialism and the nationalist commitment to establishing the USSR as a global superpower with the influence and prestige that are requisites of that status—in order to justify the sacrifices demanded by the leadership (or, to put it less kindly, the failure of that leadership to manage the domestic economy in a reasonably efficient fashion) and to broaden popular support for the regime. As Thomas Wolfe pointed out in a rather prescient essay written in 1974, while the value of ideological argument in the context of legitimation may be "running down, it is nevertheless clearly evident that an energy and enthusiasm for playing the role of a great power in world affairs is not wanting in the Soviet case."[12] Indeed, the Brezhnev period would appear to have been one of growing reliance on traditional symbols of national power and prestige to legitimize the regime, rather than on the appeal to Marxist-Leninist universalism.

Once again, while popular legitimacy is a more or less permanent problem, the degree to which it is pursued through foreign expansion may vary over time. In the mid and late 1950s, and again in the mid and late 1960s, the Soviet leadership managed to sustain rates of growth sufficiently high to allow considerable improvement in living standards. The legitimizing imperative for expansion was not strong. It was this economic success that led Bialer, among others, to argue that the major sources of regime legitimacy in the USSR were domestic and economic and that foreign policy played a far less significant role in legitimation. He states that "the

Soviet regime has by and large been able to deliver the goods, it has generally been able to satisfy popular expectations for higher standards of living." But he also points out that "what is most important to stability are sudden changes or discontinuous drops in living standards (such as changes in work norms or sudden price increases)"[13] or, one might add, the unavailability of goods to which the consumer has become accustomed, which was a problem of growing severity in the early 1980s. Depending on the fate of Gorbachev's reform program, it may well reemerge. The character of resource allocation decisions made by Brezhnev in order to consolidate his internal power (and, notably, his increasing the share of resources allotted to the military and to agriculture while eventually reducing funds available for investment in capital goods and light industry), in conjunction with bad weather and the failure of economic detente as a substitute for economic reform, resulted in seriously reduced rates of growth, rendering the "consumerist" strategy of legitimation less promising. Many have argued that, as a consequence of the increasingly clear faltering of the Soviet model, the Soviet leadership must rely to an increasing degree on external victories, on the growth of "progressive forces" in world politics, and on expanding the global power and prestige of the Soviet state, unless it returns to mass terror as a basis of its rule.[14] Conversely, given the deteriorating international environment and the collapse of detente, the Soviet leadership could well point to imminent external threats to Soviet security in order to secure popular compliance and support. Soviet media emphasis, during the Andropov period, on the danger of war and the severity of the threat posed by the "Hitlerite" policies of the Reagan administration suggested that the regime may appreciate the merits of this approach to legitimation in the present situation.

The earlier mention of the consequences of Brezhnev's alliance with the military brings up a final element in the discussion of the basic driving forces of Soviet policy in the Third World: growing military power. The period since the mid-1960s, as noted earlier, has brought a sustained, all-service military buildup of significant proportions. Two elements of this buildup deserve mention here. The first is the attainment (some would argue the surpassing) of strategic parity in the early 1970s. The relevance of this achievement for Soviet policy in the Third World was perhaps best stated in 1962 by Raymond Garthoff:

If the Soviet Union can stalemate the United States in the intercontinental arena, the way is now clear for gradual expansion of power through any variety of methods, military and non-military, in the entire Eurasian periphery. While the optimal Soviet aim of the annihilation of the major center of hostile power remains deterred and frustrated, the sub-optimum aim of improving the Soviet power position in peripheral areas is now enhanced by the neutralization of the enemy power center.[15]

The attainment of parity meant that nuclear deterrence of Soviet probes in the periphery was no longer credible (to the extent it ever had been), as the West no longer possessed escalation dominance. In addition, the attainment of parity gave substance to the Soviet claim to global equality with the United States. From 1970 onward, Soviet spokesmen, among them Leonid Brezhnev[16] and Andrei Gromyko,[17] with increasing frequency asserted the right of the USSR as a superpower to a role in international issues throughout the globe.

More to the point perhaps was the relatively rapid growth in Soviet force projection capabilities (see Table 3-1). This growing interventionary capability was supplemented by considerable expansion in Soviet blue water naval forces. In short, the USSR was also developing the conventional means to back up its claim to equality. It was becoming possible to do what had been impossible before. As Thomas Wolfe said in 1974:

> To the extent that one's options may be broadened by having more of the physical instruments of policy, the men who will be making the Soviet Union's foreign and military policies in the next five to ten years will be able to choose from a richer menu of alternatives than their predecessors. . . . [I]f they do only reasonably well in managing the Soviet Union's interests, we can expect to see a steady expansion of Soviet political and military influence in the Third World.[18]

The point to make here is that as the USSR develops the capacity to project force in the Third World beyond the Soviet periphery, and as its resolve to stake a claim to global equality and to attempt to translate this military power into political influence strengthens, the Soviet military is faced with the necessity of acquiring reasonably reliable support facilities. This provides a further motivation for seeking influence in the Third World.

A summary of Soviet objectives in the Third World includes, therefore, national security, the spread of socialism and supplanting of capitalism, and the enhancement of the prestige of the Soviet state. These latter Marxist-Leninist and nationalist objectives may reflect genuine commitment on the part of the leadership and/or concerns about regime legitimation among the various constituencies whose loyalty and support is sought by the CPSU. The Soviet buildup of force projection capabilities with which to pursue these objectives itself provides an impetus to expand, not only because when one has developed a capability, there is a temptation to try it out, but also because the effort to project force into remote regions requires to some extent supporting facilities close to the target.

What policy preferences or interests follow from these considerations? Briefly, along the Soviet periphery, the Soviet conception of security dictates efforts either to control contiguous states or to deny Western military access to them. Considerations of security also favor attempts to deny Western access and to enhance the Soviet presence in regions farther afield that are or may be used by the West as deployment areas for strategic weapons or that contain resources important to Western readiness. Soviet interest in the Middle East and in the Indian Ocean Basin may be accounted for largely in these terms.

Marxist-Leninist and nationalist commitments, coupled with considerations of regime legitimation, require that the world revolutionary process be seen to progress in the Third World at the expense of capitalism through expansion in the numbers of socialist-oriented regimes; that, through these regimes, Soviet influence throughout the periphery continues to grow; and that, conversely, revolutionary gains and positions of influence be defended where they are threatened. Finally, the necessity of supporting facilities for the USSR's growing force projection capabilities adds a military dimension to the quest for influence, in the sense that the Soviets attempt to exploit their influence in order to obtain bases, ports, and landing rights. Military power is used to gain political influence, which in turn is used to enhance military power.

This summary of objectives and policy implications leads naturally to the question of whether Soviet policy in the Third World is defensive or offensive in character. With regard to motivation, it would appear that the answer is both. Moreover, in policy the two categories are not analytically distinct one from another, since, as is arguably the case in Afghanistan, concerns about peripheral security in unstable regional conditions may induce actions that would normally be considered offensive or expansionist. Given the ambiguities inherent in this supposed dichotomy, it is more useful in political argument than it is in scholarship.

It should be stressed that these are tendencies in Soviet behavior, and not absolute imperatives. The intensity with which they are pursued depends not only on the internal and external pressures of the moment, which have already been noted, but also on the risks faced by the Soviets in the pursuit of these objectives, the degree to which opportunities for Soviet expansion present themselves, and the degree to which the instruments available to Soviet policymakers are appropriate to the opportunity concerned.

INSTRUMENTS AND CONSTRAINTS

In pursuing its interests in the Third World, the USSR has a number of instruments at its disposal: ideology, diplomacy, economic assistance, arms transfers, and various degrees of force.

Historically, ideological affinities with radical Third World nationalists, coupled with the attractiveness of the Soviet model, may have had some utility for the Soviets in gaining influence within the anti-colonial movement and in the new states that grew out of that movement's success.[19] However, the increasing stagnation evident in the Soviet economy and polity, the growing stratification within Soviet society, and the evident inapplicability of much of the Soviet experience in Third World conditions have dissipated this original appeal. Some have argued that the spread of self-styled Marxist-Leninist regimes in the Third World in the late 1970s was a continuing testament to the appeal of Soviet ideology to radical movements in the less developed countries. Certainly, the socialist commitment of many of the leaders of these states has some substance, although the degree to which they might be considered "Marxist-Leninist" in any meaningful sense may be questioned. One suspects that much of the echoing of Soviet Marxist doctrinal formulations by Third World radicals reflects not so much ideological affinity as the sentiment that this is one means of assuring Soviet support.[20]

It is true that Leninist doctrine on organization and political structure may remain attractive to Third World revolutionary movements concerned with consolidating their control after a seizure of power. But this in and of itself by no means necessarily constitutes a basis for Soviet influence. Indeed the opposite could be argued. If domestic vulnerability strengthens the dependence of Soviet clients on their external patron, then to the extent they are successful in implementing a Leninist solution to the problem of concentrating and institutionalizing their power, this dependence is weakened.

Even those states whose leaders would certainly be considered Marxist-Leninist (e.g., Vietnam and Cuba) seem motivated in their foreign policies as much by nationalist aspiration as by missionary zeal. More than occasionally, they have shown themselves willing to risk Soviet displeasure in their pursuit of nationalist objectives. In the cases of Cuba and Vietnam, loyalty is bought with weapons and money, not by appeals to a common ideological heritage.[21] Perhaps the last significant remaining ideological advantage of the USSR in the Third World is the proclivity, all other things being equal, for the Soviets to support rhetorically and to sympathize with revolutionary challenges to Western positions and conservative regimes. This puts them in an advantageous position in adapting to the frequent upheavals associated with the process of modernization in Third World states. However, revolution in the Third World is not inevitable, and such a posture carries costs in relations with conservative regimes as well. Most notably, it can create openings for the United States to expand or consolidate influence in key regions with states that view Soviet activities with suspicion. The Soviet-Saudi relationship is perhaps the best example of this.

The role of diplomacy in the pursuit of Soviet objectives in the Third World is often overlooked. In the first place, however, the projection of force is not the only means by which to establish the Soviet claim to a role in Third World affairs or to equality as a global power. Soviet behavior since the Geneva conference on Indochina in the mid-1950s and Khrushchev's proposal for a five-power conference on the Middle East in 1958 suggest an appreciation of the fact that Soviet diplomatic initiatives on regional security questions are one means of pursuing the quest for equal status in global affairs. Where successful, as with Kosygin's initiative on the Indo-Pakistani war in 1965, they may carry considerable prestige for the mediator. Moreover, Soviet diplomatic initiatives that pander to the desires of their clients (namely, advocacy of the Palestine Liberation Organization's participation in a reconvened Geneva conference on the Middle East and the inclusion in the Soviet Middle East peace plan of a stipulation concerning respect for the national rights of the Palestinian people) are a means of acquiring and preserving influence.

More broadly, since the Soviet-Afghan, Soviet-Persian, and Soviet-Turkish treaties of 1920–21, the USSR has sought to stabilize relations with Third World states along the periphery of the USSR through the negotiation of treaties of nonaggression and mutual security, the principal aim apparently being to limit the possibility of foreign military access to the territory of states contiguous to the USSR. Parenthetically, though the weight of Soviet military power no doubt lurked in the background of the discussion of these early treaties, they corresponded to the interests of the other signatories as well. Afghanistan and Turkey, for example, signed their original treaties with the RSFSR in order to counterbalance what they believed to be British threats to their sovereignty.

This applies a fortiori to a more recent variety of Soviet diplomatic instrument—the treaty of friendship. If my count is correct, since 1970 the USSR has signed friendship treaties with some eleven Third World countries (Egypt and India in 1971, Iraq in 1972, Somalia in 1974, Angola in 1976, Mozambique in 1977, Vietnam, Ethiopia, and Afghanistan in 1978, South Yemen in 1979, and Syria in 1980). The purpose of such treaties from the Soviet perspective is at least sevenfold:

1. the cementing of client relationships by formal agreements;

2. the deterrent effect of such a relationship vis-à-vis regional adversaries of the client;

3. the legitimation through a legal instrument of a Soviet role in the region concerned;

4. the legitimation of possible subsequent interventions (in this sense, the Soviet refusal to accept Iranian abrogation of Article

6 of the 1921 treaty—providing for Soviet intervention in case of prior foreign intrusion into Iran, or the creation there of a "centre of action for attacking Russia," and in case the Iranians are insufficiently strong to repel this danger—is significant[22]);

5. the symbolization of Soviet emergence as a global power;

6. some assurance of client support for Soviet initiatives elsewhere as a quid pro quo for Soviet assumption of limited security responsibilities in behalf of the client;[23] and,

7. in a related vein, some assurance that the client will avoid security cooperation with adversaries of the USSR.

Despite these diplomatic initiatives, it bears stressing that the USSR, relatively speaking, continues to be seriously disadvantaged in diplomatic competition, particularly in areas removed from its borders. Serious Soviet attempts to influence events in noncontiguous areas began only in 1953–55. The Soviets lack the rather tight nexus of historical, cultural, economic, and political ties enjoyed by the ex-colonial powers and to some extent by the United States.[24] Though the Soviets may to some extent have been making up this disadvantage, it continues to constrain the effective use of diplomacy as an instrument with which to pursue Soviet objectives in much of the Third World. It might be argued that this lack of a historical connection to the ex-colonies is compensated for by the tradition of anti-colonialism, which exempts the Soviets from the colonial stigma attached to the metropolitan countries. But as the memory of the colonial era fades, the political utility of this tradition of sympathy is eroded. What matter are the economic and political problems of the day, and here the old colonial powers along with the rest of the capitalist world often have much to offer.

Moreover, the diplomatic gains for the USSR mentioned above are just as much reflections of the success of other instruments of Soviet policy as they are instruments in their own right. For the most part, these treaties are manifestations, indeed outgrowths, of aid relationships of long standing.

Soviet material assistance to Third World states has taken three principal forms: economic aid, arms transfers, and more direct forms of military involvement. Economic aid played a far more important role relative to military assistance in the late 1950s and early 1960s than it has since the ouster of Khrushchev, though it remains important in some specific relationships (e.g., India, Nigeria, Vietnam, and Cuba). In 1955–64, for example, the ratio of economic to military assistance was approximately 60:100. In 1965–74, the analogous ratio was 34:100, and in 1975–79, 26:100.[25] Moreover, although total economic assistance grew in each of these periods in nominal terms ($2,566 million in 1955–64, $5,595 million in 1965–74, and $7,268 million in 1975–79), these figures greatly overstate real growth, and it is almost certainly the case that foreign economic assistance declined as a proportion of Soviet GNP.

The apparent shift from economic to military assistance may be explained in a number of ways. First, as early as 1962, Soviet development economists were criticizing Soviet assistance programs as misdirected and wasteful, given the limited absorptive capacities of recipient economies.[26] The kind of economic assistance that the Soviets were willing and able to give was in many respects quite unsuited to the needs of and conditions in less developed countries. The value of such assistance became questionable on political grounds as well in the mid-1960s, when many of the radical regimes courted by the Soviets fell prey to military coups (e.g., Indonesia, Ghana, Algeria, and, somewhat later, Mali) and again in the mid-1970s when, despite massive Soviet assistance on the Aswan Dam and the Helwan steel complex, Egypt rather unceremoniously cut its ties with the USSR. The result was that the Soviets came to consider trade and aid with Third World countries far more in terms of potential economic benefit to the USSR than as a source of influence.[27]

Beyond this, after a half century of intense effort, the USSR has achieved a GNP equal to roughly half that of its principal competitor. Even were its economy organized differently, it would have difficulty competing with the United States in the area of economic assistance. Moreover, its economy is one in which output is planned on the basis of identified needs and priorities and in which a rather high proportion of national income has traditionally been allotted to capital investment and military expenditure. As such, surplus goods available for use in aid programs are not easily available.[28] Moreover, they are already largely spoken for as a result of substantial commitments to a small number of allies such as Vietnam and Cuba. The inconvertibility of Soviet currency and the Soviets' own tight foreign exchange situation make it difficult to provide credits for goods that are not of Soviet origin.

All of these factors constrain rather severely the Soviet capacity to use economic assistance as an instrument to secure influence and position in the Third World. The Soviet capacity to use economic instruments as a lever in its relations with Third World states is limited also by the minimal role that the USSR plays in the North-South trading and financial relationship and by its incapacity to present a credible alternative to participation in the international capitalist economy. One might well argue here that Cuba and Vietnam are the exceptions that prove the rule.

It has often been noted that as a result of these various limitations on the Soviet capacity to take advantage of cultural, political, and economic leverage, Soviet policy in the Third World is much more heavily dependent on military instruments than is that, say, of the United States.[29] This is the only ground on which the USSR can compete massively and effectively. The principal form of Soviet military involvement in the Third World historically has been the transfer of arms. In this sphere, it might well be argued that the USSR possesses a number of advantages. Given the nature of its arms procurement process, large stocks of transferable weapons are usually at hand. Moreover, the decisionmaking process is subject to few domestic political constraints of the type that have bedeviled American arms transfers to Latin American and moderate Arab regimes. Finally, this process is a secret one. The result is that the USSR can deliver large quantities of weapons at short notice and with little embarrassing publicity.

The value of Soviet arms transfers has been growing steadily since the first sales to Egypt in 1955. If one excludes China, the Democratic People's Republic of Korea, Vietnam, Laos, and Cambodia (these two after 1975), and Cuba, the 1955–74 total was $13.5 billion; the 1975 figure, $2 billion; 1976, $3.1 billion; 1977, $4.7 billion; 1978, $5.4 billion; and 1979, $6.6 billion.[30] In 1979 the USSR bumped the United States out of first place as an arms supplier to the Third World.[31] Although arms transfers have been a significant component of Soviet influence-building strategies in a number of countries (e.g., Indonesia, Vietnam, India, Iraq, Syria, North and South Yemen, Egypt, Sudan, Libya, Algeria, Guinea, Mali, Ghana, Nigeria, Angola, Ethiopia, Somalia, Cuba, Peru, and Grenada), the degree to which they are an effective and reliable instrument in the quest for influence may be questioned. Their effectiveness appears to depend on the following factors:

1. the stability of the client regime;

2. the degree of dependence of the client on Soviet support, that is, the presence or absence of alternative sources of diplomatic support and arms supplies;

3. the degree to which the Soviets' policy in the region is dependent on their relationship with the client concerned, that is, the degree of leverage possessed by the client;

4. the sufficiency of Soviet assistance in addressing the security needs of the client;

5. the degree to which the arms transfer relationship is embedded in a broader nexus of ideological, political, and economic ties; and, on a more abstract plane,

6. the extent to which the client's policy is dominated by particularistic rather than internationalist concerns; that is, the extent to which client policymakers are "nationalists first" and/or the extent to which their foreign policy concerns are dominated by regional conflicts not easily susceptible to external control.

The Egyptian, Somali, and Iraqi cases suggest that the Soviet record of success in pursuing its objectives by means of arms transfers is a rather spotty one. This instrument would appear to be particularly unreliable when arms transfers constitute the essential substance of the relationship. The Middle Eastern cases suggest, moreover, that dependence may well be a two-way street. Arms-transfer relationships with uncontrollable allies may lead to situations where the USSR is faced with the choice of escalating its involvement in dangerous situations or losing its investment.

It is perhaps for reasons such as these that Soviet policymakers to an increasing extent see arms transfers as a source not so much of influence as of hard currency (an increasing number of transactions being on a cash-and-carry basis) or as a barter item to be traded in return for needed commodities (as was possibly the case with Soviet offers of arms assistance to Argentina during the

Falklands War). That is to say, Soviet arms transfers appear to be taking on an increasingly commercial rather than political character. Grants or concessionary long-term credits to finance arms appear to be confined increasingly to states considered ideologically reliable (i.e., the vanguard party regimes[32] and states recognized by the Soviets as socialist, such as Vietnam and Cuba).

The increasing Soviet reliance on intervention as an element of military policy in the Third World may also have been a product of the recognition of the shortcomings of less radical means. In general, Soviet intervention in combat situations in the Third World has been "cooperative" in character,[33] in that it involves use of non-Soviet forces (usually Cuban, though in Ethiopia some South Yemen units were used), with the Soviet role being confined largely to logistical support, as in Angola, and/or command and control, as in Ethiopia. Soviet regular forces have on occasion been directly involved in conflict situations beyond the Soviet periphery—as with air support missions in North Yemen in 1967, Sudan and Ceylon in 1970–71, and Iraq in 1973–74, and air defense deployments in Egypt in 1970–72 and from 1982 to the present in Syria.

The first four of these instances involved very limited deployments. The Egyptian action—which ultimately included some 12,000–15,000 missile crewmen and 200 pilots—was apparently an act of desperation in the face of Egyptian threats to cut their ties with the USSR, was purely defensive in character, and again involved only very limited involvement in combat.[34] The Syrian instance, also involving several thousand air defense personnel, has involved no combat action. Indeed, Soviet personnel are probably there just as much to ensure nonuse of Soviet long-range surface-to-air missiles by the Syrians as they are to underline the seriousness of the Soviet commitment to Syria. In all of these instances, Soviet use of force was limited, was a complement to local or other external forces, and was risk averse.

The only recent instance in the Third World where the Soviets have intervened massively and unilaterally and have engaged in prolonged combat in order to occupy and hold foreign territory and to impose a political and social system was in Afghanistan. It was the qualitatively distinct character of this action that made it particularly alarming, with one observer going so far as to assert that "the decision to invade Afghanistan marks a watershed in

Soviet policy, inasmuch as the Soviets have chosen to resort to new means—direct military intervention—to pursue an old goal, the extension of political power abroad."[35]

The action in Afghanistan was indeed the first time in recent memory (though not the first time ever, given Soviet actions in Mongolia and Iran in the early 1920s) that Soviet military power was employed in this particularly brazen fashion against a Third World country. This suggests to many not a disturbing new trend in Soviet policy toward the Third World as a whole but an indication that Soviet policymakers view instability along their periphery in quite a different light than they do the same phenomenon elsewhere in the Third World. This is small comfort where Persian Gulf issues are concerned but is significant nonetheless in gauging the dimensions of the current Soviet challenge in the Third World.

Growing Soviet interventionism was not merely a product of the shortcomings of other instruments and asymmetries in the Soviet capacity to compete with the West. The growth in Soviet force projection capacities, as noted above, was a critical permissive condition, not so much for action along Soviet borders (though airborne troops and air transport played a significant role in the initial Afghan operation) as for action further removed from the USSR. Soviet IL-76s apparently aided significantly in ferrying Cuban troops to both Angola and Ethiopia. Much of the equipment provided to Egypt and Syria during the critical stages of the 1973 war, to Angola in the early days after independence, and to Ethiopia in the crucial initial stages of the war with Somalia was transported aboard An-22s. Neither of these aircraft existed prior to the mid-1960s. As the stock of such aircraft grows, so too does the Soviet rapid deployment capability. As Soviet amphibious transport capabilities expand, so too does the capacity to sustain such deployments. As such, trends in Soviet military procurement appear to favor increasing Soviet use of force.

The Soviets' reliance on military instruments to expand their influence in the Third World gives them an interest in fostering situations in which such instruments are useful. Put differently, it gives them an interest in fostering and sustaining conflict and instability in the Third World. One should not, however, take this point too far. The more these Third World countries establish positions of their own that may be threatened by conflict and instability, the more this general interest in instability is balanced by specific interests in the limitation of conflict. In Southern Africa, for example, the Soviets' situation is paradoxical. Too strong a South African challenge to Angola might well face them with a choice of mounting a dramatic escalation, with its attendant dangers, or seeing their client disappear or defect. On the other hand, a peace settlement would considerably reduce Angolan dependence on the USSR, open the door to U.S. influence, and shift the ground of the competition to economic assistance and investment, where the Soviets would be at a distinct disadvantage. Moreover, along their own periphery, instability associated with religious extremism carries the danger of affecting minority populations within the USSR and is potentially quite damaging.

Recalling the point that expansion in Soviet force projection capabilities favors a growth in Soviet interventionism, one should not ignore the regional, global, intrabloc, and domestic contexts in which this expansion is occurring. These place important constraints on the utility and effectiveness of force as an instrument of Soviet policy in the Third World. In the first place, and this is no great novelty, Soviet use of force in the Third World is opportunistic.[36] It is a response to emergent local conflict, where involvement carries potential for political rewards. Involvement in Angola was a response to the April 1974 coup in Portugal and the sudden Portuguese decision to liquidate its African empire and also to the subsequent power vacuum in this strategic region.

The intervention in Ethiopia was an outgrowth of the 1974–77 revolution and the rather rapid deterioration in Ethiopian-American relations associated with the radicalizing trend evident in Ethiopian politics and Ethiopian abuse of human rights. This deterioration culminated in a suspension of the American arms assistance program at a moment when the government was engaged in a full-blown civil war in Eritrea, a developed guerrilla war in the Ogaden fueled by an irredentist and well-armed Somalia, and incipient insurgencies in Tigre and in the north central portion of the country along the Sudanese border—that is to say, when Ethiopia needed immediate and massive foreign military assistance.

In Afghanistan, the coup of 1973, followed by the revolution of 1978, created an opportunity for substantial expansion of Soviet influence, particularly as the needs of the revolutionary regime for foreign military assistance in dealing with a budding insurgency grew in 1979. Since the Afghan invasion, there have been few opportunities as attractive as these for the Soviets to take advantage of, and this is one plausible explanation for Soviet passivity in the Third World since their action in Afghanistan.[37]

The second regional constraint on Soviet policy in the Third World, and one that has already been mentioned in passing, is the nationalism of the parties with whom the Soviets have to deal in order to further their interests. The particular commitments even of self-avowed Marxists-Leninists contribute a considerable element of uncertainty and risk where the Soviets have not actually occupied and assumed direct control of a target state, as is evident from the cases of China, Egypt, Somalia, Sudan, and to some extent Cuba. Even in cases where no break has actually occurred, the concern of radical elites with maintaining sovereignty as well as making the revolution has occasionally inconvenienced the USSR to no small degree. Despite frequent requests, both Mozambique and Angola have reportedly refused to provide the Soviets with bases.[38] Although the Ethiopians have been somewhat more forthcoming than their Southern African brethren, the granting of port rights in Eritrea and limited naval privileges in the Dahlak Islands have by no means compensated in strategic terms for the loss of Berbera and other bases in Somalia.[39] The Soviet image problem in much of the Third World after the Afghan invasion was seriously compounded by this general sensitivity about national independence. One effect of the Afghan action was presumably to strengthen this impediment to the expansion of Soviet influence, though such effects weaken over time as people's memories fade and as circumstances change.

Perhaps more important are the global constraints faced by the USSR in the pursuit of its objectives in the Third World—principally American nuclear and conventional military power. In contemplating the use of force in the Third World, the Soviet leadership must assess the risk that their actions may result in counterinvolvement by American conventional forces. In this context, although Soviet force projection capabilities have grown dramatically since the mid-1960s, they remain quantitatively (see Table 3–2) and in some cases qualitatively inferior to comparable American capabilities. Soviet force projection into areas removed from Soviet borders could not be sustained in the face of American

Table 3–2. Comparison of Soviet and U.S. Force Projection Capabilities, 1984–85.

	USSR	United States
Long-range air transport	280[a]	322[b]
Amphibious shipping	33[c]	61[d]
Aircraft carriers	3[e]	13
Helicopter carriers	2	—[f]
Airborne divisions	7	1
Marines	16,000	186,000

a. Includes military but not civilian IL-76s and An-22s.
b. Includes C5 and C141; excludes 218 C130s.
c. Includes Ivan Rogov, Ropucha, and Alligator classes.
d. Includes Blue Ridge, Tarawa, Iwo Jima, Austin, Raleigh, Anchorage, Thomaston, Newport, and Charleston classes.
e. One more in trials.
f. Included under amphibious shipping.

Source: International Institute for Strategic Studies, *The Military Balance*, 1984-85 (London: IISS, 1984).

military opposition. Second, they must assess the possibility that such a confrontation might escalate to general war. Again, the strength of both of these constraints varies over time. To judge from Soviet behavior, American activism in the Third World encourages Soviet restraint, and it is oscillation in American military policies that accounts in large part for the cycles of activism and quiescence in Soviet policy since the mid-1960s.

It has been argued, for example, that one source of the low profile adopted by the Soviets in much of the Third World in the mid-1960s was Soviet concern about the intensity of the American military response in Vietnam.[40] The gradual expansion in the Soviets' conception of their own role in Third World conflicts, evident in the Soviet military literature in the late 1960s and early 1970s,[41] may be explained in terms not only of the growth in Soviet conventional force projection capabilities but also of the weakening of the American military establishment during the Vietnam era along with domestic U.S. political difficulties that arose from the Vietnam War and greatly impeded American's defense of its Third World interests.

At the time of the Soviet decision to intervene in Angola, the United States gave the USSR a significant indicator of the extent of danger of confrontation in the Third World when it failed to support its South Vietnamese ally in the last stages of the Vietnam War. Later in the same year, by voting to prohibit further American involvement in Angola, Congress gave the Soviets carte blanche to settle the Angolan War on their terms. In short, one source of Soviet activism in the Third World in the mid-1970s was the failure of American conventional deterrence.

Likewise, although one should not underestimate the continuing strength of domestic constraints on American use of force, one can account for relative Soviet passivity in the Third World in the early 1980s not only in terms of diminished opportunity but also because the change in American administration and arguably in the mood of the American public with regard to the assertion of American prerogatives as a superpower have to some extent increased the perceived risks associated with Soviet force projection.

With regard to escalation, Soviet military commentary from the late 1960s and early and mid-1970s displays a gradual decline in concern about general war growing out of local conflict.[42] This presumably reflected the Soviets' attainment of parity, as noted above, but also may have been based on their assessment of the unlikelihood in the atmosphere of the mid-1970s of confrontation resulting from an American military response to a Soviet initiative. Again, given current American rhetoric, the nature of current procurement, the use of American forces in Lebanon and Grenada, and the sustained program of exercises in Central America and the Caribbean, there is reason to expect a rethinking of this Soviet position. Along these lines, a reading of the party press suggests a growing concern about the possibility of nuclear war arising from conflict in Third World "hotbeds of tension."[43]

One further aspect of American policy deserves mention here. Increasing American investment in European conventional and theater nuclear forces and the renovation of the strategic nuclear arsenal are forcing the Soviets to refocus their attention and resources on dangers at the center of global politics, pushing Third World issues down the list of priorities.

With regard to intrabloc concerns, the severe economic problems encountered in the late 1970s and early 1980s in much of

Eastern Europe along with the political spillover in Poland create a climate of uncertainty and potential instability among the Soviet satellites that was not evident in the mid-1970s. It can be argued that this new array of problems also favors a refocusing of the attention of Soviet policymakers away from Third World issues.

Finally, several aspects of the current Soviet internal situation place constraints on their activism in the Third World. Most notable among these are new military demands associated with the rapid expansion in American defense spending that coincide with considerable economic difficulty and low growth. The need to marshal limited Soviet resources to deal with domestic economic difficulties and the looming American threat arguably discourage adventurism in areas of less than immediate strategic interest to the USSR.

The other domestic factor that may have operated as a constraint on aggressive Soviet behavior is the succession problem. One aspect of the process of transition from one set of leaders to another may well have been a certain degree of *immobilisme* in foreign policy, no single leader possessing a level of power sufficient to push through an ambitious foreign policy program. The relevance of this factor has diminished, however, since Gorbachev's accession to power and his rapid consolidation of control over the foreign policy apparatus.

In a more general sense, some have argued that the transition from the rather rigid old guard to a more managerially oriented and pragmatic younger group of leaders will bring with it growing moderation in foreign policy. The other side of this coin is that the next generation of leaders is less experienced in foreign policy issues and thus lacks an appreciation of the prudential limits imposed on Soviet international behavior in a bipolar system graced with a surfeit of nuclear weapons. Moreover, given the highly structured character of political socialization in the USSR, it might be premature to attempt confident conclusions about the greater pragmatism of the younger generation. It is difficult, therefore, to draw confident conclusions with regard to the long-term impact of the succession process on Soviet foreign policy.

In short, although the direction of Soviet behavior may to some extent be organically determined, that behavior does not occur in a vacuum. Its characteristics are shaped by calculations of cost and benefit. This balance of cost and benefit in turn is at least partially shaped by the policies and actions of external actors and, most notably, those of the United States. Moreover, the USSR is constrained in its expansionism by the necessity of maintaining stability in those territories that it already controls and by the intensity of its own political and economic problems, both of which pose significant difficulties in current conditions.

PROSPECTS

What then are the prospects for Soviet foreign policy in the Third World? At the most basic level, there is little reason to expect any change in the competitive and revisionist essence of Soviet foreign policy in the Third World. Moreover, it is true that a gradually worsening economic situation in the USSR may push the Soviet leadership toward more adventurist policies in the Third World. However, the USSR's economic situation appears to have stabilized for the moment. Even if Gorbachev's efforts at reform fail and the decline resumes, one should not overestimate its potentially noxious consequences for Soviet international behavior. One might just as well argue that a growing economic squeeze will render the Soviet leadership loath to assume new commitments.

In addition, many of the pressures pushing the Soviets toward radicalism in the Third World have dissipated. The Chinese are no longer the problem they were. The disappearance of detente has removed the need for "compensatory activism." The apparently growing seriousness of the external threat provides an alternative source of legitimacy. Beyond this, the risks associated with Soviet use of force have grown, while opportunities lending themselves to such use have diminished. Finally, the balance of cost and benefit perceived by the Soviets to be associated with previous force projection in the Third World may well contribute to Soviet ambivalence about such activity.[44]

While the argument cuts both ways, therefore, on balance there are good grounds to expect a period of relative moderation in Soviet foreign policy in the Third World. The initial phase of Gorbachev's tenure in office—which was marked by a concern to maintain and consolidate established positions in the face of growing American pressure, an emphasis on the cultivation of state-to-state relations with major Third World actors, and little evidence of willingness to take risks to expand Soviet influence in the context of a reduction in the priority accorded to Third World issues in Soviet foreign policy—appears to support this conclusion.

NOTES

1. Intervention is defined here as coercive interference in internal and regional conflicts involving combat deployments and affecting "authority structures." See James Rosenau, "Intervention as a Scientific Concept," *Journal of Conflict Resolution* 13, no. 2 (1969): 161, 165.

2. Caution should be exercised in the discussion of Soviet policy in the Third World, since the latter term is in large part a Western concept and one that is treated with a certain ambivalence in the Soviet literature. Nonetheless, many Soviet categories, such as the "East," the "underdeveloped countries" (*slaborazvitye strany*), the "colonial and semi-colonial countries," and the "national liberation move-ment," refer to a group of countries that correspond geographically to what Western analysts would consider to be the Third World. I am indebted to Dr. Herbert Ellison for reminding me of this important methodological point.

3. Zbigniew Brzezinski, "The Soviet Union: Her Aims, Problems, and Challenges to the West," in *The Conduct of East-West Relations in the 1980s, Part I*, Adelphi Paper no. 189 (London: International Institute for Strategic Studies, 1983), p. 4.

4. This is of course not a uniquely Russian trait. A sense of mission for one's own people and a sense of moral superiority over others is perhaps integral to nationalism as such. It would appear, however, to be particularly well developed in the Russian case.

5. For a discussion of the meaning of legitimacy, see Seweryn Bialer, *Stalin's Successors* (New York: Cambridge University Press, 1980), p. 183.

6. A similar division of internal constituencies is made by George Breslauer in *Khrushchev and Brezhnev as Leaders: Building Authority in Soviet Politics* (New York: George Allen and Unwin, 1982), p. 8, n. 14; and Bialer, *Stalin's Successors*, p. 185.

7. On this point for the Brezhnev period, see Harry Gelman, *The Brezhnev Politburo and the Decline of Détente* (Ithaca, N.Y.: Cornell University Press, 1984), p. 156.

8. Colin Legum, "Angola and the Horn of Africa," in Stephen Kaplan, ed., *Diplomacy of Power* (Washington, D.C.: The Brookings Institu-tion, 1981), pp. 578, 592.

9. Joan Barth Urban, "The West European Communist Parties," in Roger Kanet, ed., *Soviet Foreign Policy in the 1980s* (New York: Praeger, 1982), p. 181.

10. Ibid., pp. 181–82.

11. Bialer, *Stalin's Successors*, p. 146, notes also the important legitimizing role in the specific Russian context of the provision of order.

12. Thomas Wolfe, "Soviet Global Strategy," in Kurt London, ed., *The Soviet Impact on World Politics* (New York: Hawthorne, 1974), p. 238.

13. Bialer, *Stalin's Successors*, p. 154.

14. For a discussion of the advent of pessimism within the Soviet elite and its implications for Soviet foreign policy, see Edward Luttwak, *The Grand Strategy of the Soviet Union* (New York: St. Martin's Press, 1983). Although I am not as sure as he seems to be about the seriousness of the threat posed to the Soviet regime by economic stagnation and demographic change, he may be right in pointing to an increasing reliance on the "appeal of Russian nationalism," given the possibility of a growing economic frustration among the ethnic Russian community.

15. Raymond Garthoff, *Soviet Strategy in the Nuclear Age* (New York: Praeger, 1962), p. 13.

16. Leonid Brezhnev (1970), as cited in R. Kolkowicz, "The Military and Soviet Foreign Policy," in Kanet, *Soviet Foreign Policy in the 1980s*, p. 17.

17. Andrei Gromyko, *"Rech' Tov. A.A. Gromyko,"* Pravda, 4 April 1971, p. 8.

18. Wolfe, "Soviet Global Strategy," p. 239.

19. Nehru, for example, in his autobiography noted how strongly he had been affected by a visit to Moscow in 1927. Jawaharlal Nehru, *Autobiography* (London: The Bodley Head, 1953), pp. 166, 302.

20. On this point, see Kenneth Jowitt, "Scientific Socialist Regimes in Africa," in C. Rosberg and T. Callaghy, eds., *Socialism in Sub-Saharan Africa* (Berkeley, Calif.: Center for International Studies, 1978), p. 137.

21. For an opposite view of the strength and significance of ideology as an instrument of Soviet foreign policy, see the summary of Charles Fairbanks' paper in *Soviet/Cuban Strategy in the Third World after Grenada* (Washington, D.C.: The Woodrow Wilson International Center for Scholars, 1984), p. 41.

22. E.H. Carr, *The Bolshevik Revolution*, vol. 3 (Harmondsworth, UK: Penguin, 1977), p. 294.

23. Zafar Imam, "Soviet Treaties with Third World Countries," *Soviet Studies* 36, no. 1 (1983): 66.

24. A similar point is made by I.W. Zartman in "The USSR in the Third World," *Problems of Communism* 31, no. 5 (1982): 76–80.

25. Derived from statistics presented in Gu Guan-fu, "Soviet Aid to the Third World: An Analysis of Its Strategy," *Soviet Studies* 35, no. 1 (1983): 72, 74.

26. On this point, see Elizabeth K. Valkenier, "Soviet Economic Relations with the Developing Nations," in Kanet, *The Soviet Union and the Developing Nations* (Baltimore: Johns Hopkins University Press, 1974), pp. 225–27.

27. Ibid., pp. 219–21.

28. Bialer also makes this point in *Stalin's Successors*, p. 261.

29. Though, to be fair, American forces historically have been far more heavily involved in force projection in the Third World, while until quite recently the dollar value of American arms transfers exceeded that of Soviet transfers.

30. *Communist Aid Activities in Non-Communist Less Developed Countries, 1979 and 1954-79,* CIA, Er-80-10318U (October 1980), as cited in Barry Blechman et al., "Negotiated Limitations on Arms Transfers," in Alexander George, ed., *Managing US-Soviet Rivalry* (Boulder, Colo.: Westview, 1983), p. 282.

31. If one counts in aid to communist countries, the USSR presumably unseated the United States somewhat earlier.

32. For a relatively authoritative discussion of the "vanguard party regime," see Yu. Irkhin, *"Avangardnye Revolyutsionnye Partii Trudyashchikhsya Osvobodivshikhsya Stran," Voprosy Istorii,* no. 4 (1982).

33. "Cooperative intervention" is a term coined by Stephen Hosmer and Thomas Wolfe in *Soviet Policy and Practice Toward Third World Conflicts* (Lexington, Mass.: Lexington Books, 1983), pp. 79–108.

34. Kaplan, *Diplomacy of Power*, p. 170.

35. Bialer, *Stalin's Successors*, p. 1.

36. S.N. MacFarlane, *Soviet Intervention in Third World Conflict* (Geneva: Graduate Institute of International Affairs, 1983), p. 26; Hosmer and Wolfe, *Soviet Policy*, p. xviii; Gelman, *The Brezhnev Politburo*, pp. 38, 42.

37. Ibid., p. 42.

38. For the Angolan case, see John Marcum, "Angola," in Gwendolen M. Carter and Patrick O'Meara, ed., *Southern Africa: The Continuing Crisis* (Bloomington: Indiana University Press, 1979), pp. 193–94.

39. MacFarlane, *Soviet Intervention*, pp. 31–32.

40. Karen Dawisha, *Soviet Foreign Policy Towards Egypt* (London: Macmillan, 1979), pp. 36-37.

41. For a useful chronicling of this trend, see Mark Katz, *The Third World in Soviet Military Thought* (Baltimore: Johns Hopkins University Press, 1982), pp. 57–59, 84–86.

42. Ibid., pp. 67–69.

43. S.N. MacFarlane, "The Soviet Conception of Regional Security," *World Politics* 37, no. 3 (April 1985), pp. 309–10.
44. For an argument along these lines, see MacFarlane, *Soviet Intervention*.

4 EASTERN EUROPE

Robin Alison Remington

Any attempt to analyze East European relations with the Third World faces major obstacles.[1] Even if one limits the topic to East European members of the Warsaw Pact and the Council for Mutual Economic Assistance (CMEA), there are 6 East European states relating to more than 100 countries in Africa, Asia, Latin America, and the Middle East. The sheer number of political actors and interactions is intimidating and in itself complicated by a series of arbitrary choices. For "Third World" is a residual, ideological category, a convenient catchall for those countries that are neither East nor West but implicitly presumed to be at some embryonic stage of development that could tilt toward either ideological/political/economic model.

This raises a definition problem. What does one do about those Third World countries that have explicitly opted for Marxist-Leninist modernization strategies? And for that matter, where does one put the Third World national liberation movements—those non-state actors struggling for real estate and recognition in the international system? There is the nonaligned political movement (NAM) that clocked in at 101 members, 10 observers, and 12 guests at the Eighth Nonaligned Summit in Harare, Zimbabwe, September 1986, overlapping—if by no means identical—with the Third World. Or there is the nonideological category known as the South, organizationally represented by the Group of 77 (which had grown to 120 members at last count). In short, for the purposes of this kind of analysis, it is much easier to agree on what to include as East European actors than on what to count as their Third World counterparts.

As used in this analysis, the Third World includes countries with varying degrees of socialist orientation—to use Leonid Brezhnev's term at the 26th Soviet Communist Party (CPSU) Congress in 1981—on "the noncapitalist path of development."[2] It does not include countries accepted by the Soviet Union and Eastern Europe as engaged in "building socialism."[3]

Unfortunately, the problem of definition is only the start of one's troubles in attempting to sort out East European policies toward the Third World. Such research is severely hampered by lack of systematic country-specific research on East European foreign policy.[4] Those studies that do exist tend to be general overviews, primarily concerned with the extent of deviation from Soviet policies and priorities.

Although the virtual blackout on East European Third World connections throughout the 1970s, described by Roger Kanet in an article summing up research needs in the area of East European foreign policy,[5] has begun to lift in the 1980s,[6] there is no coherent body of literature on this topic. Data are fragmentary and hard to come by.[7] CMEA sources do not exist on some areas and may or may not be reliable on others. Western sources frequently are contradictory, and often Soviet and East European figures are lumped together and cannot be disaggregated. The line between fact and journalistic rumor is often blurred. Chapters in the same book can disagree with no clues as to which author is the more reliable.[8]

In the 1980s it is clear that the amount of East European action regarding the Third World is steadily increasing, and two tentative propositions emerge from an investigation of the fragmentary sources available on East European interests, capabilities, and objectives toward less developed countries (LDCs):

1. In the 1980s the Third World connection is becoming simultaneously more important and higher risk for East European policymakers.

2. As a corollary, even when East European commitments appear to reflect Soviet-defined objectives, the very nature of increasing East European involvement with the LDCs of the Third World tends to undermine fundamental, long-term Soviet interests.

ASSUMPTIONS CONCERNING THE NATURE OF THE EAST EUROPEAN BLOC

This is not the place to rehash the conceptual debates that divide scholars of Eastern Europe over the respective explanatory value of imperial versus hierarchical, systemic models or dependency theory for understanding Soviet-East European relations, nor to get bogged down over whether or not those relations can be appropriately described as "organic."[9] Nonetheless, one's position on such questions does influence one's perception of East European relations to the Third World. Certainly, there is an implicit assumption of those who collect aggregate Soviet-East European data vis-à-vis the LDCs that Eastern Europe operates essentially as an instrument of Soviet policy in this regard. Indeed, the very designation "Eastern bloc" refers to ideological/political boundaries separating those countries in East-Central Europe that underwent Communist revolutions at the end of World War II from their European identities, implying shared Communist objectives and priorities. This analysis focuses on the East European members of what once without a second thought would have been considered the "Soviet bloc."

This focus becomes problematical. While the existence of a Soviet bloc in East-West terms has some utility, most scholars think the East European members of Communist alliance structures do not operate as a bloc in relation either to their own superpower or to the West, never mind in terms of their still more diverse interactions with the Third World. There are six East European members of the Warsaw Pact and CMEA representing a wide range in terms of size, natural resources, level of economic development, historical patterns, cultural orientation, nationality composition, language, and religion. East European Communist systems took root in enormously different environments and developed restraints leading to very different options. This analysis, therefore, assumes that country-specific situations and pressures influence East European policymakers as national actors in terms of both objectives and the ability to accomplish them in the Third World.

In addition, as members of the Soviet-East European alliance structures, East European nations are subject to interbloc obligations that may or may not be defined by Moscow and that may coincide or compete with their own national interests. Moreover, a third potential cleavage exists with respect to any individual East European country's perceived interbloc commitments and that country's place in the intra-Communist subsystem.[10] Take, for example, what appears to be the influence of the Romanian-Chinese connection on how Bucharest chooses to allocate its resources in the Third World.[11] It is within these potentially conflicting frameworks that interests underlying East European expanding contact with the Third World must be considered.

East European Interests

Broadly speaking, scholars differentiate between those East European states that coordinate with Moscow's expressed interests in the Third World (the German Democratic Republic, Czechoslovakia, and Bulgaria) and Romania with its actively independent Third World policy. If these positions are considered to be a continuum, Poland and Hungary do fall somewhere in the middle. However, since Poland has consistently ranked second in the total amount of both exports and imports to the LDCs for three decades and more than double the extent of Hungarian involvement in 1980,[12] it is difficult to agree with Vernon Aspaturian that Poland and Hungary should be grouped together under the label of "relative abstention" from assistance activities.[13] Whether or not such trade is an "assistance" can be argued; that it represents a different order of involvement cannot.

In terms of political interests, all East European states share the felt need to be more visible as national actors in the international system and have an interest in the degree to which their Third World activity contributes to such visibility and prestige. These states differ over their Third World involvement vis-à-vis the Soviet Union. Bulgaria, Czechoslovakia, and the GDR consider their activity as a positive demonstration of alliance (interbloc) obligations that gains points and perhaps more tangible rewards as well in terms of bilateral relations with Moscow. Romania deliberately cultivates the Third World as an alternative to closer interbloc relations. Here, indeed, perhaps "in-betweens" is the best we can do to classify Poland and Hungary, at least given the lack of country-specific data.

As members of the international communist movement, East European policymakers have a shared ideological interest in the revolutionary potential of the Third World. They are in principle committed both to winning the hearts and minds of Third World elites to Marxism-Leninism and to strengthening "noncapitalist" aspects of Third World economies.[14] And there is no doubt that "socialist/proletarian" solidarity played and plays a role in channeling East European economic as well as political involvement toward those Third World countries perceived as being on a "noncapitalist path of development" with a "socialist orientation." Thereby East European-Third World relations become a component of image-building in the intra-Communist world that, from the in-system perspective, contributes to changing the balance of forces between communism and capitalism. In this sense, East European interests remain tied to Soviet global objectives, and the Third World functions as an ideological/strategic resource in East-West competition. Nonetheless, there is a considerable gap between rhetoric and reality when it comes to such ideological interests, and it is exceedingly difficult to separate out ideological and economic considerations.

Not surprisingly, East European economic interests vis-à-vis the Third World vary according to their natural resource base. From this perspective the relatively less well endowed countries (the GDR, Czechoslovakia, Hungary, Bulgaria) could be presumed to have more incentive to seek needed raw materials abroad. However, all East European countries have a growing need for energy resources, especially since the 1975 CMEA pricing-mechanism shift to a "moving average" for Soviet oil, which had fallen well below world market prices. That need can be expected to increase as the Soviet supply becomes less available and, in any case, must be paid for with hard currency. Hence, East Europeans come to the Third World as buyers. They also come as sellers looking for markets for products that frequently still do not meet Western standards. Where they look and what sort of incentive packages are involved depend largely on what they want to see and who is interested and able to buy. Nor does the composition of trade turnover stay the same over time, as indicated by V.D. Chopra's comments on Indian-Bulgarian trade.[15]

There is also the virtually unexplored dimension of political-culture-policy linkages in relation to specific East European target areas in the Third World. Romanian is a Romance language. It is at least plausible that the Romanian perception of itself as a Latin culture played a role in the extent of Bucharest's activity in the Western hemisphere, or indeed facilitated Bucharest's major political commitments in Latin America and Latin American receptivity to such contacts.[16]

From a historical perspective, there has been some attention to the possible relationship between former German ties to Africa and the heavy GDR focus on African Third World nations.[17] A still more provocative domestic–foreign policy linkage to be explored is the possibility that the institutional interests of the GDR military and security apparatuses may function to reinforce Soviet policy needs.[18] This aspect should not be discounted, although it would unquestionably be problematical to research. The East German National People's Army (NVA) is a military in search of a mission. To whatever extent morale needs and the imperatives of professional advancement are satisfied in Africa, the NVA's role becomes less of a potential domestic, interbloc, or even European problem.

Finally, the personal preferences and situations of East European policy elites are indigenous factors that influence the degree of country-specific involvement around the world. One does not need a biographical profile to conclude that Ceausescu finds his extensive Third World summit diplomacy gratifying, contributing to his personality cult as well as to Romania's identity as "a developing socialist country," structurally similar to much of the Third World.[19]

The Capability Factor

If we understand capability to refer to the ability of any set of policymakers to expend resources in such a manner as to achieve objectives, then the capabilities of East European actors in the Third World are a function of three variables: the amount of resources available, the political/technical skill in utilizing them, and the receptivity of Third World target areas. Conversely, capabilities may be seen as extent and type of actual engagement in various regions, such as the number of East German military forces abroad. In terms of dollars, weapons, and military/technical personnel, there is obviously a counting problem, and sources disagree.[20] Moreover, even if we had a perfectly accurate picture of the extent of such involvement, it would reveal discouragingly little about the political efficacy for the East European country involved. Therefore, capabilities as a function of resources, skill, and receptivity need to be considered.

The question of resources is inevitably tied to the state of East European economies, for although the percentage amounts may be small, if we take official U.S. figures for 1954–84, Eastern Europe provided $14.9 billion (in U.S. dollars) in assistance to LDCs, which in absolute terms is certainly significant for the countries paying the bill.[21] Relatively speaking, the total amount would be slightly less than half that provided by the Soviets. Indeed, looking at the 1984 figures of $1.7 billion and $2.3 billion, respectively, it seems that for that year East European collective contributions surpassed the halfway mark in terms of Soviet aid.

For East European economies, as with the Soviet economy itself, the 1970s were a time when it was possible to avoid the hard choices.[22] Eastern bloc economies appeared stronger than they were. Western bankers needed to recycle OPEC petrodollars. East European planners faced increasing energy costs and declining Soviet willingness to subsidize their growing energy needs. Albeit ultimately illusory, detente legitimized more independent East European foreign policies and facilitated East-West economic deals. In such circumstances, the loans were virtually inevitable. It is always less painful, in the short run, to live on borrowed money than to cut back on domestic consumption or investment.

Conversely, the 1980s have become a time of agonizing reappraisal for East European economic planners. Western economic recession, high interest rates, and economic insecurity added up to bad news for East European policymakers and ordinary citizens alike. There is a price to pay for interdependence. Whatever pleasure party ideologues may have taken in these "contradictions of capitalism," East European economies increasingly dependent on new loans suffered. To make matters worse, the political climate soured in the backlash that followed the Soviet December 1979 intervention in Afghanistan. The hard choices could no longer be ignored.

Although economic data on Eastern Europe do not always agree, it is clear that debt servicing crises limit East European economic options to varying degrees that will undoubtedly affect these countries' capabilities in the Third World.[23] Poland's debt servicing ratio may have improved substantially in 1982, but the Polish economy is still in deep trouble. It is not surprising that after three decades of ranking second in both imports from and exports to less developing countries, Poland's imports in 1982 were almost one-third of the 1980 total, and Poland ranked last in terms of the East European six. Whether or not we have supportive data, it is probably safe to say that other forms of Polish interaction with the Third World also reflected declining Polish economic capability. There is an understandable effort to hold the line on imports while exporting as much as possible, and although imports have gradually increased since 1981 while exports dropped from the peak $1.5 billion to an estimated $1.2 billion in 1985, the overall balance of trade remains in Warsaw's favor.

Conversely, despite its own declining growth rate, Romania's Western debt has dropped to $6.5 billion in 1985. Bucharest's trade turnover with LDCs remained substantially higher than that of all other East European countries. This is so notwithstanding growing internal criticism of the extent or perhaps the nature of Bucharest's economic commitments in the Third World. Ceausescu has personally responded to such grumbling by reminding Romanian economists of the political dimension of these ties.[24]

Although East Germany has the second largest Western debt in absolute terms ($13.9 billion in 1985), the GDR economy is under considerably less strain than that of most of its East European neighbors. And while it is also true that a substantially higher percent of that economy is devoted to defense spending (7.7% of GNP in 1984), it is likely that the size of the GDR deficit budget reflects the cost of keeping East German military and security personnel in Africa. There is no sign that they will be coming back, but the number of East Germans stationed in Africa appears to be decreasing.[25] This decrease parallels a drop in East German trade with the Third World; by 1985 GDR exports ranked fifth.

While the East German economy certainly has more resources available, Bulgaria has benefited from better economic management than much of Eastern Europe. Although Sofia's Western debt is thought to have jumped back up from the 1984 low point of $2.2 billion to $3.1 billion in 1985, it is still among the lowest in Eastern Europe. Data on the Bulgarian growth rate indicate that there may be problems in the future, if the projected drop from 2.7 percent in 1984 to a -.8 percent for 1985 actually took place.[26] We do not yet know what that fluctuation might mean for the 3.9 percent of Bulgarian GNP going to defense expenditures in 1984, for example.

Without a doubt, Bulgaria is the most understudied East European country from all perspectives.[27] This academic blindness is particularly shortsighted in terms of East European capabilities in the Third World. Bulgaria may, in fact, be the most interesting of the six countries, not from the perspective of absolute amount or potential resources to devote—although even these indicators are not negligible—but in Sofia's steadily increasing involvement. Bulgarian exports moved from sixth place in 1960 and 1970 to third place in 1980. In 1981 and 1982, Bulgaria was second only to Romania and surpassed the East German absolute amount in 1984 and 1985 figures. On the other hand, Bulgarian imports, while generally increasing, are well under the export figure, indicating a strongly favorable balance of trade from the Bulgarian perspective.

Hungary has the third highest Western debt ($11.7 billion in 1985), and the Hungarian economy is projected to continue to grow only at 0.8 percent in 1985. Hungarian defense spending rose sharply from 2.2 percent of the GNP in 1983 to 3.9 percent in 1984. Hungarian trade with LDCs has declined since 1982, with a less favorable export-import ratio than in the case of Bulgaria.

Czechoslovakia has a range of problems stemming from 1968 that influence both prospects for economic reform and decisions about resource allocation. Prague's Western debt is relatively low ($2.8 billion in 1985). Its projected annual growth rate for 1985 was 1.4 percent. Conversely, Czechoslovak defense expenditures are relatively high (4.0% of GNP in 1984). The likelihood is that this is determined by domestic and European concerns. Despite the reportedly still flourishing arms trade, there is no substantiated evidence to indicate that the Czechoslovak army is militarily involved in the Third World to any significant extent.[28]

On the issue of arms transfers as a component of capability, the data, albeit contradictory, indicate rising absolute amounts subject to fluctuation. According to one estimate, East European arms accounted for perhaps 8 percent of the 1983 world's arms trade and roughly half of those arms going to the Third World.[29] To what extent these arms were intended for, or actually succeeded in, buying political influence or facilitating access to needed raw materials or favorable trade terms is simply unknown. This analysis tends to agree with David Albright's conclusion that the influence-building involved is just as likely targeted toward Moscow as toward the Third World recipient.[30] Although Albright is correct in observing that Warsaw Pact coordination exists in terms of what appears to be "a socialist division of labor" vis-à-vis the Third World, putting it that way is somewhat misleading. Given that such coordination extends beyond the pact in terms of Cuban involvement, this is much more likely an intra-Communist than an interbloc affair. Whether or not the bottom line is the same, such considerations determine policy channels and institutional instruments. And here, there seems to be some agreement that the alliance mechanism is not involved.[31]

As to the question of political/technical capabilities, very little can be said with certainty; what we think we know may be a function of traditional national stereotypes. Nonetheless, it is not farfetched to assume that the infrastructure of prewar commercial and diplomatic contacts in Asia, Africa, and Latin America contributed to Czechoslovakia's prominent Third World role in the 1950s and 1960s. Past experience provided a cadre of skilled personnel, presumably with a higher level of understanding of how to operate effectively in Third World cultures. That advantage was reinforced by Prague's long-term reputation in the international arms trade. Even in the 1920s and 1930s, the Skoda works were one of the major weapons producers in the world.

In the postwar period, the new Communist regime aggressively exploited opportunities in the Third World, while Czechoslovak United Nations diplomacy seems to have effectively buttressed the country's Third World objectives.[32] It is not surprising that Prague became the mecca of Third World students seeking technical training to assist their countries on the road to modernization and industrial development. This combination of political and technical ability made Czechoslovakia number one among the East European countries in the Third World for almost two decades.

Despite strenuous efforts to win friends and recognition in the Third World, East Germany had little luck until the signing of the Basic Treaty with the Federal Republic of Germany in December 1972, which removed the pressure on Third World countries to choose between the two Germanys.[33] This freed East German political capabilities to play a major role just at the time when Czechoslovak political and economic capabilities were reeling under the impact of the 1968 invasion by its "fraternal allies." To the extent that the sparse literature we have agrees on anything, it is that among the countries of "real socialism," the GDR has taken over Czechoslovakia's position, at least in terms of supplying military assistance. Whatever may be the long-run evaluation, there is little doubt in the short run that the East Germans are sought out by Third World governments because they are seen as having significant technical capabilities in this regard. That perception may well be the reality in terms of the education that a Third World student can get at an East German university or institute.

The issue of political capability can be measured broadly by the extent of activity, in which case the GDR presence appears to be alive and flourishing. The fact that economic involvement has been cut back does not indicate much about political skills.

Finally, although Romanian technical skills do not have the reputation of those available in Czechoslovakia and East Germany, the sustained Romanian efforts in the Third World have demonstrated impressive political capabilities. This is particularly so with regard to Bucharest's interactions with the nonaligned movement, where Romania has a truly unique status despite the barrier to membership because of its participation in the Warsaw Pact.[34] Romania's ability to portray Bucharest as a consistent friend of the Third World and, indeed, to stay on good terms with both sides in a range of Third World conflicts where other East Europeans have been forced to choose, demonstrates political skill, even if Romania does benefit from being less visibly tied to Moscow.

With respect to accessibility, those East European societies with former Third World ties that could be reactivated did have an advantage. However, more broadly, East European access to the Third World has not been burdened with the suspicions of newly independent nations concerning Eastern or Western superpower intentions. Even Czechoslovakia and East Germany, commonly regarded in the West as the most faithful Soviet surrogates, have fared well. This relatively easy access is partly a function of the sheer power discrepancy involved when most Third World countries deal with the Soviet Union and partly a perception of Third

World policymakers concerning their own potential freedom of maneuver. But in either case, those East European regimes interested in expanding their Third World involvement benefit from the receptivity of their target areas. This does not mean to imply that the situation is intrinsically contrary to Soviet interests. There is some reason to think that contacts begun with a more acceptable East European partner may facilitate Soviet access that might otherwise be more difficult to achieve.[35] And certainly Soviet decisionmakers see advantages to having their East European allies share the bill for Soviet global objectives.

Sorting out actual East European resources disbursed to the Third World is complicated by the problem of aggregated Soviet and East European data. However, we can say that between 1975 and 1981, East European military agreements with non-Communist LDCs almost tripled from $635.0 million to $2.5 billion and accounted for more than one third of the Soviet $6.5 billion commitment. Since 1981 such East European agreements have dropped off dramatically to an estimated U.S. $845.0 million in 1984.[36] East European economic credits to LDCs totaled $14.9 or $16.1 billion in the 1954–84 period using Department of State and CIA data, respectively. In either case, the amount equals roughly half the Soviet effort. Unfortunately, this aid is broken out by recipients, not by East European senders. The pattern of recipients, however, shows some interesting deviations from Moscow's spending in the Third World. In Latin America, for example, both State Department and CIA sources agree that the East European six invested more heavily than the Soviet Union itself over the last twenty years. Brazil is a major East European partner, while by 1984 what appeared to be steadily rising support for the Sandinistas dropped sharply despite the upward trend of Soviet credits.[37] Indeed using the State Department's total of $14.9 billion, only $1.5 went to "Marxist client states."

More than twice as many East European economic technicians work in developing countries as do their Soviet counterparts, 86,390 and 39,570, respectively. According to earlier CIA data, between 1965 and 1979 the number of academic students being trained in Eastern Europe grew almost five times to reach 24,024. But by 1984 we have only aggregate data of 92,950 Third World students studying in the Soviet Union and Eastern Europe. In 1984 some 21,335 Soviet and East European military technicians reportedly worked in the LDCs—interestingly, more than twice as many in Syria (5,300) as in Afghanistan (2,025). From 1955 to 1984, reportedly some 78,445 military personnel from the Third World trained in the Soviet Union and Eastern Europe—including more than 9,000 from Indonesia, a higher figure than for Afghanistan, if it is correct.[38]

In short, the statistics are conflicting. We know that the number of LDC students studying in Eastern Europe is probably growing, as is the combined number of LDC military men training in Warsaw Pact countries. There is no systematic breakdown for making USSR-East European comparisons or for charting internal East European trends.

The fragmentary data that we have indicate that the country-specific pattern essentially corresponds with the more multi-dimensional definition of capabilities. In both senses, Czecho-slovakia's capabilities have declined. East Germany's expanded until 1982 and then appeared to drop back. Romania's capabilities are substantial but may be increasingly overextended economically. Keeping in mind that capabilities are integrally related to objectives, we can now draw some conclusions about the country perspectives.

COUNTRY-SPECIFIC OBJECTIVES

Bulgaria

Without questioning the image of Bulgaria as a "faithful ally"/ Soviet surrogate,[39] in a range of Sofia's Third World connections (i.e., interactions with those LDCs currently defined as having a socialist orientation and being in support of liberation movements), we can tentatively say that Bulgarian objectives in the Third World are becoming increasingly economic. In 1982, for example, there were five Bulgarian-Kuwaiti agreements: a trade agreement with the United Arab Emirates; Bulgarian parliamentary delegations to Iraq, Jordan, and Syria; and a trade agreement with Nigeria.[40] In 1983 Libya remained Bulgaria's largest Third World trading partner, and much of Bulgaria's activity was with potentially "revolutionary" prospects; but even here the cooperation focused on the economic dimensions such as "further exploitation of mineral resources."[41] These dealings have not displaced the ideological/ political objectives symbolized by Bulgarian support of the PLO; the estimated 300 Bulgarian specialists in Angola; arms aid to South Yemen; and 1985 hospitality in Sofia to the Libyan Foreign Minister Ali Abdel Salam Turayki, Zimbabwe Prime Minister Robert Mugabe, and Nicaraguan President Daniel Ortega. But in the context of the sagging Bulgarian economy, there is at least the possibility that Sofia's economic needs have caught up with its revolutionary fervor as an incentive for expanding Third World contacts.

Czechoslovakia

Prague is perhaps the clearest case of the rhetoric being out of tune with the reality. Although Czechoslovakia's verbal support for "progressive forces" in the Third World is still strong, as is the traditional Czechoslovak arms trade, Czechoslovak initiative and trade with the Third World have not recovered from the trauma of 1968. When arms are sold to both sides, as in the case of the Ethiopian government and the Eritrean rebels, there is some reason to question the ideological purity of motives.[42] Pressures from the declining Czechoslovak economy, increasing energy needs, and dwindling foreign exchange appear to have more to do with Prague's choice of trading partners than does ideology. In 1978 the number of foreign technical personnel being trained in Czechoslovakia reportedly had declined to roughly 1,000.[43] There are no recent figures, but Czech and Slovak specialists currently working in the Third World are probably being paid in hard currency.

Certainly during those euphoric days of the Prague Spring, some observers blamed the poor condition of the Czechoslovak economy on overextending in terms of Third World commitments. This was part of the impetus for a "national foreign policy." Today, the country's deepening economic crisis[44] makes it all the more likely that Czechoslovakia's primary objectives in the Third

World are to cut costs and gain access to needed energy resources—what we might call political disengagement in favor of what in 1968 was termed "our real possibilities."[45]

East Germany

Although the urgency that drove East Germany to search for international recognition in the Third World declined with the signing of the 1972 Basic Treaty between the two Germanys, the GDR still bears the scars of the more than twenty years of rejection by the international community. Consequently, the need for international status felt by East German policymakers is more intense, and the Third World becomes an arena within which the GDR can overcome the lingering image of being "the other Germany." Indeed, note the references to Berlin as the capital of the GDR that appear in some of the East German Treaties of Friendship and Cooperation with Third World countries of "socialist orientation," despite Berlin's international status under the 1972 Quadripartite Agreement.[46]

Moreover, the objective of distinguishing itself as the good, socialist Germany, as opposed to its neocolonialist, capitalist West German rival, establishes a firm coincidence of interest between Moscow and Pankow in terms of targeting East German activity in support of revolutionary potential and Marxist-Leninist regimes, symbolized by increased East German-Nicaraguan high-level visits and economic assistance in 1985. The portrayal of the GDR as a Soviet surrogate oversimplifies a complex symbiotic relationship within which the East German objective includes not only the interbloc dimension of meeting alliance obligations but an agenda of intra-Communist image-building as well.

Nor are economic objectives irrelevant. By 1982 roughly one-third of GDR exports to the Soviet Union were needed to cover the cost of Soviet oil.[47] Since East Germany has an increasingly massive Soviet debt as well as Western debt servicing, it is not surprising that its trade pattern departs from its military commitments and the rhetoric of fraternal solidarity. According to Brigitte Schulz, in 1980, 73 percent of GDR exports went to only fifteen LDCs. Of that amount, the oil-exporting countries of Algeria, Iraq, Iran,

Libya, and Nigeria received almost half, as opposed to roughly the 16 percent that went to Angola, Mozambique, and Ethiopia.[48] In such circumstances, the GDR undoubtedly shares the general East European objective of access to needed raw materials, energy, and hard currency payments for technical services.

Hungary

Hungarian objectives in the Third World are visibly more limited than those of other East European actors. Although there is some agreement that this amounts to "relative abstention" when it comes to assistance activities, that abstention does not apply to economic activity more broadly defined.[49] By the early 1980s, Hungary had developed trade relations with some 86 developing countries.[50] Notwithstanding preliminary 1985 figures, which indicate a decline, Hungary has generally moved forward as an importer from the Third World. Indeed, by 1983 Hungarian imports edged above those of the GDR in absolute dollar figures, making Hungary the second largest importer in the Eastern bloc for 1983–84. Yet Hungarian exports to the Third World in the 1980s are consistently in sixth place. If one balances high-level 1982 Hungarian visits to Burma, the Philippines, Kuwait, and Brazil against the hospitality granted to Yassir Arafat in February 1982, it is hard not to agree with Scott Blau that Budapest's objectives in the Third World are primarily economic and essentially pragmatic.[51] Less persuasive is his conclusion that such trade relations are of limited domestic significance. While that may have been the case before Moscow cut back on its subsidies to the East European energy needs in the form of below world market CMEA prices, since the mid-1970s the Hungarians have faced increasing costs for Soviet oil that must be paid for in hard currency. It is likely that Hungary's recent memberships in the International Finance Cooperation and the International Development Association, officially to facilitate Hungarian "participation in Third World development projects," are connected to just such energy needs.

Rhetorically, Hungarian support for Soviet Third World positions should be seen as a part of a consistent trade-off by Budapest that involves the appearance of foreign policy conformity in return for substantial domestic autonomy in the form of the Hungarian economic reform. However, it is not out of the question that Hungarian support for the PLO is intended to win points with Arab energy suppliers as well as with Moscow.

Poland

Although it falls among Gilberg's "in-betweens" and Aspaturian's "relative abstainers" from assistance to the Third World, for three decades Poland ranked second among the East European six in both imports and exports from LDCs. At the same time, the number of African students studying in Poland more than doubled between the 1960s and 1970s, reaching 3,000 by 1977. Throughout the 1970s, Poland provided military aid to Algeria, Angola, and Mozambique, although at a level likely below that of the East Germans. In addition, "many" Polish experts worked in Ethiopia and Ethiopian military delegations met with Polish officers.[52] (Given Poland's collapse into martial law on December 13, 1981, it is a moot point as to who was influencing whom in such discussions.) Still, the pattern is reasonably clear in terms of a mix of ideological/political objectives that did not stray significantly from Moscow's order of priorities.

Nonetheless, like Hungary, Poland's primary objectives in the Third World, even before Warsaw's troubles in the 1980s, appear to have been economic. Currently, these objectives are dominated by the search for needed raw materials (which became particularly urgent as the Western debt grew because Third World clearing agreements made it possible to receive the needed imports without expending hard currency) and the need to sell domestic products. Scientific and technical cooperation are seen as mutually beneficial, as are joint economic ventures, although there is scant information on the extent of such collaborations.

Given the disastrous state of the Polish economy since 1980, it is not surprising that Polish imports to the Third World dropped sharply, nor that Warsaw's primary objective has become the search for hard currency, symbolized by some 8,000 Polish technicians reported to be working in Iraq.[53] Overall, the Polish balance of trade with LDCs in the 1980s is clearly in Warsaw's favor.

Romania

Romania's political objectives in the Third World flow from Bucharest's self-defined status as a socialist developing country. Romania has assiduously cultivated the acceptance of its developing identity through mounting a campaign to become a de facto member of the nonaligned movement, joining the Group of 77, and establishing extensive bilateral ties throughout the Third World. Since Romania first attended the Nonaligned Foreign Ministers' Meeting in Lima in 1975 as a guest and then the 1976 NAM Summit in Colombo,[54] Romanian guests have become a permanent feature at nonaligned summits, foreign ministers' meetings, and other ad hoc sessions.[55] Romanian speeches appear in conference proceedings, and articles written by Romanians are published in *The Nonaligned World*, an international journal devoted to the Nonaligned Movement.

Since the second NAM Summit, held in Cairo in 1964, the Romanian head of state has sent a personal message to each summit conference, a practice begun by Gheorghiu-Dej and turned into a fine art by Ceausescu. Indeed, according to Romanian data, between 1965 and 1982 Ceausescu personally visited seventy-seven nonaligned states, while heads of state of forty-three nonaligned nations paid eighty-five official visits to Romania, thereby creating a substantial political/legal infrastructure. By 1982, twelve treaties of friendship and cooperation/collaboration in areas of mutual interest had been signed.[56]

Another unique political objective can be seen in Bucharest's sustained efforts to assist in the peaceful settlement of disputes that wrack the nonaligned movement. Although the attempts to play a mediating role in the Iran-Iraq war have apparently fallen on deaf ears, Romanian shuttle diplomacy designed to de-escalate the Lebanese civil war received considerable international recognition and appreciation. Bucharest's peace initiatives in the Middle East serve the practical purpose of allowing Romania to maintain good relations with Israel as well as with the PLO and with its Arab supporters. Such a political balancing act is no mean trick.

This is not to imply that Romanian Third World activity has no ideological agenda. There appears to have been substantial military involvement with those African states of socialist orientation in the 1970s, even reports that Romanian officers trained tank crews in Mozambique in the use of Soviet-made T-34 and T-54 tanks.[57] However, if we consider that Romania reportedly supplied weapons to all three of the liberation movements in Angola and that it signed the 1978 Treaty of Friendship and Cooperation with the Khmer Rouge, Romania's ideological agenda takes on a Byzantine complexity. To sort it out would require case-by-case analysis that is beyond the scope of this chapter. Nonetheless, in the most general terms, we can say that Romania takes both its socialist and developing identities seriously and that Third World involvements reflect a desire to maintain intra-Communist credibility while gaining acceptance of Romania as a developing country.

It is also quite possible that a range of Romanian Third World activity is motivated by the need for pro-Soviet trade-offs in the interbloc political game that Romania plays by virtue of its East European identity. In short, the Third World may well be still another arena in which Bucharest's political objective is to blur the lines between anti-Soviet, autonomous, and supportive activity in order to prevent polarization that would increase the risk of Moscow's retaliation.

Finally, although Romanian economic objectives in the Third World have clearly taken second place to political considerations, economic imperatives have played and most likely will play an increasingly important role in that country's relations with the developing countries around the world. Romania's joint ventures focus on development of needed raw materials, and its peace efforts are simultaneously aimed at preventing interruption of desperately needed resources. Whether we take Romanian or Western figures, Romania's foreign trade with the Third World has increased from less than 10 percent in 1970 to almost 30 percent in the 1980s. Notwithstanding a shift back in the direction of intra-CMEA trade in the preliminary 1985 figures, the reportedly more than 130 economic projects that have been commissioned or are now being constructed with Romanian technical assistance are largely a reflection of mutual economic advantage as calculated in Bucharest. And quite likely, many of the approximately 15,000 Romanian engineering specialists working in the Third World are doing so as much for hard cash as for solidarity.

PROBLEMS AND PROSPECTS

State Department and CIA data indicate that East European military sales to Third World countries almost tripled between

1980 and 1981, then fluctuated with continued high delivery rates. Economic credits and grants from Eastern Europe, after rising steadily for three decades, dropped in 1981 to roughly half of the 1980 figure and declined steadily for another two years before surging back in 1984 to an estimated U.S. $1.7 billion.[58] Despite fluctuations in East European LDC imports and exports in the 1980s, the absolute amounts are substantially greater than such exchanges in the 1960s or 1970s.

This picture reflects the troubled state of East European economies and ever-rising energy needs throughout the region. To whatever extent Moscow cannot or will not continue to subsidize East European energy needs (or demands hard currency to do so), the East Europeans are forced to look elsewhere. The only place to look in terms of raw materials, which can sometimes be obtained in complex barter arrangements instead of for hard cash, is in the Third World. This inevitably tilts East European objectives toward economic rather than ideological considerations. Indeed, even the East Germans may be increasingly pressed to calculate profits instead of revolutionary prospects. This is not to say that East European activity, particularly in the Middle East, will be any less problematical from a Western point of view. Arms sold for economic benefit can be just as destabilizing regionally as those transferred for ideological payoffs.

If the increasing economic importance of the Third World to East Europeans is self-evident, the higher risk factor hypothesized in this analysis is perhaps somewhat less so. However, this too is rooted in the painful economic dilemmas facing planners throughout the region. During the 1970s Western scholars talked about "mature communism," while Western bankers certainly assumed that East European socialism had created stable enough authoritarian systems to make attractive credit risks. It was a time of optimism that obscured the fact that those East European Communists who rode to power on the coattails of the Red Army still faced endemic crises of legitimacy. Soviet liberation and scientific socialism are no substitutes for indigenous revolutionary myth. The rational legal basis of legitimacy embodied in East European constitutions is visibly stronger on form than content. Nor, with the exception of Ceausescu, can the present generation of political elites take comfort in their own charisma. Whatever the official party line, East European leaders know that they are often perceived as the lesser of many evils by large parts of their populations.

It is not surprising that East European Communist parties fell back on legitimacy through performance in the form of high growth rates, social mobility, and steadily rising standards of living. Tactically, Communist leaders tried to improve their image with mixtures of cautious nationalism, consumerism, and cooptation of technical/cultural intelligentsia. Poland provides a graphic example of what can happen if performance slips too far. And as with Malenkov's New Course in the 1950s, East European systems are much more vulnerable than the Soviet Union itself, although Moscow certainly faces some of the same dilemmas.

To the degree East Europeans find the daily food shortages more difficult or feel that they are backsliding or sense that the door to tomorrow is slamming shut, there will be less public patience with funds siphoned off into Third World adventures. This is probably true even of those joint enterprises that actually are based on mutual advantage, in that the rhetoric of solidarity obscures the hardnosed economic reasons for much East European Third World activity at home as well as abroad. Moreover, engaging in honest discussion of why escalating Third World involvement may be necessary would border on public anti-Sovietism and would carry a range of other undesirable consequences. Thus, even as East European policymakers are pushed toward expanding their Third World economic activity, the danger of domestic backlash and instability grows. It is this dilemma that accounts for the ongoing resistance to Mozambique's efforts to gain membership in the CMEA.

Finally, the trade-offs Moscow faces in pressing its East European allies into supporting its commitments economically are also higher risk. Czechoslovakia in 1968 provides a negative model. To the extent that Czechoslovak overcommitment in the Third World undermined that country's economy, it was a factor in events leading to the Prague Spring. Czechoslovakia was badly burned again when Soviet efforts at influence-building collapsed as Anwar Sadat set out on the road to Camp David in the mid-1970s.[59] We do not know the role played by Third World adventures in the economic morass out of which Solidarity emerged to challenge the leading role of the Polish United Workers' Party. However, it is quite clear that political pressures generated by the Soviet intervention in Afghanistan contributed to the sense of urgency that led to Gierek's fatal attempt to cut back on Polish food subsidies in the summer of 1980. Whatever short-term-plus advantage the Soviets derive from even the most supportive East European conduct in the Third World, if it comes at the cost of major destabilization of the East European country involved, it is a long-run minus. The price of East European proxies may be the political viability of these regimes.

Indeed, even when such economic/political destabilization does not occur, there is an intangible long-term cost. By definition, such activity erodes the cohesion of the Soviet bloc and leads to boundary disintegration between the socialist and the developing worlds. To the degree that it succeeds, it increases the sense of efficacy of the East European countries as national actors. There is a very human tendency of East European leaders to take credit for success. If efforts fail, as did Czechoslovak investments in Egypt, Moscow gets the blame. Whether or not such hostility is openly expressed, it undoubtedly influences subsequent intra-CMEA bargaining. Indeed, there is a double edge to East European interbloc obligations in this regard. Even after the Soviets had been expelled from Somalia, for example, the GDR maintained youth brigades there, a move that could be variously interpreted as keeping a foot in the door for Moscow's return or as a lack of solidarity.[60]

As for the prospects, it would seem that East European involvement in the Third World is rather like Pandora's box. The lid is off; it is not at all clear what will come out. After all, the Third World is a highly unstable environment. East European capabilities aside, objectives often depend on opportunities. For East European policymakers, as for their comrades in the Kremlin, it is not always easy to tell whether one is winning or losing today, much less tomorrow.

NOTES

1. In my search for sometimes nonexistent data and in the struggle to sift through the often contradictory material available, I gratefully acknowledge the research assistance of Brigitte H. Schulz, the indispensable resources of the Harvard Russian Research Center and the Boston University African Studies Library, and the helpfulness of Documents Librarian Claire Loranz at the Margaret

Clapp Library, Wellesley College. Schulz's selected bibliography of English language, West German, and East European sources is included in the original working paper, "Proxies, Partners, or Competitors? The East-South Connection" (Washington, D.C.: Woodrow Wilson International Center for Scholars, International Security Studies Program, 1986).

2. Leonid Brezhnev, "Speech at the 26th Communist Party Congress," *Pravda*, 23 February 1981; *Current Digest of the Soviet Press*, 25 March 1981, p. 7.

3. For a more elaborate categorization scheme, see Michael Radu's introductory chapter in his pioneering collection, *Eastern Europe and the Third World: East vs. South* (New York: Praeger Special Studies, 1981).

4. Hannes Adomeit and Robert Boardman, eds., *Foreign Policy Making in Communist Countries* (New York: Praeger, 1979) underlines this problem, as does Roger E. Kanet's straightforward critique, "Research on East European Foreign Policy: Other Needs, Other Areas, New Directions," in Ronald H. Linden, ed., *The Foreign Policies of Eastern Europe: New Approaches* (New York: Praeger, 1980), pp. 311–12.

5. Kanet, "Research on East European Foreign Policy," p. 313. Robert and Elizabeth Bass's fine analysis of early East European involvement in Africa in Zbigniew Brzezinski's *Africa and the Communist World* (Stanford, Calif.: Stanford University Press, 1963), pp. 84–115 is a notable exception. The norm was for books on East European countries to have one chapter summerizing foreign policy in which the Third World was seldom so much as mentioned.

6. See Daniel N. Nelson, "Eastern Europe and the Non-Communist World," in Stephen Fischer Galati, ed., *Eastern Europe in the 1980s* (Boulder, Colo.: Westview Press, 1981); Vernon V. Aspaturian's detailed analysis, "Eastern Europe in World Perspective," in Teresa Rakowska Harmstone, ed., *Communism in Eastern Europe*, 2d ed. (Bloomington: Indiana University Press, 1984); and Edwina Moreton's chapter, "Foreign Policy Perspectives in Eastern Europe," in Karen Dawisha and Philip Hanson, eds., *Soviet-East European Dilemmas: Coercion, Competition, and Consent* (London: Heinemann, 1981). Perhaps not surprisingly, attention has focused on the areas of immediate policy concern: see Trond Gilberg, "East European Military Assistance to the Third World," in John F. Copper and Daniel S. Papp, eds., *Communist Nations' Military Assistance* (Boulder, Colo.: Westview, 1983); Roger E. Kanet, "Military Relations Between Eastern Europe and Africa," in Bruce E. Arlinghaus, ed., *Arms for Africa: Military Assistance and Foreign Policy in the Developing World* (Lexington, Mass.: D.C. Heath, 1983); and

"East European States," in Thomas H. Henriksen, ed., *Communist Powers and Sub-Saharan Africa* (Stanford, Calif.: Hoover Institution Press, 1981).

7. Note the discrepancies between the U.S. Department of State, *Conventional Arms Transfers in the Third World, 1971–1981* (Washington, D.C., August 1982) and U.S. Department of State, *Soviet and East European Aid to the Third World* (Washington, D.C., February 1983), or more recently, between the U.S. Department of State, *Warsaw Pact Economic Aid to Non-Communist LDCs, 1984* (Department of State Publications, May 1986) and *CIA Handbook of Economic Statistics, 1986* (U.S. Government Printing Office, September 1986).

8. For a case in point, see the chapters of Condoleeza Rice and Jonathan Dean in David Holloway and Jane M.O. Sharp, eds., *The Warsaw Pact: Alliance in Transition?* (Ithaca, N.Y.: Cornell University Press, 1984).

9. For a general overview, see Andrzej Korbonski, "Eastern Europe," in Robert F. Byrnes, ed., *After Brezhnev: Sources of Soviet Conduct in the 1980s* (Bloomington: Indiana University Press, 1983), pp. 290–344. For elaboration of the hierarchical model, see William Zimmerman, "Hierarchical Regional Systems and the Politics of System Boundaries," *International Organization* 26, no.1 (Winter 1972): 18–36; as applied to the 1980s, William Zimmerman, "Soviet-East European Relations in the 1980s and the Changing International System," in Morris Bornstein, Zvi Gitelman, and William Zimmerman, eds., *East-West Relations and the Future of Eastern Europe* (London: Allen & Unwin, 1981), pp. 88–104.

10. In this sense, I am going somewhat beyond the classification scheme of John Van Oudenaren, *The Soviet Union and Eastern Europe: Options for the 1980s and Beyond* (Santa Monica, Calif.: Rand, 1984). He is concerned primarily with the East-West dimensions without reference to either the intra-Communist dynamic or the Third World.

11. See Michael Radu, "Romania and the Third World: The Dilemma of a 'Free Rider,' " in Radu, ed., *Eastern Europe and the Third World*, p. 249 regarding facilitating Bucharest's relations with Zimbabwe.

12. Tables IV and V in Robin Alison Remington, "Proxies, Partners, or Competitors? The East-South Connection," Working Paper (Washington, D.C.: Woodrow Wilson International Center for Scholars, December 1986).

13. Aspaturian, "Eastern Europe in World Perspective," p. 24.

14. Kanet, "East European States," p. 27.

15. V.D. Chopra, *India and the Socialist World* (New Delhi: Allied Publishers Private Limited, 1983), pp. 166–67.

16. Radu, "Romania and the Third World," p. 241.

17. See Melvin Croan, "A New Afrika Korps?" *The Washington Quarterly*

3, no. 1 (Winter 1980): 21–37, and Jiri Valenta and Shannon Butler, "East German Security Policies in Africa," in Radu, *Eastern Europe and the Third World.*

18. Valenta and Butler, "East German Security Policies in Africa," pp. 148–50.

19. Ceausescu report to the 1972 National Conference of the Romanian Communist Party. This results in a certain ideological sleight of hand when it comes to the Cuban position that the "socialist countries are the natural allies of the nonaligned." See Radu, "Romania and the Third World," pp. 242–43. It also conveniently allows Bucharest to argue that "developed" socialist countries should do their share in terms of the contributions sought in the North-South dialogue without taking on that responsibility for itself, although this view is not always so consistently expressed. See Ionitza Oltenau and Ileana Inoescu, "The New International Economic Order: A Romanian Perspective," in Ervin Laszlo and Joel Kurtzman, eds., *Eastern Europe and the New International Economic Order: Representative Samples of Socialist Perspective* (New York: Pergamon Press, 1980), pp. 45–63.

20. Note the significantly lower German figures for arms sales in the 1970s in Kanet, Tables 10 and 11, "East European States," pp. 44–45. Also Gilberg cites sources that put the number of East German military personnel in Africa in the late 1970s somewhere "between a few hundred and ten thousand." "East European Military Assistance to the Third World," p. 83.

21. U.S. Department of State, *Warsaw Pact Economic Aid to the Non-Communist LDCs, 1984*, p. 2.

22. See Paul Marer, "East European Economies: Achievements, Problems, Prospects," in Teresa Rakowska Harmstone, ed., *Communism in Eastern Europe*, pp. 283–328; also Sarah Meikelejohn Terry, *Economic Stringency, Political Succession and Stability in Eastern Europe,* Occasional Paper 187 (Washington, D.C.: Woodrow Wilson International Center for Scholars, Kennan Institute, April 1984).

23. U.S. Department of State, *CIA Handbook of Economic Statistics, 1986*, p. 2.

24. *Scinteia*, 3 August 1978, quoted in Radu, "Romania and the Third World," p. 257.

25. According to Ruth Leger Sivard, *World Military and Social Expenditures, 1985* (Washington, D.C.: World Priorities, 1985), GDR forces stationed abroad came to 2,290, down from 3,790 in her 1982 edition. Her 1985 figure is very close to that of the IISS, *The Military Balance 1985–86* (London: IISS, 1985), whose 2,370 included 75 East Germans in South Yemen and another 5 in Guinea. However, the direction is not the same because *The Military Balance, 1982–83*

(London: IISS, 1982) identified only 2,270 East German military personnel abroad. Neither source mentions the Reagan administration's reported figure of 60 East Europeans in Nicaragua.

26. U.S. Department of State, *CIA Handbook of Economic Statistics, 1986*, p. 40.

27. Articles on Bulgarian foreign policy are rare, and there is no Bulgarian chapter in Radu's otherwise excellent collection. Gilberg, "East European Military Assistance to the Third World," pp. 77–81, in Copper and Papp, eds., *Communist Nations' Military Assistance*, explicitly deals with Bulgaria, but he also includes Vietnam, which clearly belongs in the category of intra-Communist dealings.

28. Condoleeza Rice, "Warsaw Pact Reliability: the Czechoslovak People's Army (CLA)," in Daniel N. Nelson, ed., *Soviet Allies: The Warsaw Pact and the Issue of Reliability* (Boulder, Colo.: Westview Press, 1984), p. 139.

29. Thomas H. Snitch, "East European Involvement in the World's Arms Market," *World Military Expenditures and Arms Transfers, 1972–1982* (Washington, D.C.: U.S. Arms Control and Disarmament Agency, April 1984): 117-21.

30. David E. Albright, "The Communist States and Southern Africa," in Gwendolen M. Carter and Patrick O'Meara, eds., *International Politics in Southern Africa* (Bloomington: Indiana University Press, 1981), pp. 3–44.

31. For example, Aspaturian quotes a "knowledgeable East German" to the effect that Soviet bloc policy in the Third World is "coordinated in terms of general objectives through the foreign ministries of the respective countries"; see Aspaturian, "Eastern Europe in World Perspective," p. 24.

32. Vratislav Pechota, "Czechoslovakia and the Third World," in Radu, ed., *Eastern Europe and the Third World*, p. 81.

33. See Michael Sodaro, "The GDR and the Third World: Supplicant and Surrogate," in Radu, ed., *Eastern Europe and the Third World*, pp. 106–40.

34. A detailed discussion of this is provided by two Romanian scholars at the Institute of Political Science, University of Romania, Bucharest. Constantin Vlad and Nicolae Calina, "The Nonaligned Movement, the International System, and Romanian Foreign Policy," *The Nonaligned World* (New Delhi), April-June 1984, pp. 260–72.

35. This is one of the few aspects of East European Third World relations to receive attention in the West as early as the 1950s; see Jan Wszelaki, *Communist Economic Strategy: The Role of East Central Europe* (Washington, D.C.: National Planning Association, 1959), p. 91.

36. U.S. Department of State, *Warsaw Pact Economic Aid to the Non-Communist LDCs, 1984*, p. 19. It depends very much on how one looks at it, for at the same time East European deliveries were high, specifically U.S. $1.8 billion. According to CIA preliminary data for 1985, the combined East European military new commitments equaled those of Moscow at $2.1 billion for the first time. U.S. Department of State, *CIA Handbook of Economic Statistics, 1986*, p. 111.

37. Unfortunately, the otherwise very useful comparison provided by the CIA statistics cannot be made in the case of Nicaragua, because the table on East European aid to less developed countries by recipient includes only nine Latin American countries, and Nicaragua is included in a residual "other" category. U.S. Department of State, *CIA Handbook of Economic Statistics, 1986*, p. 113.

38. U.S. Department of State, *Warsaw Pact Economic Aid to Non-Communist LDCs, 1984*, p. 21. Although it is not broken out, we can assume that the Indonesians were there during the Sukarno period, prior to the 1965 coup attempt that ended in the destruction of the PKI.

39. Gilberg, "Eastern European Military Assistance to the Third World," p. 81.

40. According to Kanet, "East European States," p. 29, Nigeria ranks seventh among Bulgaria's Third World trading partners.

41. John D. Bell, "Bulgaria," in Richard F. Staar, ed., *Yearbook on International Communist Affairs* (Stanford, Calif.: Hoover Institution Press, 1984), p. 310.

42. Radio Free Europe Research, *Czechoslovakia*, 16 April 1975.

43. See Pechota, "Czechoslovakia and the Third World," in Radu, ed., *Eastern Europe and the Third World*, p. 98.

44. Whether or not David Binder's quote from Czechoslovak Prime Minister Lubomir Strougal is apocryphal—"If things go on this way we will have to put up signs at the frontier saying, 'Entering Czechoslovakia, the Museum of an Industrial Society' "—it captures the state of affairs. David Binder, "Czechoslovakia, the East's New Economic Casuality," *New York Times*, 8 November 1981, p. A 21.

45. J. Hanak, in *Reporter* (Prague), 27 March-3 April 1968, quoted in Pechota, "Czechoslovakia and the Third World," p. 90.

46. Sodaro, "The GDR and the Third World," p. 134.

47. Brigitte H. Schulz, "Solidarity or Self-Interest: Socialist Germany in Africa" (Boston University, Walter Rodney African Studies Seminar, 15 October 1984): 10.

48. Ibid., p. 12.

49. Aspaturian, "Eastern Europe in World Perspective," p. 24.

50. Scott Blau, "Hungary and the Third World: An Analysis of East-South Trade," in Radu, ed., *Eastern Europe and the Third World*, p. 170.
51. Ibid., p. 172.
52. Gilberg, "East European Military Assistance to the Third World," p. 85. The extent to which Poland supplies arms to the Third World remains unverified, although Howard Frost notes "rhetorical support" for a number of liberation movements as well as the PLO. "Poland and the Third World: The Primacy of Economic Relations," in Radu, ed., *Eastern Europe and the Third World*, p. 202.
53. U.S. Department of State, *Soviet and East European Aid to the Third World, 1981* (Washington, D.C., 1983).
54. A success that, according to Radu, Bucharest owed to its Latin American connections. "Romania and the Third World," p. 241.
55. Such as the International Roundtable on Nonalignment in the Eighties, held in Petrovaradin, Yugoslavia, August 28–31, 1981, where the Romanian participants' remarks were duly included in the English-language version of the Roundtable proceedings. Cristian Popisteanu, "A Few Remarks Concerning Non-Alignment Policy and Movement in the Struggle for Ensuring International Problems in the '80s," *Nonalignment in the Eighties* (Belgrade: Institute of International Politics and Economics, 1982), pp. 77–85.
56. Vlad and Calina, "The Nonaligned Movement," p. 270.
57. Gilberg, "Eastern European Military Assistance," p. 87.
58. U.S. Department of State, *Warsaw Pact Economic Aid to Non-Communist LDCs, 1984*, p. 2.
59. Condoleeza Rice, "Defense Burden Sharing," p. 82.
60. Edwina Moreton, "Foreign Policy Perspectives in Eastern Europe," p. 190.

5 NEAR EAST

Charles Tripp

INTRODUCTION

In the Near East the persistence as well as the causes of interstate conflict lie in the domestic politics of the states themselves. Both are to a large extent seized by sharply opposed visions of what the state or the region should look like. The issues at stake between the rival parties bring into question their very survival and identity as political communities, and in doing so, raise the troubling questions of the principles upon which the community is to be organized and the territorial extent of its authority. In many respects, therefore, the thrust of politics in these newly established and insecure states is explicitly revolutionary. This tends to equate compromise with betrayal and the forfeit of authority. Violence and force become alternatives to compromise and the necessary adjuncts of revolutionary policies aimed at reshaping the state and the region. When war is not in progress, armed truce becomes the dominant mode of regional relations in an effort to stave off the compromises that regional order would demand.

This general outline, insofar as it points to the depth of the conflicts at issue in the Near East and to the attitudes with which those conflicts are approached, justifies the concern felt when assessing the propensity of the region to conflict. For it would suggest that the persistence of conflict in the area is a structural feature of the politics of its component states and of the political choices of their respective governments.

This chapter will argue that the political condition of a significant proportion of the parties to conflict in the Near East is such that there exists a greater incentive to maintain a readiness, both material and ideological, for war than there is to seek a workable common basis for regional order. This argument is based on the observation that maintaining a readiness for war, while not necessarily indulging in open conflict or doing so only sporadically when regional or domestic circumstances seem to demand, requires fewer profound sacrifices than does determinedly pursuing peace.

This may seem paradoxical or even perverse given the sacrifices required by war. Nevertheless, it will be argued that the sacrifices demanded by the effort to sustain a comprehensive peace are of a different order. In essence, they demand from the parties involved a willingness to abandon the security of the present for the risks of the future. More specifically, they demand from those who claim the right to rule a degree of self-abnegation that puts at stake their very survival. This seems to apply with particular sharpness in the Near East for the specific reason that the governments concerned are each engaged in different ways in the task of consolidating the states they rule by reference to a unifying but exclusive nationalism.

In many senses, this is a revolutionary project within the state and an irredentist one in the region. The pattern of the modern nation-state imposed on communities organized on quite different principles of political loyalty must necessarily do violence to those traditional and persistent bonds, as well as throw into question the validity of neighboring states' territorial limits. The task of establishing and preserving the national identity of the state puts the onus on the authorities of maintaining the cohesion and the security of the community, which defines and justifies its existence. This requires not only the obligation to live by the nationalist myth but also the determination to acquire or to defend, by force if necessary, the territory appropriate to that myth.

In the Near East this has been a peculiarly troubling undertaking—with one significant exception—for all the Arab states as well as for the Palestinians. Those in authority must cope with competing principles of power, which devalue to a large extent the validity of the given states. Those who rule must attempt to encourage loyalty to the state, of which they hope themselves to be the chief beneficiaries, while at the same time seeking to disguise the fact that their system of power, and thus the identity of the political structure itself, frequently owes more to the old ties of sectarian and tribal loyalty. At the same time, they must seek to master the challenges represented by the belief that only dedication to the idea of an Arab nation or of an Islamic *ummah* justifies the claim to rule. Inevitably, the precarious balance demanded by this effort to retain power in the state while coping with these anti-state imperatives limits the degree to which they can afford to compromise on matters of regional significance.

The exception to this pattern among the Arab states has been Egypt. The uniquely different history and political society of Egypt have allowed its rulers to escape from the frozen cycle of insecurity that besets its neighbors. This is not to say that similar forces have not been at work within Egypt and within Egypt's views of the region. Rather, they have been of a different magnitude. While Nasser may have been tempted to exploit Arabism and even Islam in an endeavor to extend Egyptian national interests, the dismal experience of these endeavors allowed his successors to subordinate them to a more narrowly defined and manageable idea of Egyptian nationalism.

The other exception in the Near East is Israel. The mix of liberal and nationalist ideals in the Zionist project makes it unique. The liberal conception of political authority has remained central to the organization of the state of Israel, and the distinctive circumstances of that state's creation and consolidation have ensured that it remained relatively free from the crises of authority that prevailed in the surrounding Arab states. However, conflicts over what Zionism should be about as a nationalist philosophy have not been so easily resolved. In this, again, Zionism has an individuality, in that the thrust of the idea of a return to Zion has been based on an irredentism that concerned territory rather than simply political community. There was thus an ambiguity from the start of the project regarding the proper limits of the state of Israel, and it is an ambiguity that has now emerged to become one of the principal crises afflicting the politics of the state.

The point to be made is that the states of the Near East are all, in some measure, involved in the difficult and often violent endeavor of seeking to define themselves as political communities. At the historical moment when they are most jealous of their nationalist myths and are made insecure by their perceptions of threats that cast in doubt their very identity, it can be argued that they are constitutionally least able to make the sacrifices demanded by peace and, conversely, that they are in some respects politically attuned to making the sacrifices demanded by war.

Peace in the Near East, if that state is envisaged as a comprehensive settlement of the issues involved and a common consent to abide by the rules of a regional order, might be a far greater political problem for those in power than maintaining the current war footing. This is not least because it would force an admission that the nationalist revolutions in which they have all been engaged were not after all the supreme value in politics they were hitherto claimed to be. In those states where it has been used to disguise a rampant and exclusive absolutism, this admission might give rise to unwelcome examination of the foundation of political power. Even where this did not apply, however, such an admission would raise the question of whether, given the prejudices and insecurities established by recent history, the government's chief constituencies would be willing to follow such a lead.

The political will and resilience needed to overcome this legacy would require the confidence of a government in its own authority, and thus in its ability to negotiate, if it became necessary to compromise, in the name of the state, while retaining the allegiance of its subjects. Lack of such confidence has undermined previous attempts at establishing a peaceful regional order, and the consequent inertia could be considered one of the chief characteristics of Middle Eastern politics.

Inertia in this sense does not imply stasis, since it can be accompanied by considerable diplomatic and political movement. It does, however, suggest that in the absence of any significant break with the past or of sustained external pressure, the forces of the region itself will tend to emphasize the risks inherent in innovation, returning the parties to their original positions of wary truce. This is not a position of equilibrium, since inertia such as this may be comfortable in the short term, but gives rise to three major causes for concern: It ill prepares the states of the region for any effective response to the sudden and inevitable crises that will erupt in domestic and regional politics, or indeed for any chance of foreseeing and preempting such crises; it reverberates throughout the region, which puts in jeopardy any piecemeal attempt at conflict resolution; and it tends to give a promise of false reassurance to interested outside powers. This neither prepares them to deal with future crises nor compels them to think seriously about how to avert such crises.

In order to examine the problem of political inertia and its underlying causes and consequences, this chapter will be divided into two parts. The first will look at the circumstances and potential of conflict in two areas of the Near East: in the Levant and in Egypt's regional security environment. The second will deal with the degree to which these conflicts have engaged the attentions and energies of the superpowers, what this has meant for the conflicts in question, and, as important, what this may yet mean for the development of East-West competition in the Near East.

REGIONAL CONFLICT IN THE NEAR EAST

The Levant

The issues at stake between Israel and its Arab neighbors revolve around the questions of political community and territoriality, which largely define the causes of conflict in the Near East and determine the strength of will behind its conduct. The determination of the Zionist movement to acquire territory in Palestine, which alone would provide physical security and national identity for the dispersed communities of Jews, met with the rejection of this project by the Arab communities or by the Arab governments which themselves claimed an exclusive right to exercise political authority in Palestine. This assertion of competing claims to the same territory in the name of mutually exclusive national ideas lies at the heart of the Arab-Israeli conflict and to some extent also explains the continuing friction between the Arab states of the Levant. The current situation engendered by these unresolved conflicts is to a large extent due to the developments brought about by the crises of the 1960s.

For Israel, the territorial gains made in the war of 1967 seriously upset the internal balance of the state and lie at the crux of its present dilemma. Acquiring the territory of the West Bank and Gaza gave Israel control over 1.3 million Palestinian Arabs. In theory, they were separated from the Israeli body politic by being placed under military rule. In practice, they could not so easily be separated since the territory they inhabited was considered by many to belong by right to the Jewish nation.[1]

The sense of the new territorial potential of Israel and the fear of sacrificing this most valuable asset of nationhood were significant contributing factors in the revival of the fortunes of revisionist Zionism. The latter was to become the governing principle of the state after the elections of 1977, and especially after those of 1981, and was to be the driving force committing Israel to war in Lebanon in 1982. This war has underlined the tensions within the state regarding its future and the best means of securing that future. For the revisionist tendency, the existence of Israel's formidable military apparatus seemed to offer an opportunity to bring about two significant alterations in the political map of the region by the application of force: the destruction of the Palestine Liberation Organization (PLO) as a focus for the national aspirations of the Palestinian Arabs under Israeli military rule and the reconstitution of a well-disposed Maronite-dominated political order in Lebanon.[2] In this, the Likud government failed to appreciate both the intractability of the two political projects to the forceful means employed and the revulsion in Israeli politics to the costs incurred in employing them.

The partial eclipse of the fortunes of the Likud and the inevitable withdrawal of troops from Lebanon that followed have left untouched the central dilemma of Israel's future, which is the fate of the occupied territories and of their inhabitants. Annexation of the territories would radically alter the Israeli political system, either by destroying its democratic foundations or by destroying the Zionist ideal of creating a specifically Jewish national political community.[3] Yet any move to relinquish these territories, either to Jordan or to a Palestinian state, would be fraught with danger for the government that sought to make such a move. It would bring the emotions of revisionist Zionism into a powerful combination with the fears for national security, bred of the experience of war, to destroy the administration concerned.

Consequently, for any Israeli government at present, and especially for one seeking to come to grips with the economic plight of the country, the attractions of regional inertia are greater than those of any other option. A determined effort to address directly the issues at stake, in a move to lay the foundations for regional order, would require a painful internal reassessment of Israel's future as a nation-state in the Near East. It would also require, as a precondition, the evident willingness of all the other parties in the conflict to make sacrifices as profound as Israel's would be in renouncing all claims to the West Bank or to East Jerusalem. Furthermore, Israel would require not only some evidence of present good faith on the part of its adversaries but also some assurance of their ability to sustain such an initiative regardless of the inevitable changes in those who exercise power. Since this touches on the troubled questions of succession, political continuity, and above all on Israeli perceptions of how these issues have destabilized the politics of the Arab world during the past forty years, this is clearly a considerable obstacle to creating the necessary conditions of confidence in Israel.

The Palestinians, who should be the most closely concerned with the opportunities offered by such a prospect of Israeli withdrawal, are perhaps the least well equipped to inspire the confidence that would make such a move conceivable. The years following the 1967 war, which witnessed the reactivation of the idea of Palestinian statehood championed by the PLO, raised three unsettling and still unresolved questions for the Palestinians: first, the definition of the national aim for which they were aspiring and on behalf of which the PLO claimed to represent the Palestinian nation. No less than Zionism, the Palestinian national movement has yet to clarify the territorial extent of the Palestinian homeland. Internally, this issue continues to divide the movement, and externally it has yet to produce a basis for negotiation with Israel. Second, this leads to the connected and equally unresolved question of the means to be employed to achieve the national goals. Third, since the Palestinians must perforce reside in Arab states that they cannot control, there is the very questionable degree of autonomy they can expect to exercise from the national security policies and territorial ambitions of those states.

For those who have pinned their hopes on a "Jordanian option," there is the problem that it does not lie in the power of Jordan to sustain an independent initiative in the Near East. The irony here is that of all the rulers in the Levant, King Hussein probably has the acutest sense of the perils of continuing inertia for his domestic order and for regional order. Yet he also has the least capacity to break out of the cycle unaided.

The Hashemites have always entertained political ambitions in Palestine, but precisely because these have been seen through the perspective of dynastic interest, rather than through the uncompromising prism of some national myth bound up with territory, they have found it easier to compromise on the particulars. However, this has largely been dependent on the authority of the monarch himself. As the bases of that authority have necessarily changed with the changing demographic and social structure of the kingdom, the dynasty has been increasingly aware that its room for independent maneuver is narrowing. If internal cohesion and the security of the regime are to be maintained, then King Hussein must take into account the Palestinian sensibilities of his subjects. The attempt to combine the two strands of Hashemite pragmatism and Palestinian nationalism lies at the heart of King Hussein's effort to bring a joint Jordanian-Palestinian delegation to negotiate directly with Israel.[4] Despite these encouraging signs of movement, it is doubtful that King Hussein will be able to sustain the momentum in the absence of substantial aid or concessions from the other interested parties to the conflict, and in the teeth of Syrian opposition.

For most of the past thirty years, successive regimes in Syria have been caught between an awareness of military weakness on one hand and a fear of the political perils of substantial compromise on the other. As a result, the radical Baathist regime that came to power in 1966, which has developed into President Hafez al-Assad's current form of government, has become adept at inaction in the Arab-Israeli conflict. This has given the regime the appearance of pragmatism, but it is a pragmatism in the service of, and severely constrained by, two supremely irredentist and perhaps unrealizable ideas, the first being the ideal of Greater Syria and the second that of the Arab Nation as formulated by the ideologues of the Baath party.[5] On these two ideas Assad has sought to found the myth of his political authority, and consequently their preservation has largely shaped his views of Syrian national security.

The first idea encourages loyalty to the Syrian state in its present form and simultaneously legitimizes the actions taken to assert Syrian control over Lebanon and over the PLO. The second, more wide-ranging in its scope and ambition, serves to justify the continued hold of the Baath party on power in the name of the legitimacy claimed by the apostles of an unfinished revolution. Both are thought to deflect the open sectarian conflict that political life in Syria perennially threatens to become and to disguise the fact that power has in fact already been seized by members of the Alawi sect.[6]

For these very reasons, the regime in Syria must strive in public all the more forcefully to stress its complete commitment to these larger ideas. There is an obvious danger in merely settling for some territorial compromise on the Golan, when the raison d'être of the whole structure of power has been the dedication to the cause of regaining the territories of "lost Palestine" or "lost Southern Syria," if necessary by force. At the same time, it remains obvious enough to the regime in Syria that to seek to pursue these goals through direct military action against Israel is a hopeless undertaking. Yet it cannot afford to be seen to abandon the goals or the military instrument.

The result has been the maintenance of an armed truce with Israel, while the military buildup proceeds as evidence of the regime's seriousness of purpose. This in turn frees, or perhaps compels, the regime to pay attention to the subordination of its domestic and Arab security environment to its will. In this endeavor it has shown considerable ruthlessness and strength of purpose, as events in Lebanon since 1976 and within Syria itself since 1979 have shown.[7] The war in Lebanon and subsequent developments have merely tended to underline for the Syrian regime the risks involved in moving toward the establishment of common ground for regional order with Israel.

Egypt and the Security of Its Environment

The intractability of regional conflict in the Levant and the indivisibility of regional conflict from the unreconciled imperative of domestic politics have led to the present uneasy situation of armed truce. That the truce has not been more frequently or more catastrophically broken has been due in large part to the realization by those who would use force against Israel that such action could have little hope of success without the participation of Egypt.

For Egypt, the 1967 war also marked a turning point in its relationship with Israel, demonstrating not that the imperatives of domestic politics were any less relevant to Egypt's attitude but rather that Egypt's political history and character separate it qualitatively from the Levantine nexus. The 1967 war coincided with and contributed to the internal collapse of the Nasser revolution. It set Egypt on the interior-oriented course that was to find full expression during Sadat's presidency. Although two more wars with Israel were to follow—the War of Attrition and the War of Yom Kippur—these were to give impetus to the reaffirmation of a sense of specifically Egyptian nationalism. Combined with the strength of the Egyptian state, Sadat was able to abandon the irredentist claims to which Nasser had inextricably committed himself in championing the cause of Arabism.[8] This in turn laid the foundation for the territorial compromise with Israel that began in the disengagement agreements of 1974 and 1975 and ended in the evacuation of Sinai by Israel in 1982.

Mutual recognition of the principle that territorial compromise can act as the basis for order in the relationship between states is clearly an optimistic development within the context of the Arab-Israeli conflict. However, there are particular features of this settlement that caution against an overoptimistic assessment of its potential as a model to be followed in the Levant.

Unlike the other Arab parties in the conflict with Israel, Egypt is a nation-state. Although the country has been troubled by questions of identity with and ambition in the Arab world, Egypt's government can plausibly claim that it is a nation, defined by the common historical experience of the society currently occupying the territory of the modern state. Nasser's successors have deliberately eschewed the temptation to define the nation in a way that integrates the territory of Israel into a wider scheme. Sinai could be and was represented as part of the Egyptian homeland. Gaza, historically part of Palestine and inhabited by non-Egyptian Arabs, was omitted.

For its part, the Israeli government responsible for negotiating with Egypt had not incorporated the territory of Sinai into its revisionist idea of the proper aims of Zionism. Nor had such an idea gained currency in Israel except among a very small minority. Consequently, bargaining over the return of Sinai to Egypt did not touch on the core of nationalist legitimacy in the way that similar bargaining over the West Bank and East Jerusalem might have done. On both sides, therefore, there was an ability to conceive of and to sustain the kinds of compromises that would underpin orderly relations between the two states. This formed the basis of the Washington Treaty, and the resilience of the order encapsulated in it is commensurate with the resilience of the political systems of the two states that are party to that treaty.

Precisely because Egypt's situation has been fundamental in affecting the potential for open conflict in the Near East, it is necessary to understand how that situation may in turn be affected by the security of its environment. In this respect, Egypt is faced by the two disturbed states of Libya and Sudan. The instabilities generated by the internal politics of these two states have a potential for regional disruption that might yet affect Egypt. Although the forces at work within the two are particular to their individual histories, nevertheless, as in the Levant, the basic problems revolve around the unresolved questions of the political community and territory of the state, the impulses of irredentism and social revolution, and the utility of force in carrying through the goals of politics.

For Libya, Egypt holds a special place in Qadhafi's diagnosis of the region's ills and in his proposed remedies. The continued failure of the Egyptian government to behave in the only way he believes it should behave has convinced him that the peoples of Egypt have been ill served by their government and would welcome the radical change he promises. The single-minded pursuit of Arab unity is, for him, both a good in itself and the only effective means of facing up to and defeating the challenge represented by Israel. From his perspective, this is a truth that can be immediately grasped by the Egyptian masses and therefore constitutes a legitimate political yearning denied them by their rulers. As a result, it has become a moral imperative for Libya to banish false consciousness and to help in the overthrow of the successors to Nasser.[9] This has naturally led to considerable friction in Egypt's relations with Libya.

From the Libyan side, the chief expression of these envenomed relations has been the sponsorship of subversion. The emergence in Egypt of groups willing to use violence to change society presented Qadhafi with an opportunity to act against Egypt. Ideological affinity, even if it meant merely challenging the

Egyptian state authorities, a similar unwillingness to compromise, and an identity of views on the role of violence in precipitating mass support for political change, clearly attracted Qadhafi to several of these shadowy organizations.[10]

Their activities, although irksome and violent, did not shake the Egyptian state. They did, however, provoke President Sadat into taking sudden if limited military action against Libya in 1977. Quite apart from the obscure results of this exercise, there was reportedly some adverse reaction within Egypt to the excessive nature of the response.[11] President Mubarak seems to share such an assessment and has contented himself subsequently in meeting the haphazard Libyan challenge by deploying the considerable internal security resources of the Egyptian state against Libya's agents.

Given Egypt's weight and cohesion, there is clearly a limit to the amount of damage Qadhafi can inflict on his neighbor. For its part, the Egyptian government seems determined not to let the conflict escalate. There may once have been an impulse on the Egyptian side to encourage subversion among those disgruntled by Qadhafi's revolution, but this does not appear to have been systematically pursued. Instead, a form of frozen disdain now characterizes the Egyptian side of the conflict, accompanied by a certain vigilance aimed at preempting subversion within Egypt itself.

The imperviousness of Egypt has led Qadhafi to turn his attention to more vulnerable states in the region. In this connection, the scope offered him by the turmoil of Sudanese politics has been welcome as a means both of realizing his wider revolutionary ambitions and of indirectly attacking Egypt. Qadhafi welcomed the coup that overthrew President Nimayri in Sudan in April 1985 and was quick to give his vocal support to the new regime. It was clear, however, that his enthusiasm was due not simply to the downfall of a man with whom he was waging a bitter personal vendetta but also to the radical change this seemed to portend in Egypt.[12]

The Egyptian tendency to regard Sudan as an integral part of its own national security, together with Egypt's military capability, gives it both the political will and the instruments to ensure, or to seek to ensure, that no actively hostile regime emerges in Khartoum. However, deeper involvement in the affairs of Sudan, especially in the form of military action, could be seriously counterproductive, not only in terms of the objective being sought in Sudan but also in terms of the reverberations this might set off within the politics of the Egyptian state. The caution displayed by the present government of Egypt, both in domestic and in regional affairs, is an encouraging factor in this sense.

In Khartoum, whatever form of political regime eventually emerges, there exists an awareness of the necessity for Sudan to live equally with its neighbors. It is too vulnerable a country not to do so, as the closing years of Nimayri's rule demonstrated. It is unlikely, therefore, to lend itself to the designs of another state, whether it be Libya or indeed Egypt.

These restraints on the escalation of regional conflict are, of course, dependent on the state of domestic politics. By the same token, the roots of the regional conflict lie also in the configuration of domestic politics. As far as the security of Egypt's regional environment is concerned, therefore, this will depend on the revolutions in progress in Sudan and Libya. Clearly the Egyptian response is the crucial one in determining whether the friction caused by the upheavals will erupt into interstate conflict. In defusing the potential for open regional conflict in Northeast Africa, the stability of Egypt is the predominant factor. The importance of such stability can scarcely be overestimated. Egypt has a pivotal role in reducing the likelihood of serious conflict in the Levant and in Northeast Africa. The fact that Egypt has been able to sustain a policy disengaging it from surrounding conflicts has been due to its resilient state structure, to its limited resources, and to a necessary concentration on the ills of its internal condition. If there is a cause for concern, it lies in the abilities of the Egyptian government to cope adequately with these ills.

OUTSIDE POWERS AND REGIONAL CONFLICT IN THE NEAR EAST

The conflicts depicted in the preceding section are disturbing enough in their implications for the security of the region itself. More troubling still for international order is the fact that the condition of regional security in the Near East has become enmeshed in the preoccupations and rivalries of outside powers. The disappearance of the old empires after the Second World War did not mean that the Near East had suddenly become autonomous at a stroke; nor did it mean that the Near East had suddenly ceased to be of interest to outside powers. On the contrary, substantial outside economic interests remained, and the region retained a strategic fascination for the two superpowers that had emerged from the war, both of which sought to preserve and extend the influence necessary to secure those interests from the presumed depredations of the other.

In this endeavor, the old methods of direct *imperium* had been explicitly abandoned. Instead, new means had to be worked out in order to safeguard those material, and sometimes ideological, values believed to be at stake in a historical competition between the United States and the USSR, played out in a region of independent states. This has led to a series of relationships being established with local governments, which are susceptible, precisely because the element of direct administrative force is lacking, to the changing priorities and fears of the local governments themselves. Not to recognize this is to be faced at times of stress or crisis with the stark choice either of complete withdrawal from the area or of direct commitment to force local circumstances to bend to an external will. Since neither the United States nor the USSR seems prepared to indulge in the renunciation of all interest implied by the former or to impose its control in the manner implied by the latter, a compromise must be found that will allow the pursuit of a middle way.

The pursuit of this middle way continues to characterize the relations established between the two superpowers and local states. It should not be thought of as a coherent or consistent policy. Rather, it has led to uncertainty, impetuosity, and the sometimes ill-considered use of force to address situations that would seem otherwise to have escaped control. In the Near East this has increased the capacity of the conflicts between the states concerned, and whose present alignment serves to define superpower interests, to engage the attentions of the superpowers. Yet at the same time, it seems to have weakened the capability of the superpowers either to address directly the causes of these conflicts or to prevent these states from engaging in armed struggle when this is believed vital to their survival.

The consequence of this has been to tie superpower interests into the definition proposed by local states of their own national interests and of the means regarded as imperative to secure those interests. It is, after all, the responsibility of government to exploit the given facts of the regional and the international order to achieve the most favorable possible outcome for the projects on which they are engaged. The resources and the continuing rivalry of the United States and the USSR are precisely two such facts. It has become, therefore, a major task of regional powers to ensure that these vital resources will be used in their own favor. In this they have been helped by the natural propensity of the United States and the USSR to interpret events in the developing world primarily in terms of East-West competition.

As a result, it is not easy to see how either superpower can arrive at a definition of its interests in the Near East, and how they may best be protected, that is, significantly distanced from the priorities and concerns of the client states involved. The implication of this is that both superpowers, in their respective ways, have become parties to the major conflicts in the Near East and remain vulnerable to the regionally determined dynamics of those conflicts. This is disturbing in that the eruption of open warfare between the regional states risks the escalation of that conflict into a direct clash between the superpowers themselves.[13]

While both the United States and the USSR are undoubtedly aware of the dangers inherent in such a situation, there seems to be little prospect of either superpower escaping from such a cycle. Current East-West relations along with the pain and difficulty involved in attempting to reassess the validity of their local clients' priorities would seem to preclude, for the time being, the degree either of cooperation between the superpowers or of ruthlessness toward their local clients that would be required to impose and maintain a comprehensive regional order in the Near East. Such a regional order would leave all parties dissatisfied in some measure. It seems improbable under present conditions that the superpowers would be able to exercise the self-restraint and firmness necessary to prevent the exploitation of that dissatisfaction.

The ways in which these processes have worked out in practice in the Near East illustrate the general observations that can be derived from the foregoing. First, the workings of domestic politics within the states concerned seem not to be amenable to effective and consistent superpower management. Second, the superpowers must perforce deal with the given political structures of the area. Their eagerness to retain the allegiance of these states tends to make them generally uncritical of the interpretations of regional events formulated by the governments in power, however colored these may be by an intensely local political mythology. Third, this gives them a view of regional conflict in which their own strategic priorities become engaged, without giving them the control they are able to assert over bilateral East-West relations. Finally, this troubling perspective and the fears it evokes add the weight of the superpowers to the "crisis of inertia" in the Near East.

Lebanon

In Lebanon in 1976 the USSR was obliged to follow the Syrian version of what was at stake in the country, despite deep misgiving about the Syrian decision to intervene.[14] This stemmed from the Soviet realization that there was no point in jeopardizing its relationship with Syria over something that the Syrian government regarded as vital for its national security. The USSR's uneasiness about the liability it had been obliged, de facto, to accept was emphasized throughout the years that followed by consistent refusal to give Syria the kinds of security guarantees for its presence in Lebanon that it so persistently demanded.[15]

This, however, was forced upon the USSR by the war of 1982. Israeli and American intervention, combined with the material losses suffered by the Syrian armed forces, clearly changed Soviet perceptions of what was at stake. It activated a Soviet interest in the area that had more to do with countering the moves of its superpower rival than with any intrinsic interest in Lebanon itself. Precisely to prevent the deterioration of the relationship with Syria, which it regards as vital to maintaining those interests, the USSR came to Syria's aid in lending its support to the latter's defiant posture in Lebanon.[16]

The unique Israeli-American relationship makes it difficult for any U.S. administration to override the requirements of Israeli national security as defined by the elected government of that state.[17] In 1982 this led the Likud government to believe that it had tacit American endorsement for its aims in Lebanon. Faced with the fact of the invasion and its consequences, the United States found itself committing American troops, first as part of the plan to guarantee the evacuation of the PLO forces from Beirut and then—with the multinational force—in an attempt to ensure that the atrocities committed in the aftermath of that evacuation were not repeated.

The problem then arose that, having sent troops to Lebanon with one rather ill-defined mission, the United States chose at the same time to champion the more ambitious cause of reconstituting the Lebanese state. Naturally, the American forces in the area came to be regarded as the instruments by which this "reconstitution" was to take place. They lost their initial aspect of mediators and took on the colors of protagonists in the Lebanese melée.[18]

This apparent American commitment to a specifically Lebanese policy was encouraged not only by the Israeli government but also by President Gemayel in Lebanon itself. He was desperate to enlist American aid to help him reestablish the Lebanese state in a form he did not have the power to impose himself. Without apparently giving serious thought to what was involved or to the American interests being advanced thereby, the U.S. government found itself embarked on this questionable project. It took the violent events of 1983 and 1984 to convince the U.S. administration that it would be more prudent to leave the Lebanese to work out their own destiny than to increase American involvement. In essence this meant a recognition that the shape of the Lebanese state was an irrelevance to the national interests of the United States.

Palestine and the Palestinians

As the Reagan peace plan demonstrated, the United States was not so willing to follow the revisionist idea that the future of the West Bank should lie in Israeli annexation. In this reluctance, the U.S. relationship with Jordan constitutes something of a moderating factor. Evidence that elements of the Hashemite interpretation of events have found some credence in the United States lies both in the Reagan peace plan itself and in the encouragement for King Hussein to bring at least part of the PLO into acceptance of the plan. Jordan is working with a greater sense of urgency than the other states involved, and it has tried to persuade the United States of the eventually detrimental effects of Near East inertia. Nevertheless, despite American concern about the security of the Hashemite monarchy, it seems unlikely to lead the United States to compel Israel to accept the form of autonomy for the West Bank that King Hussein regards as crucial to the future survival of his kingdom.

Both Jordan and Israel are competing to persuade the United States to see things through their conflicting perspectives. At present it seems that the Israeli interpretation is set to dominate. Partly because of the nature of the relationship with Israel and partly because of continuing uncertainties about the nature and authority of the PLO, the United States will probably continue to follow the Israeli lead. This means awaiting an Israeli initiative that would allow the United States to play a mediating role such as it continues to play in the Israeli-Egyptian relationship. In order for this to happen, the Palestinians would have to emerge with a commonly acknowledged, central authority willing to make major concessions on the status and territorial extent of Israel. For its part, an Israeli government of convincing authority would have to design an imaginative plan for the West Bank and Gaza that would allow the kind of autonomy for which the Palestinians would be prepared to negotiate. It seems doubtful that the United States is equipped to provide either of these preconditions.

As far as the USSR is concerned, the fate of the Palestinians is clearly subsidiary to its relationship with Syria. It may have been dismayed at the vigor with which Syria pursued its ambitions within the PLO during the past three years, but it evidently did not feel moved to prevent this.[19] Insofar as these activities have reinforced Syria's claim to be a necessary negotiating partner in any settlement of the Palestinians' future, this action is indeed welcome from the Soviet point of view. Keeping Syria, and thus itself, in the game of Levantine politics appears to be the main Soviet preoccupation. The rearming of Syria, along with the political support implied by Assad's desired "strategic relationship," is a price the USSR is willing and able to pay in order to ensure that this remains the case. In doing so it does not risk much. Furthermore, it can be reassured by the fact that the United States finds itself in a similar position. The USSR can be confident, therefore, that its interests are maintained in the region, allowing it to turn its attention to other, more pressing questions in East-West relations.

Egyptian Security

The security and alignment of Egypt must be key factors in the way the superpowers view the Near East. These factors are central both to the Arab-Israeli conflict in the Levant and to the different order of problems that beset Northeast Africa. Should the inherent instabilities of domestic politics in the region reach such a pitch that they once again throw into doubt Egypt's political future, this would profoundly affect the potential of the Arab-Israeli conflict. Dissatisfaction with the results produced by the newly established order in its relations with Israel is an important current in Egyptian politics and finds an echo among those who have other reasons for dissatisfaction with the state.[20] Although awareness of this dissatisfaction has caused a certain coolness in relations between the two states, it is as yet insufficient to destroy the bases on which that order is founded. The capacity of the United States to diagnose and to act upon the effects that regional frustrations will have upon Egypt's future direction, especially when combined with the many internal frustrations of Egyptian politics, is an unknown quantity. However, there are some grounds for concern since it touches upon the two weakest elements in the U.S. repertory: the indecision evident in inducing Israel to extend the peace process and the more general inability of a superpower to determine the course of domestic politics in the states of the Near East.

In Libya, Qadhafi has a great capacity for provocation, and he has succeeded in touching a raw nerve in the current U.S. administration. Nevertheless, as past years have shown, there is little the United States can do to alter the impulse behind Libya's haphazard and frequently violent forays, since that depends on the nature of a revolution still in progress. Recent attempts to affect the security of Qadhafi's position itself have had mixed, and in some senses negative, results. It would, therefore, appear to be more effective for the United States to return to its previous policy of seeking to prevent or to preempt as much as possible the externally disruptive effects of Libyan policy.[21] In this sense, Libya's already limited capability to affect seriously the regional order can be reduced still further.

Attempts to read into Qadhafi's designs an East-West dimension have only partial relevance. The chief determinant is the impulse of domestic politics. It does not appear that there is sufficient

Soviet control to justify the claim that Soviet interests are being remorselessly advanced thereby. Qadhafi has his value for the USSR, both as a consumer of Soviet arms and as a subscriber to the anti-American rhetoric believed useful to the USSR in the developing world. Similarly, his techniques of subversion and their targets may not be unwelcome to the USSR. However, insofar as they are capable of provoking sharp reactions and of stimulating a form of beleaguered anti-Libyan solidarity among his troubled victims, with which Libya itself is at a loss to cope, they have a perturbing effect upon the more cautious style and timetable of other Soviet projects in the Near East.[22] Qadhafi seems to epitomize the kind of independent and unreliable Third World leaders whose experimental and disruptive policies tend to make the USSR distance itself from their effects.

CONCLUSION

It might be argued that the view of the Near East put forward here does not after all suggest too bleak a prospect for the future of regional order. The inertia depicted as characterizing the region's states has already established a kind of de facto order in their relations. The imperatives of domestic politics may prevent the states concerned from reaching workable compromises to settle the issues at stake between them, but against this must be set the fact that the existing truce is in some sense due to their doubts about the utility of force. This would appear to indicate that the parties to these conflicts have reached a stage in which they have recognized the limitations of war as a means of solving their problems. If this were the case, then a reassessment of alternative solutions might be in the offing, however painful the compromises required might be.

Similarly, since the attitudes of the superpowers have been influenced in part by the exhaustion of their clients and in part by their own inclination to recoil from the prospect of direct confrontation in the Near East, their very inaction would seem to be a prelude to an attempt to think in concert about the prerequisites of order in the region; or at least it might suggest that the superpowers are relaxed enough to wait until the local states have reassessed their own situations and have themselves conceived proposals that would allow superpower mediation.

There is evidence that at least some elements of this more hopeful side to Near Eastern conflict do in fact exist. King Hussein has pursued his initiative with determination, seeking first and unsuccessfully to bring the PLO into an acceptance of the need for a negotiated settlement and subsequently to persuade Israel, directly and indirectly, to reciprocate. Egypt, as well as encouraging these moves and injecting new warmth into its hitherto frozen relations with Israel, has at the same time reacted to the sudden change of regime in Sudan with a certain equanimity. Syria, having reasserted its influence in Lebanon, seems to have little interest in allowing the situation there to provoke further Israeli intervention. In the Vienna conversations in February 1985, the superpowers showed a willingness to discuss Near Eastern issues. Nothing concrete emerged from these talks, but the sense that a dialogue should be maintained seems to have won some favor.

However, to develop these various elements into an agreed formula for a regional order requires all the parties involved to take considerable risks, not simply with the relative importance of their regional positions but in some cases with their national security and political survival. If these steps are to be taken, an unprecedented degree of political resolve and flexibility would need to be demonstrated by the parties involved, as well as a measure of external reassurance that would presuppose a hitherto elusive superpower collusion. The danger is that both the timing and the political will of the parties will be fatally out of synch, leaving them to fall back on the old, comforting postures of inaction.

On both the regional and the superpower levels, the current situation of armed and wary truce testifies to the persistence of old patterns of insecurity and mistrust. This is no less the case in domestic politics than in regional relations. Even in the absence of open conflict, the combination of the two may serve to drive local states into ever closer links with the superpowers in whose resources and support they see some protection from the threats besetting them. This process is unlikely to encourage the superpowers themselves to see the region in terms that escape from the tyranny either of local projections or of their own continuing concern that their rival should not secure for itself an unacceptable advantage in the region.

The longer-term implications of this state of affairs are worrying. Regional inertia has its price. The lines of conflict remain drawn up, although the parties involved may see no immediate advantage in activating them. On the one hand, this means that the unresolved issues retain their power to move others in the immediate region and beyond who have some stake in the causes of these conflicts. On the other hand, politics cannot remain static. Over time, forces animated by the sensed inadequacies of their predecessors may push for new and extreme interpretations of the obligations of the state in the region. In this respect, the lack of present attention to the basic issues of contention both contributes to causing future radicalization and also, by providing emerging radicalism with a regional agenda, tends to direct it toward a more violent prosecution of the conflicts inherent in those issues.

The superpowers, whose interests are already planted in the given dispensation of states, will run the risk of being drawn into these more radical interpretations of the imperatives of war, with the prospect of finding themselves locked into direct confrontation as a consequence. It may well take a threat as unmistakable and as grave as this to give the superpowers the incentive to reassess their relations with one another and with the states concerned in the Near East.

One of the chief problems of the "do nothing" attitude is that, superficially at least, it seems eminently comfortable and free of risk. Security becomes equated with whatever can be held, if necessary by force, in the short term. There seems to be little chance of controlling other people's revolutions, and therefore it appears less dangerous merely to wait until they exhaust themselves, while maintaining sufficient force to deter attack. In these conditions a sense of urgency by one party can be seen as weakness by others, providing an opportunity to reinforce their relative positions rather than to negotiate a compromise for the future.

One way of weakening this cycle would be to establish some form of guaranteed regional order, removing the option of direct interstate conflict whatever the impulses of domestic politics. Even if this means placing unpalatable constraints on the independence of all the states concerned, in the sense that they would be restrained either from pursuing the maximalist goals of their nationalist revolutions or from arming themselves accordingly, it would be preferable to the continued cycle of conflict that will otherwise be the outcome. In present circumstances, it seems that neither the local states nor the superpowers have reached such a stage of willing self-restraint. The irony is that the realization that this may after all be a more tolerable solution than a further round of war is most likely to dawn once war has broken out.

NOTES

1. Moshe Ma'oz, *Palestinian Leadership on the West Bank: the Changing Role of the Mayors under Jordan and Israel* (London: Frank Cass, 1984), pp. 85–90, 160–205.
2. Ze'ev Schiff, "Lebanon: Motivations and Interests in Israel's Policy," *The Middle East Journal* 38, no. 2 (Spring 1984): 223–27.
3. For an illustration of some of the dilemmas raised thereby, see the essays in D.J. Elazar, ed., *Governing Peoples and Territories* (Philadelphia, Penn.: Institute for the Study of Human Issues, 1982).
4. See, for example, the texts of the Jordan-PLO agreement of February 11, 1985. "The Palestinian/Jordanian Agreement Text," *Al-Sharq al-'Awsat*, 24 April 1985, p. 9.
5. Itamar Rabinovitch, "The Foreign Policy of Syria: Goals, Capabilities, Constraints and Options," *Survival*, July/August 1982, pp. 175–80.
6. Nikolaos van Dam, *The Struggle for Power in Syria* (London: Croom Helm, 1981), pp. 109–29.
7. *The Observer*, 9 May 1982.
8. Adeed I. Dawisha, *Egypt in the Arab World* (London: Macmillan, 1976), pp. 50–59; Fouad Ajami, *The Arab Predicament* (Cambridge: Cambridge University Press, 1981), pp. 94–106.
9. "To Build Unity and Defeat the Enemy," *Al-Zahaf al-'Akhdar*, 22 January 1982, p. 1; and "From the Minaret," *Al-Zahaf al-'Akhdar*, 19 March 1982, p. 7.
10. "New Anti-Egypt Libyan Offensive," *The Egyptian Gazette*, 28 February 1977, p. 3, "Libyan Saboteurs tried to wreck Cairo Summit," *The Egyptian Gazette*, 18 March 1977, p. 1, "Life imprisonment for Libyan Agents," *The Egyptian Gazette*, 18 August 1981, p. 1; and "Egypt says it uncovered a Libyan Plot," *The International Herald Tribune*, 2 April 1985, p. 2.
11. *Arab Report and Record*, 1977/14, July 16–31, 1977, pp. 580–84.
12. "Gadaffi demands Mubarak overthrow," *The Times of London*, 20 May 1985, p. 7.

13. Malcolm Mackintosh, "The Impact of the Middle East Crisis on Superpower Relations," in *The Middle East and the International System, I. The Impact of the 1973 War*, Adelphi Paper no. 114 (London: International Institute for Strategic Studies, 1975), pp. 3–5.

14. Galia Golan, "The Soviet Union and the Israel Action in Lebanon," *International Affairs* 59, no. 1 (Winter 1982/83): 9.

15. *Strategic Survey 1982–83* (London: International Institute for Strategic Studies, 1983), pp. 64–65.

16. C.A. Roberts, "Soviet Arms-transfer Policy and the Decision to Upgrade Syrian Air Defences," *Survival*, July/August 1983, pp. 154–58.

17. Ze'ev Schiff and Ehud Yaari, *Israel's Lebanon War* (New York: Simon & Schuster, 1984), pp. 74–92.

18. William B. Quandt, "Reagan's Lebanon Policy: Trial and Error," *The Middle East Journal* 38, no. 2 (Spring 1984): 237–50.

19. Golan, "Soviet Union and the Israel Action in Lebanon," pp. 9–16. In this she is referring to Soviet behavior during the 1982 invasion of Lebanon. The principles she outlines, however, as well as the reactions of the USSR to PLO appeals for aid apply equally well to the events around Tripoli in late 1983 and to the events in Beirut in May 1985.

20. See, for example, Pierre Savin, "Israel vu d'Egypte," *Politique Etrangère*, June 1981, pp. 427–36.

21. See P. Edward Haley, *Qaddafi and the United States since 1969* (New York: Praeger, 1984) for a detailed account of the development of the relationship. This study is especially good on the period of the first Reagan administration.

22. O. Ogunbadejo, "Qaddafi's North African Design," *International Security* 8, no. 1 (Summer 1983): 154–78.

6 PERSIAN GULF

Shaul Bakhash

The West has a broad interest in the security of the Persian Gulf region. Despite changes in sources of supply, the industrial states require access to stable and reasonably priced supplies of Persian Gulf oil. The Persian Gulf states constitute an export market worth tens of billions of dollars a year. It is in the interest of the industrial states that the Persian Gulf governments handle their considerable foreign exchange holdings in a manner that will not disrupt currency markets. It is also in the interest of the Western powers to deny this strategic region to the Soviet Union.

To the pursuit of these interests, the West can bring certain assets. Historically, the region has been closely linked to England and, more recently, to the United States. It is to the West that the countries of the region primarily turn for their import requirements and, with one or two exceptions, for arms. Despite the anti-American posture of some states in the region, the elites of the Persian Gulf states are trained largely in the West. In countries like Iran and Saudi Arabia, there exists a traditional suspicion of the Soviet Union.

On the other hand, the industrial states also suffer from certain handicaps. At the moment, the United States is seen as the intrusive, outside power. Close identification of the ruling families with the United States means that the unpopularity of a regime can easily be translated into anti-American or anti-Western feeling. A reaction has developed against what is seen as excessive Westernization, and the Islamic resurgence, which is in part an exercise in

Research and writing of this paper were completed when the author was a fellow at The Woodrow Wilson International Center for Scholars in Washington, D.C. Research assistance was provided by Kathryn Babayan.

cultural self-assertion, reinforces this anti-Western tendency. U.S. support for Israel makes military cooperation with America difficult for Gulf regimes.

The states of the region, moreover, are buffeted by powerful domestic, regional, and international currents. Under the impact of oil revenues, individual states are undergoing an immense transformation whose political and social consequences are unpredictable. Ruling families and governments are divided by traditional rivalries, territorial claims, and conflicting ambitions and ideologies.

Radical regimes in South Yemen and Iran, and in an earlier context in Iraq, challenge the more traditional states in the region. The Soviet Union remains a potentially threatening intruder, having established a presence in the Horn of Africa, in South Yemen, and in Iraq. However the intentions of the Soviet Union in Afghanistan are assessed,[1] the Soviets are better placed from that position to pressure Iran and to threaten Persian Gulf and Indian Ocean shipping.

The security of the Persian Gulf thus involves much more than troops, arms, and military alliances. It is intimately linked to regional politics and to the internal condition of the individual states.

THE INTERNAL DIMENSION

The Persian Gulf states are in the throes of a major social and economic transformation. Oil money is rapidly changing demography and patterns of settlement. New classes are emerging. Oil revenues permit general prosperity but also produce skewed patterns of wealth distribution. Urbanization is rapid and ill planned. Economic boom has brought to the Gulf huge numbers of migrant workers; a considerable portion of the population, whether in Saudi Arabia, Kuwait, Abu Dhabi, or Qatar, is made up of foreigners, among whom the Palestinians are a major cohesive and politically conscious group. Shi'ite minorities and majorities are also an important element in many Gulf states.

The ruling classes pursue a life-style that is often at odds with publicly professed Islamic norms. Rightly or wrongly, corruption is perceived to be widespread. Although opportunities for political participation and public debate are limited, people in the Gulf states are touched by the ideological currents that affect other parts of the Middle East and Arab world—Arab nationalism, Islamic fundamentalism, Islamic radicalism, liberalism, socialism. The Islamic Republic in Iran, with its emphasis on revolutionary militancy, Islamic law, economic justice, and intransigence toward the United States, is the latest in a series of revolutionary Middle East regimes that challenge the legitimacy of traditional Persian Gulf rulers.

All this is well known, and the changes and challenges that the Persian Gulf states must confront have often been catalogued. But there is little agreement on the significance of these developments for the stability of Persian Gulf societies. In the aftermath of the Iranian revolution, there was an understandable tendency to view the Arab governments of the Persian Gulf as threatened entities, soon to be swept away by revolution and radical change.[2] Other observers have been impressed by the ability of the Persian Gulf states to cope, to muddle through despite manifold problems.[3]

What is certain is that the consequences of the developments now taking place in the Persian Gulf states are only dimly understood, both in the region itself and by outside observers. Iran may serve as an example. Between them, England and the United States had accumulated over 150 years of intimate diplomatic, economic, and political involvement in Iran. Yet at every juncture in the developments that led to the overthrow of the Pahlavi dynasty, the process of change under way in Iran was misunderstood.

The Nixon administration encouraged the shah to undertake a responsibility for the security of the Persian Gulf for which the country was ill equipped and for which there was little popular support. In the scramble for lucrative contracts, Western governments and companies promoted an ill-considered attempt at overnight industrialization that gravely undermined the legitimacy of the regime. The shah was not the strong, decisive ruler he was believed to be. The revolution was not anticipated. A large and well-equipped army, police force, and security apparatus could not save the monarchy. When the revolution came, the nature of the successor regime was misjudged, and there was a widespread assumption that the post-shah government would be moderate, pro-West, and even a source of stability in the region.

The obvious lesson is that security studies in an area as volatile as the Persian Gulf must devote considerable attention to internal political, social, and economic developments in the regional states. At least as much importance must be attached to political ideologies as to military tactics, to demography as to counting troops, to political structures as to the balance of military forces. The same stricture applies to regional politics and developments. Of the two major upheavals in the region over the last decade, one, the Iranian revolution, was rooted in domestic politics and the other, the Iran-Iraq war, in regional politics.

THE REGIONAL DIMENSION

Relations between the states of the Arabian Peninsula and the Persian Gulf have been troubled by a range of disputes.[4] These disputes have been territorial and have often involved a scramble for the control of valuable economic assets or strategic land- or sea-based positions. They have centered on traditional family, dynastic, or historical rivalries or pitted peoples of different religious persuasions against one another. They have involved rival ideologies. They have often involved outside powers or their surrogates, including Egypt, Jordan, the People's Republic of China, Cuba, the Soviet Union, England, and the United States.

In practice, the major powers in the region—Saudi Arabia, Iran, and Iraq—have often used their superior power to settle territorial disputes in their own favor, employing various forms of pressure, financial inducement, and force. In the 1960s and 1970s Saudi Arabia secured territorial concessions from Abu Dhabi, Qatar, and Oman. In 1971 the shah of Iran seized by force of arms the Greater and Lesser Tumbs, two small islands in the Persian Gulf also claimed by Ras al-Khaimah; he persuaded the ruler of Sharjah, in return for a financial settlement, to acquiesce in the Iranian occupation of the island of Abu Musa.

These actions fed suspicions and created resentment among the smaller Gulf states. In the case of the Iranian seizure of the Tumbs and Abu Musa, this resentment came to be expressed in the traditional language of Iranian-Arab hostility. (Iraq sought to profit from this by claiming it intended to free the islands from Iranian control when it made war on Iran in 1980.)

There were defensible claims on both sides, and the territorial rearrangements were not always of great moment. Moreover, Iran and Saudi Arabia acted with responsibility in other ways. Saudi Arabia did not press territorial claims against Kuwait once that country was threatened by Iraq. The shah gave up Iran's historical claim to Bahrain. (Although after the overthrow of the monarchy, one Iranian cleric, in a widely reported case, asserted his right as a Shi'ite leader to interfere in the affairs of Bahrain, the Tehran government never officially revived the Iranian claim to the island.) Saudi Arabia, and Iran under the shah, provided financial assistance to the poorer Gulf states, acted to secure Gulf regimes, and cooperated on regional security. Until the Iranian revolution the smaller Gulf states had learned to look to the two countries for protection even as they played them off against one another to guard their own independence.

Iraqi territorial ambitions against Kuwait, on the other hand, were met with firm resistance, both by the regional states and by outside powers. In 1961 British troops, later replaced by a joint Arab force, manned the Iraq-Kuwait border following an Iraqi threat to Kuwait. When Iraq moved troops into northern Kuwait in 1973, Saudi and Iranian troop movements and intense diplomatic pressure forced Iraq to make at least a partial withdrawal.

Two other conflicts have involved the regional powers and outside states in military conflict. The Dhofar rebellion in Oman was supported both by South Yemen and Iraq. It was suppressed with the assistance of British, Iranian, and Jordanian troops and considerable infusions of Iranian and Saudi money. The rebellion is unlikely to be renewed, although the possibility cannot be ruled out, given the ideological thrust of the South Yemen regime; its previous history of involvement in Dhofar; its military arsenal; and the presence in South Yemen of Cuban, East German, and Soviet military advisers.

The civil war in North Yemen in the 1960s involved Egypt and Saudi Arabia in major roles and a number of other states less prominently. As many as 70,000 Egyptian troops eventually fought on the republican side. Saudi support for the royalists was supplemented by assistance from Iran and Jordan. In 1963, after

Egyptian aircraft strafed Saudi villages, a squadron of U.S. aircraft was deployed as a show of support. The conflict ended only when Israel's defeat of Egypt in the 1967 war forced Nasser to withdraw his troops and to reach an understanding with Saudi Arabia.

Relations between Saudi Arabia and North Yemen remain uneasy, and some Saudi involvement in Yemen's internal affairs appears inevitable. The troubled politics of both Yemens, the radical image they project, their links with the Soviet Union, the fact that they invite the involvement of outside powers by their erratic politics, and the new link between revolutionary Iran and South Yemen all mean that this will remain a potentially disruptive corner of the Arabian Peninsula. At the moment, however, the Yemens do not appear to pose a serious threat to the rest of the Gulf.

A number of conclusions can be drawn from the conflicts in Yemen and Oman and the crises in relations between Iraq and Kuwait. First, Gulf conflicts can attract non-regional states, and second, the major states in the region are prepared to commit troops and provide support in local conflicts where they believe major interests are threatened. Third, the settlement of such conflicts may often require the support of outside powers. Fourth, settlement of conflicts has often depended on fortuitous circumstances, such as the defeat of Egypt by Israel in 1967 or the overthrow of Abdul Karim Qasim in Iraq in 1963. Finally, outside involvement notwithstanding, the regional states up to now have on the whole been successful in containing the potential damage inherent in regional conflicts.[5]

THE IRANIAN REVOLUTION AND THE IRAN-IRAQ WAR

Much more serious have been the repercussions of the Iranian revolution and the Iran-Iraq war. Although there have been marked continuities in Iranian foreign policy across the watershed of the revolution, the change in regimes has nevertheless brought about a sharp reorientation in Iranian foreign policy.[6] Iran saw itself as a guardian of Persian Gulf stability under the monarchy; since the Islamic revolution, it has often been in the business of destabilizing Gulf regimes and exporting revolution. The United

States, once a close ally, is now treated as an arch enemy and depicted as the Great Satan. Iran sided with moderates on the Arab-Israeli issue; it is now a vocal member of the rejectionist front and speaks of carrying its war first to Baghdad, then to Jerusalem. Arab states with which Iran maintained close relations under the monarchy, such as Morocco, Jordan, and Egypt, are now regarded with hostility. It is Libya and Syria that, among the Arab states, are Iran's closest allies.

The war has exacerbated relations with the Arab states of the Persian Gulf that, fearful of an Iranian victory and sensitive to Iraqi pressure, provided Iraq with up to $35 billion worth of "loans" and allowed Iraq the use of their ports and overland trade routes. The Gulf states have on occasion found themselves involved in the hostilities. Iranian aircraft attacked targets in Kuwait on a number of occasions. During the "tanker war" initiated by Iraq in 1984, Iran on occasion reacted to attacks on Iranian shipping by attacking shipping plying Saudi and Kuwaiti ports. Because Iraq used Kuwait as a transshipment point for arms imports, Iran stepped up attacks on Kuwaiti tankers in 1987. In June 1984 Iranian and Saudi aircraft engaged in a dogfight in which an Iranian fighter was downed.

The war also reinforced the propensity of the Khomeini regime to try to export revolution.[7] The revolution from the beginning tended to be seen by its leaders as the model and spark for revolutions throughout the Gulf region and elsewhere that would be Islamic and anti-imperialistic and would favor the "disinherited" classes. Clerics and other revolutionary propagandists from Iran were involved in spreading the message of the Iranian revolution in the Gulf states. In the aftermath of Iran's dramatic victories in the first half of 1982, Khomeini appears to have seen the possibility of establishing an Islamic state, similar to Iran's, at Baghdad and making this the nucleus of a string of Islamic governments throughout the Gulf region.[8] Iran's insistence on continuing hostilities until the overthrow of Saddam Hussein is rooted in part in this long-term goal.

Iran, moreover, has sought to export a revolutionary Islamic ideology through the agency of the annual *hajj* pilgrimage to the Holy Places in Saudi Arabia. To the same end, it hosts an annual conference in Tehran of Friday prayer leaders from various Islamic states. It provides a base for the Supreme Assembly of the

Islamic Revolution of Iraq, led by members of the Shi'ite al-Hakim clerical family of Iraq, who actively work for the overthrow of the Baath regime. Iran sent a contingent of Revolutionary Guards to participate in the Arab struggle during the Israeli invasion of Lebanon. The Revolutionary Guards contain a special "liberation brigade" that is in theory prepared to participate in liberation struggles outside Iran.

Revolutionary rhetoric, Islamic propaganda, and the sponsorship of Islamic or revolutionary organizations do not always reflect the realities of foreign policy, however. There are moderates as well as radicals, doves as well as hawks, in Iran's revolutionary coalition. The revolutionary impulse has been tempered by the need to trade, export oil, secure technology, and maintain correct diplomatic relations with a range of countries. Since 1985, a greater degree of pragmatism has characterized Iran's relations with both Europe and the Gulf states. Nevertheless, the radical streak remains a powerful component in Iranian ideology and will continue to color aspects of its foreign policy.

Due to three factors, the Iran-Iraq war has been successfully confined to the two principal belligerents. First, although Iraq in 1984 showed signs of seeking to end the war by expanding it—by involving other Gulf states and even outside powers—both Iran and Iraq have on the whole displayed restraint in their treatment of nonbelligerents. Second, the Gulf states followed a policy of placating both sides but standing firm against attempts to widen the war.

Saudi and other Gulf money presumably helped induce Iraq to refrain from unduly provocative acts during the "tanker war" in 1984. While relations between Iran and Saudi Arabia have been strained, Kuwait and the Gulf sheikhdoms have taken care to remain on reasonably friendly terms with Tehran. Iran was allowed a relatively large share of OPEC production quotas. Iran has also been allowed to compensate for the loss of Khorramshahr port, which was destroyed by Iraqi shelling early in the war, through the use of transshipment facilities at ports on the Arab side of the Gulf. Until Iran began to attack Gulf shipping in 1984, the Gulf states were restrained in their criticism of Iranian war policy.

At the same time, the Gulf states have taken steps to strengthen their own defenses. Following the discovery of the Iranian-backed coup attempt in Bahrain in December 1981, the countries of the

Gulf Cooperation Council agreed to cooperate more closely on matters of internal security. Saudi Arabia asked for and received U.S. AWACS aircraft to guard against Iranian air attacks, and in 1984 the Gulf states voted in the United Nations to condemn Iran for its attacks on shipping in the Gulf.

Third, external powers have been able to play some role in containing the fighting and bolstering Iraq against the Iranian threat. Iraqi defenses were strengthened through the supply of French aircraft, missiles, and other equipment. Jordan and Egypt aided Iraq with troops. The United States generally succeeded in 1984 in inducing its allies and friends not to resupply Iran with arms, thus reducing the chances of a new Iranian offensive. An American "tilt" toward Iraq was signaled by the resumption of diplomatic relations with Baghdad late in 1984, a development that did not go unnoticed in Tehran. The provision of air support to Saudi Arabia helped persuade Iran that there was a limit to its ability to pressure the Gulf states by attacking Saudi-related shipping. The Reagan administration's willingness to supply Iran with arms in 1985 and 1986 thus represented something of a break with the U.S. position. However, the move was dictated much more by a desire to secure the release of American hostages in Lebanon than by a carefully considered policy change. The arms-for-hostages initiative was in any case abandoned following public disclosure and the strong, negative reaction in Congress and the country at large.

From the outbreak of hostilities, the Soviet Union, too, took the position that the war was harmful to the interests of both sides and should be brought to an early end. Early in the war, the United States and the Soviet Union agreed jointly to remain neutral. Moscow suspended major weapons supplies to Iraq at the outbreak of hostilities; arms deliveries were resumed only in 1982, when Iran recovered most of its own territory and seemed poised to carry the war into Iraqi soil. The USSR has continued to urge a peaceful settlement of the war.

A number of considerations help explain the Soviet position. Moscow has viewed the anti-American military position in Iran in 1979 as one of the positive achievements of the revolution for the USSR. It has wished to avoid any developments that would see the reintroduction of an American military presence into Iran and has criticized Iranian persistence in prosecuting the war precisely because the Iranian threat is causing the Gulf states to seek closer military ties with the United States. Moscow reacted positively but cautiously when invited to lease Soviet-flagged tankers to Kuwait in 1987. The Soviet Union may have wished to avoid being forced to come to Iraq's defense under its treaty arrangements with the Baghdad regime. It has desired to retain the friendship of both Iraq and Iran, and has thus continued to maintain correct trade relations with Tehran despite increasing Iranian criticism of the Soviet presence in Afghanistan and despite the Iranian suppression of the Tudeh (Communist) party.

Iran's war aims, particularly its demand for the overthrow of Saddam Hussein and the Baath regime, make a negotiated settlement of the war unlikely in Khomeini's lifetime. Even if the war were to be settled or a stalemate were allowed to endure without further serious fighting, Iran-Iraq relations are bound to remain a disruptive factor in Gulf politics. The war has been immensely destructive of life and property on both sides and has left the seeds of a bitterness and suspicion that will take years to overcome. If peace comes, both sides will wish to rebuild their arsenals, and this renewed "arms race" may prove unsettling to the regional balance of power. Iran under the Islamic Republic has proved as intent on achieving a dominant position in the Gulf region, a position to which it lays claim by virtue of its size and historical role, as it was under the shah. In a postwar period, it will continue to pursue this goal in the name of a revolutionary and Islamic ideal.

Nor will a postwar Iraq necessarily emerge as a force for regional stability. It is only in the light of the Iranian threat that Iraq is now perceived as a moderate element, deserving of European military support and American diplomatic recognition. Yet until very recently, Iraq was a key member of the rejectionist front on the Arab-Israeli issue and provided support to one of the most extreme of the Palestinian terrorist/guerrilla organizations. The State Department listed it as one of the countries supporting international terrorism.

Iraq made territorial claims against Kuwait in 1961 and sought to force Kuwait to cede the islands of Warbah and Bubiyan in 1973. Until 1975 Iraq supported the rebellion in Dhofar. The Iraqi desire for more secure access to outlets on the Persian Gulf may lead to renewed claims against Kuwait territory or a renewed attempt to overturn the 1975 Algiers agreement, which established the prewar Iran-Iraq land and water frontiers. And while the Iraqi failure to achieve a quick victory over Iran in 1980 dashed Saddam Hussein's hopes of establishing Iraqi primacy in the Gulf region, such ambitions could easily be revived if the circumstances appeared favorable.

THE GULF STATES AND REGIONAL SECURITY

Saudi Arabia and the other Gulf states reacted to the threat to their security and stability posed by the Iranian revolution and the Iran-Iraq war in the multifarious ways they have reacted to similar threats in the past: They sought to thwart a perceived danger through diplomacy, financial largesse, cooption, and a playing of one side against the other. They increased cooperation in the security field, stepped up development of their armed forces, discussed means of coordinating their defense planning, and cautiously sought outside assistance.

The formation of the Gulf Cooperation Council (GCC) in May 1981 was itself a response to the Iranian revolution and the Iran-Iraq war.[9] Following the coup attempt in Bahrain in December that year, Saudi Arabia signed internal security cooperation agreements with five of the six GCC states. Some intelligence-sharing has taken place. There has been discussion on establishing a joint military command. Joint maneuvers were held in October 1983.

The internal security arrangements appear adequate for dealing with most low-level threats to the regional regimes, although problems clearly remain. The 1979 incident at the Grand Mosque in Mecca took the Saudi authorities completely by surprise, although the Bahrain coup attempt was uncovered and neutralized. The Saudis have dealt with Iranian attempts to use the annual *hajj* pilgrimage for purposes of political agitation by a combination of firmness (arrests, expulsions) and conciliation. Iranians have been expelled from, among other places, Kuwait. Nevertheless, it remains uncertain whether the Persian Gulf states are equipped to deal with broader challenges to authority or with large-scale protest movements.

The military forces being developed, which often double as internal security forces, face a similar problem. They are judged adequate for low-level external attacks but probably inadequate to counter a major external threat.

The problems are numerous.[10] Only Saudi Arabia has a large enough population to field a sizable army. Only in Oman does the army have battle experience, and then only as a counterinsurgency force. Skilled manpower is in short supply, and in both military and internal security forces, large numbers of foreigners are employed in training, advisory, and perhaps even active capacities. In addition to the foreign advisers and training officers who come with new weapons systems, there are large numbers of Jordanians and Pakistanis at various levels in most Gulf states. The experience in Iraq, and even in Iran, suggests that training indigenous forces and creating depth in skilled military manpower are long-term processes.

Moreover, mindful of the experience of other Arab states, Gulf rulers have sought to guard against coups or army interference in politics in ways that limit the effectiveness of those military forces that do exist. They employ the techniques of divided commands (as in Saudi Arabia), diversify weapons systems and sources to prevent coordination between different units, keep a tight check on ammunition, promote on the basis of loyalty as well as merit, and recruit their armed forces from among loyal bedouin tribes who may not necessarily make the best fighting material. They utilize foreign advisers and officers, and they have traditionally displayed great caution in deploying their armed forces at all. Cooperation between the military forces of the various GCC states is still in the preliminary stages.

A recent study would suggest that the Gulf states, as in the past, will continue to need outside support to deal with a major military threat coming, for example, from Iran or Iraq.[11] Assistance could come from such traditional sources as Pakistan, Jordan, and possibly Egypt, all Islamic countries. Britain may be willing, as in the past, to send troops for duty in Oman. The United States could be called on to interdict a major land or air attack.

Although in 1987 Kuwait turned to the USSR, the United States, and other great powers to protect its tanker shipping against Iranian attacks, Gulf rulers have been reluctant to call on outside powers for military assistance. When they have done so, they have preferred regional Islamic states (Pakistan, Jordan) to the Western powers. Oman aside, they have refused to permit the establishment in their countries of military staging facilities or to allow the pre-positioning of supplies. They have been hesitant even to enter into discussions to plan for such contingencies. In this they have been sensitive to domestic and regional repercussions. They are anxious not to be seen as tools of the United States or its allies nor to be identified militarily too closely with the country that is seen as Israel's primary supporter. They wish to avoid the criticism that would be leveled at them, irrespective of the merits of their action, by rival Arab leaders. They may judge that a visible American presence in the region can only invite Soviet hostility and countermeasures.

Kuwait's 1987 invitation to the superpowers to help protect its shipping was nevertheless a reminder that a local state in difficulty may, however reluctantly, seek to involve outside powers in a regional conflict, if only to end it more quickly. The immediate consequences were threefold. One, the Iraqi invitation strengthened the Soviet presence in the Gulf, although the long-term consequences of this development are difficult to evaluate. Second, it caused the Reagan administration to try to counter the Soviet presence by offering to reflag Kuwaiti tankers, although Congress was extremely reluctant to allow the United States to be drawn into the Iran-Iraq war. Three, it emphasized the pressing need to find a solution to the conflict.

THE SECURITY OF OIL SUPPLIES

Some projections of the oil import requirements of the industrial states continue to emphasize the heavy dependence of Japan, Europe, and the United States on OPEC and Persian Gulf oil.[12] In these projections, the recent oil glut and falling oil prices are seen as a temporary phenomenon, due primarily to economic recession in Europe. A market characterized once again by rising consumption and prices is projected for the near future. Whatever the accuracy of these projections, undeniably the dependence of the industrialized states on OPEC and Persian Gulf oil, at least in the short term, has greatly diminished. The industrial states have improved the efficiency of energy use. They have reduced the share of oil in the total mix of fuel and energy sources they utilize. By drawing on new sources of supply, they have reduced the share of OPEC in the total crude that they use. OPEC's production has not only fallen in absolute terms; it has fallen as a share of total world production.

A recent Brookings study, moreover, suggests that these changes are structural, in the sense that they are of longer-term duration than is generally supposed.[13] Changes in consumption patterns, the switch to alternative fuels, and similar changes will take years to reverse. The development of a futures market and the changing role of the spot market reduce the need for consumers to stockpile, simplify the allocation of oil supplies in a crisis, and make unlikely the sudden spiraling of oil prices that has occurred during crises in the past. Furthermore, Saudi Arabia and the richest OPEC producers aside, individual OPEC states have developed expenditure patterns that make them highly dependent on oil revenues, and this dependence is reinforced by falling prices and excess supplies. The glut in world oil supply and the fall in prices in 1985–86 appeared to confirm the findings of the Brookings study.

While supplies may yet be disrupted as a result of political upheaval and military conflict, these developments suggest, according to the Brookings study, that such disruptions are unlikely to be of long duration or to lead to the panic buying witnessed in 1979–80. The withdrawal of Saudi supplies under tight market conditions could prove serious. But even a successor regime in Saudi Arabia will need to sell oil and to earn revenues.

Although Saudi Arabia remains a special case, by virtue of its small population and considerable foreign exchange reserves, the Iranian example bears out the view that there will be considerable pressure on even radical Persian Gulf regimes to continue selling oil to meet pressing revenue needs. After the overthrow of the monarchy, Iran initially withdrew over 2 million barrels a day from the oil market, but as revenue needs mounted and foreign exchange reserves were depleted, it began aggressively to market its oil. There has been some change in Iranian trade patterns, but the revolutionary government continues to buy the bulk of its heavy machinery, raw materials, and high-technology goods from its Western trading partners and Japan.

However, even where political change does not threaten the security of oil supplies, it may lead to considerable political damage. The West may have retained Iranian markets and Iranian oil. But, as already noted, the United States lost important military assets in Iran as a result of the revolution. The Soviet invasion of Afghanistan might not have occurred had the shah remained on the throne. Revolutionary Iran has proved to be a disruptive force in the Persian Gulf region, and the Iran-Iraq war, a direct outcome of the Iranian revolution, has been another source of regional instability and uncertainty.

The Iranian case thus suggests that, even if oil supplies remain secure, there is little cause to be sanguine about the repercussions of political upheaval in the Persian Gulf states. It underlines once again the importance of the internal and regional dimension in any analysis of Persian Gulf security.

CONCLUSION

The security of the Persian Gulf is of great moment to the regional states themselves. The Gulf is also a region that is strategically and economically important to the West. This remains the case even though Western reliance on Persian Gulf oil and the chances of major disruption of oil supplies appear considerably diminished. In the long term, Persian Gulf sources of supply remain important. In addition, a range of other Western interests may be damaged by upheavals or unfriendly regimes in the region.

If in the 1970s the settlement of a number of disputes, general conflict management, and a nascent cooperation between Iran, Saudi Arabia, and Iraq, the three strongest states in the region, aroused hopes for continued stability in the region, these expectations have been quickly dissipated. The Iranian revolution and the Iran-Iraq war have emphasized once again the volatility of the area and the potential for major upheavals in individual states and in the region. Huge oil revenues, rapid industrialization and modernization, social and economic change, inflexible political structures, old and new regional rivalries, and the intrusion of outside powers and interests feed this inherent instability.

This means that while indigenous and external military and police power have a role to play in reinforcing regional order, security in the broad sense is not primarily a matter of arms and armies. The abilities of governments to manage orderly change, to develop mechanisms for the resolution of regional disputes, and to secure the outside support they may require without undermining their position with their own people are likely to prove as crucial as the need to provide for protection against internal subversion and external attack.[14]

The United States and Western powers concerned with Gulf stability will also need to emphasize flexibility and a broad range of responses in their dealings with the Persian Gulf states. It will be important to pay close attention to the broad and deep changes that are taking place in Persian Gulf societies, to try better to comprehend their political consequences, and to encourage states to make changes in political structures commensurate with social and economic development. While the United States and its Western allies cannot tell Persian Gulf governments how to spend their own money, they can show some restraint in encouraging a hectic pace of economic development and arms acquisition. The desire for close and well-defined security arrangements with the Gulf states is understandable, but the sensitivity of the regional states to excessively close identification with the West in this sphere should be respected. A number of alternative military options can be developed and explored. The regional states themselves need to be encouraged to develop regional institutions and other forms of cooperation.

NOTES

1. There is lack of agreement on ultimate Soviet aims in Afghanistan. A widely held view is that the Soviet Union seeks a face-saving exit that would also secure basic Soviet interests. See, for example, Jagat S. Mehta, "A Neutral Solution," *Foreign Policy* 47 (Summer 1982): 139–53. A less sanguine view of Soviet intentions is suggested in Anthony H. Cordesman, *The Gulf and the Search for Strategic Stability* (Boulder, Colo.: Westview Press, 1984), pp. 804–6.
2. Avi Plascov, *Security in the Persian Gulf III: Modernization, Political Development and Stability* (Totowa, N.J.: Allanheld, Osmun for the International Institute for Strategic Studies, 1982).

3. Peter Mansfield, *The New Arabians* (Chicago/New York: Ferguson/ Doubleday, 1981).

4. These disputes are described in Robert Litwak, *Security in the Persian Gulf II: Sources of Inter-State Conflict* (London: Gower for the International Institute for Strategic Studies, 1981).

5. These conclusions are succinctly drawn in Thomas L. McNaugher, "Arms and Allies on the Arabian Peninsula," *Orbis* 28, no. 3 (Fall 1984): 519.

6. Change and continuity in Iranian foreign policy are discussed in Shahram Chubin, "The Foreign Policy of the Islamic Republic of Iran," in *Three Case Studies: India, Iran, Vietnam*, of *Negotiations in Asia* (Geneva: Center for Applied Studies in International Negotiations, n.d.), pp. 1–29.

7. See especially, R.K. Ramazani, "Iran's Revolution and the Persian Gulf," *Current History*, January 1985, pp. 5–8, 40–41.

8. Shaul Bakhash, *The Reign of the Ayatollahs: Iran and the Islamic Revolution* (New York: Basic Books, 1984), pp. 232–33.

9. On the GCC, see Shireen Hunter, ed., *Gulf Cooperation Council: Problems and Prospects* (Washington, D.C.: Center for Strategic & International Studies, Georgetown University, 1984).

10. See the analysis in McNaugher, "Arms and Allies on the Arabian Peninsula," pp. 501–5.

11. See McNaugher's fuller development of these ideas in *Arms and Oil: U.S. Military Strategy and the Persian Gulf* (Washington, D.C.: The Brookings Institution, 1985).

12. For example, see the projections cited in Cordesman, *The Gulf*, pp. 3–5; and Bijan Mossavar-Rahmani, "The OPEC Multiplier," *Foreign Policy* 52 (Fall 1983): 136–48.

13. Douglas R. Bohi and William B. Quandt, *Energy Security in the 1980s: Economic and Political Perspectives* (Washington, D.C.: The Brookings Institution, 1984).

14. A number of recent studies on the Persian Gulf have emphasized the need for sensitivity to the weakness of local governments, local priorities and conditions, and the broad variety of considerations that must come into dealings with the Persian Gulf states. See, for example, Bohi and Quandt, ibid., pp. 46–51, and McNaugher, "Arms and Allies on the Arabian Peninsula," pp. 523–26. Similar considerations are voiced by Cordesman in *The Gulf*, despite his emphasis on security arrangements.

7 SOUTH ASIA

Stephen P. Cohen

South Asia consists of the states bounded by the Himalayas and
Hindu Kush mountains to the north and west, and the Indian
Ocean to the south, and includes India, Pakistan, Sri Lanka,
Bangladesh, Nepal, Bhutan, Afghanistan, and the Maldives.[1]
Collectively, the region constitutes one-quarter of the human race,
with a population equal to that of Latin America and Africa
combined. Culturally, it is as diverse as all of Europe, the social
distance between Pathan and Tamil being about the same as that
between Turk and Swede. Economically, the span is greater, as
South Asia contains the world's largest concentration of the very
poorest of the world as well as components of a developed, thriving
modern economy, especially in India.

It is a disservice to speak of South Asia as a "Third World"
region, given the ambiguity of that term, the diversity of states in
the region, and the internal heterogeneity of the region's largest
state.[2] Such terms are ambiguous, and even the Indian government claims membership in the Third World, but Jawaharlal
Nehru's vehement criticism of the idea of a "Third Force" (the
precursor to Third World) bears repeating:

> What the Third Force means I have been wholly unable to
> understand. . . . Numbers do not make a force. It will not make the
> slightest difference to the great military powers of today if the
> militarily weak countries band themselves together. If it takes the
> shape of banding together, even the ability to exert moral pressure
> goes into the background, and the physical side comes up. . . . We

The views expressed in this chapter do not necessarily reflect the views or policies of the
U.S. government.

have, therefore, opposed the idea of a Third Force. The moment we talk in these terms, we adopt to some extent the cold war approach and language of hostility. . . . We have enough problems of our own, and such influence as we have in the world is because of our modesty, not because of our shouting.[3]

Strategically, the region was often thought to be vulnerable and weak, as indeed it was during the great Islamic invasions from Central Asia in the fourteenth century onward and from the European invasions (by sea) since the sixteenth century. Earlier history recorded the invasion of Alexander the Great. More recently, the Japanese invaded in 1943, the Chinese in 1962, and the Soviets occupied Afghanistan in late 1979. But this picture of vulnerability is not entirely accurate: Much of Southeast Asia was under Indian cultural influence from the seventh to the thirteenth centuries A.D., and the Indian Chola Kingdom conducted naval raids in the Malacca straits in the eleventh century; parts of Tibet and Afghanistan were frequently entered and ruled by Indian and British forces. Indeed, the British, Portuguese, French, and Dutch all used their South Asia territories to support their activities in East and Southeast Asia.

British domination of South Asia was made possible by control of the sea, which they maintained twenty years after they left India, and careful attention to the limitrophe regions of Tibet and Afghanistan. At first overreaching themselves, they settled on a policy of keeping these two regions out of the hands of hostile czarist or imperial Chinese forces.

The popular media would now have it that South Asia was "the Jewel in the Crown" and that the British reluctantly departed because of exhaustion. This is inaccurate. India had been a treasure trove of silk, jewels, and spices through the nineteenth century, but its value declined just as the Raj was at its peak. First, the Royal Navy came to be fueled by oil, increasing the relative importance of the barren lands between India and the Mediterranean; second, India's spices and exotica were less than vital to an industrializing society. Indeed, as Indian manufactured goods began to compete with those from Britain, India became something of a threat. By the twentieth century, the South Asian possessions became of instrumental importance and the Indian army began to play a supporting role in the Middle East, the Far

East, and Southeast Asia. The defense of India remained important but was also part of an overall imperial defense system.[4] From being the jewel in the crown, India was relegated to a position of marginal equality with other regions.

The structure that had kept the peace in South Asia for 150 years was shattered by the coming of independence in 1947, and a dominant India found itself faced by a smaller but ideologically potent Pakistan. Yet the region as a whole was not threatened from the outside. Tibet remained a buffer for several years, Afghanistan was a weak state, and the ocean was in safe Western hands. India and Pakistan could afford their 1947–48 conflict since no outside power could take advantage of their mutual obsession.

This changed quickly. Tibet was lost to China in 1949, with Nehru's acquiescence, enabling the Chinese to confront and defeat India in 1962; the British withdrew from the Indian Ocean in 1968, and the United States, distracted by Vietnam, failed to make a smooth transition; and finally, Afghanistan became linked to the Soviet Union after the 1978 coup. Gradually, the conflict between India and Pakistan has been played out under new rules as one major power after another has been established on the region's Kashmir periphery. Today, it features not only indirect involvement by the United States, the Soviet Union, and China but a potential nuclear breakout. Further, other regional conflicts—stemming largely from ethnic and religious causes—have sprung up, providing new opportunities for the intervention of outside powers.

REGIONAL CONFLICT AND EXTERNAL INVOLVEMENT

Excluding Afghanistan, what are the most important regional conflicts in terms of their potential for the induction of outside powers? Chief among these must be the India-Pakistan dispute, which at various times has involved the United States, China, Great Britain, the Soviet Union, and several Middle Eastern states, and which may soon assume a nuclear dimension; other important regional conflicts include those between India and Sri Lanka and

India and China. Finally, there are several intrastate conflicts that have the potential of involving one or more outside and regional states.

The India-Pakistan Conflicts

India and Pakistan have fought one minor and two major wars, in 1947–48, 1965, and 1971. The latter led to the destruction of the old Pakistan and the creation of a new state, Bangladesh. These wars have involved hundreds of thousands of troops and millions of dollars of military equipment, most of it imported. Indo-Pakistani conflict has a special quality about it: More than one general on either side has characterized these struggles as "communal riots with armor." The very identities of Pakistan (an avowedly Islamic state) and India (a predominantly Hindu but secular state with a large Muslim minority) stand as a challenge to each other. The continuing struggle over Kashmir, with its predominantly Muslim population, is widely described as either one of the main causes of conflict between the two states or a consequence of their mutual distrust; it may be both at the same time.[5]

India and Pakistan have maintained most of their armed forces in opposition to each other since their initial conflict over Kashmir in 1948. Interestingly, even before they went to war in 1947–48, and even before India was partitioned and given independence, there were attempts by regional leaders to involve major external powers in regional affairs. Stressing the threatening nature of the Soviet Union, Indian officials suggested that they would like to receive the assistance from America that the British could not or would not provide. Six months before independence, Nehru's ambassador, Asaf Ali, told the Americans that India could "become a bastion for the world against the great northern neighbor which now casts its shadow over two continents, Asia and Europe."[6]

By October 1948 both India and Pakistan had made formal requests to the United States for military assistance; the Pakistani request was particularly large. The response was cautious. America denied requests from both states and in internal documents noted the importance of maintaining good relations with both South Asian states, using U.S. support "as an instrument to effect cooperation within the region." Assistance to one country that alienated the other would be self-defeating; "therefore a regional approach is necessary," although India was recognized as the "natural political and economic center of South Asia."[7]

With four exceptions, this response fixed the pattern of American involvement in the India-Pakistan conflict. The exceptions have been significant, but have not altered basic policy. The first was the 1954–65 U.S. grant and sales program to Pakistan, which built up the Pakistan armed forces to considerable strength. The program was initiated in response to Soviet expansion in East Europe and to the Korean War but was not directed against India. India was offered military aid on the same terms but refused; it did accept a much larger economic assistance program than Pakistan.

The second exception to this American policy was the short-lived (1963–65) arms aid program to India. This was in response to the Chinese-Indian war and resulted in about $90 million in grant military aid. The third (very brief) exception occurred during the 1971 India-Pakistan conflict over East Pakistan, when the United States consciously "tilted" in favor of Pakistan but did not provide any significant amount of military assistance. The final exception, a response to the Soviet invasion of Afghanistan, was the 1981 arms assistance program (which broke the fourth arms embargo that the United States had placed on Pakistan), which will run through 1987; a follow-on program, agreed upon in 1986, could extend this to 1992.

Despite these four exceptions, the basic assumption of American policy has not changed. At no time has the United States seriously considered allying with India or Pakistan in such a way that would destroy relations with the *other*. During 1953–65, India received special economic consideration, and during the current arms sales program to Pakistan, the Reagan administration has been careful to keep open its lines of communication to New Delhi; there is considerable optimism about the future of the U.S.-India relationship.

The involvement of other major powers in the Indo-Pakistan conflict has also been guided by strategic, not regional, calculations. The Soviet Union had identified India as an important country in the mid- and late 1950s as it was emerging from its own self-imposed isolation. India was first seen as the gateway to the nonaligned world and later as an important alternative to China.

As their relationship with China deteriorated, the Soviets hesitated and then (after the 1962 India-China war) began to provide India with very modern weapons—helicopters and MiG 21 aircraft. The Indians preferred Western assistance and weapons, but when the West lost interest in South Asia after 1964–65, the Soviets stepped in. They managed to become the peacemaker between India and Pakistan after the 1965 war—with American approval—and then even entered into a limited military relationship with Pakistan, hoping to wean that state away from both America and China.

China assumed the role of major military supplier to Pakistan in 1966. Chinese and French weapons, the latter purchased on commercial terms, constituted the most modern elements of the Pakistan armed forces through 1981.

In quantitative and qualitative terms, the most significant current external involvement in the subcontinent is that associated with the Soviet arms program in India. India made a few purchases from abroad after the 1971 war with Pakistan, but the Janata government negotiated a billion-dollar arms deal that was signed by Indira Gandhi in 1981, and her government then negotiated two others that were even larger.

India's dependence upon foreign arms is in part a response to Pakistan's new American supplies but is also the consequence of the failure of its own arms industry to produce modern systems. Despite years of effort, the Indians have not been able to produce a modern fighter or an effective tank and so turned to Soviet designs. Since the terms of the Soviet arms deals are not known, it may be that, in addition to valuing India's role as a de facto balancer of China, and in addition to Indian diplomatic support in Southeast Asia and even Afghanistan, the Soviets see India as a lucrative customer for their arms. Certainly the Soviets chiefly value Indian strategic and political support, but it may well be that they also make a profit from the arms deals.[8]

To summarize, the dominant expression of external involvement in South Asia has been through arms transfers. These generally reflected American, Soviet, and Chinese calculations of broader strategic objectives, not specific regional interests. This interpretation is sustained by the behavior of the two superpowers and China during major regional crises. The 1947–48 conflict in Kashmir resulted in an American arms embargo toward both India and Pakistan, not further involvement. The 1965 Indo-Pakistan war led to another embargo of American arms to India and Pakistan, and the Soviet Union and China carefully avoided any direct role (although the Chinese increased the pitch of its rhetoric by many decibels). In 1971, when the Soviets were clearly supporting India and the United States and China were clearly supporting Pakistan, none of these powers did more than ship weapons already agreed upon. In the Soviet-Indian case, this shipment was quite substantial, but in the American case, even these weapons were not supplied because of another embargo. Despite the much heralded sailing of the *Enterprise* toward the Bay of Bengal (which it did not quite reach), Soviet and American fleets kept apart from each other. This sailing was as symbolic as its 1962 sailing into the Bay of Bengal on behalf of India during the Sino-Indian war.[9]

Both the superpowers seem to believe that no purely *regional* conflict has been important enough for them either to commit their own forces directly or to challenge the role of the other superpower. This reluctance is especially noted by Pakistan, the weaker of the two regional powers, and no issue is more sensitive than the question of whether the United States will come to Pakistan's support in case of another conflict with India. This is an important question that deserves further analysis.

Pakistan has always regarded the arms supply relationship with the United States as having vital political overtones, partly because of the excessive expectations associated with the alliance in the 1950s but primarily because of the overwhelming impact of the U.S. program on the development of Pakistan's armed forces. The arms tie was seen as central to the survival of Pakistan itself. This perception faded in the 1960s and 1970s when China and other states provided arms to Pakistan.[10]

Because of this perception of centrality, there was always an assumption that the United States would support Pakistan against its chief enemy, India, an assumption privately fostered by some American officials but that would seem to exceed the 1959 agreement upon which the current relationship now rests. Yet one administration after another has publicly stated that the U.S. arms were meant for defense against the Soviet Union, not against India. No American administration has wanted to encourage the Pakistanis to attack India or to commit the United States to an open-ended conflict. Thus the new relationship, like the old one, remains slightly ambiguous: The arms are *meant* for defense against a Soviet attack; they may be *used* for defense against an Indian attack—or even in an offensive attack against India.

Yet how far would America support Pakistan in a Soviet-Pakistani conflict or an Afghan-Pakistani conflict? Would the United States then provide American aircraft? Pilots? Advisers? Air defense forces? Ground forces? All of these would be proper within the context of the 1959 agreement, but there has been little information as to what contingency plans have been discussed.

Pakistanis also ask whether the United States would support Pakistan in case of a new *Indo*-Pakistan war. Would such support be contingent upon a defensive Pakistani strategy or on the Indian initiation of such a conflict? (The force ratios are now very much in India's favor, and Indian armed forces have for at least a decade discussed strategies of preemption and first-strike.)

There are no satisfactory answers to most of these questions. Even the 1971 American policy, in which Nixon provided limited military aid and substantial symbolic backing for Pakistan in exchange for Pakistan assisting his opening to China, may not be relevant. We simply do not know what the American response would be. Surely, this uncertainty is recognized in Pakistan, which has been wary of dependency upon the United States and which has carefully avoided steps that would compromise or limit its future defense or nuclear plans.

While Pakistan's position would be in every way more precarious during a future Indo-Pakistan war (its army is much smaller; its internal supply lines are all exposed to Indian air, ground, and even artillery attack; and it has only one easily blockaded port), India has certain vulnerabilities, almost all of them external. India must keep some percentage of its forces facing the Chinese; it may not be able to prevent outside powers, including those in the Middle East, from flying in aircraft to Pakistan during such a war. These two concerns may be balanced by the prospect of support from the Soviet Union should a new Indo-Pakistan conflict erupt.

Estimates vary, but India is not likely to seek much Soviet support in the event of a future conflict with Pakistan since it would not want the Soviets to make any claims on Pakistani territory, thus moving the Soviet line of control further toward, or even east of, the Indus River. Most Indians see a troublesome but united Pakistan as more in their interest than a defeated and truncated

Pakistan. Some Pakistanis, however, are convinced that India's long-term plans are to continue the division and destruction of Pakistan that was begun in 1971, with or without Soviet assistance. A few Pakistanis have even argued that Pakistan's true interests lie westward, in a closer, more normal relationship with the Soviet Union. This position apparently is not now held in Islamabad, but given further evidence of American unreliability, Indian hostility, and Pakistani weariness at being the hosts to 3 million troublesome and expensive Afghan refugees, one might yet see a revived form of Pakistani "neutralism."[11]

These two very divergent scenarios—the prospective breakup of Pakistan or the movement of Pakistan toward a closer relationship to the Soviet Union—probably do not figure largely in current Soviet regional policy. The Soviets have launched a number of public attacks on Pakistan for harboring "bandits," but they have also been diplomatically active in Pakistan, trying to exploit resentment of the Zia government. Their prime concern with Pakistan would seem to be Pakistan's limited support for the Mujaheddin. However, as long as the war in Afghanistan remains a violent stalemate, it is unlikely that the Soviets will greatly escalate their pressure. To do so would activate more American support, and Pakistan certainly is a more substantial power than the Soviets have faced in Afghanistan. If the time came to deal with Pakistan, they might invoke the Indo-Soviet Treaty of Peace and Friendship, but it is more likely that they will continue to regard India primarily as a balancer of China. These are calculations, not fixed policies, and a new leadership in Moscow might be tempted to exploit more actively the Indo-Pakistani conflict to its own advantage.

The superpowers have generally been at cross-purposes when they involve themselves in South Asian matters; however, this was not the case during one brief period, which showed how effective *united* superpower action could be. From about 1962 to 1965, and especially during and after the 1965 Indo-Pakistan war, both superpowers worked together to reduce Chinese influence in the subcontinent and to keep India united and strong, should there be a renewal of Chinese military pressure. After initially persuading them to accept a cease-fire, the superpowers managed to bring the two countries to the negotiating table at Tashkent and to get them to sign an agreement. The arrangement might have held if internal discontent with the agreement in Pakistan (led by Zulfiqar Ali

Bhutto) had not led to President Ayub Khan's removal and if the superpowers had not then split over the issue of Bangladesh.

We have so far discussed external involvement in India-Pakistan matters and the calculations of the two major South Asian states of their outside support versus regional threats. It is appropriate to conclude with some remarks about India's and Pakistan's reactions to regional threats from the outside. Unfortunately, these reactions provide a clear measure of the dominance of the India-Pakistan conflict over calculations of regional integrity and security.

There have been two major incursions from the outside: the Chinese-Indian war of 1962 and the Soviet invasion of 1979. The Pakistani reaction (in 1962) to the Sino-Indian war was virtually identical to the Indian reaction to the 1979 Soviet invasion of Afghanistan: Both called for diplomatic rather than military steps to remove the offender, both initially underplayed the motives and intentions of the outside state, and both had to be pressured by other outside states (in the first case, Britain and the United States; in the latter, the United States) before issuing even a grudging statement of concern. In 1962 Ayub thought the Chinese had no intention of invading India; India now tends to accept the Soviets' claims that they have no further ambitions beyond Afghanistan and that they were drawn into that country because of outside meddling.

There is some irony here. Pakistan's earlier softness against China cost it a good deal of U.S. support in 1962–65, and Kennedy in particular was furious with Pakistani indifference to the supposed Chinese threat to South Asia. The Indians apparently "learned" from their own extreme reaction to the Chinese war that external threats to the region are not as great as had been imagined and could at least be managed. Their calculation may be wrong, but they have good reasons—other than their continued dependency upon the Soviet Union for arms—to be less concerned about the Soviet presence in South Asia than the United States. Indeed, were it not for the refugee problem, many Pakistanis would also regard that presence as tolerable.

India and Pakistan: The Nuclear Dimension

One final component of the Indo-Pakistani conflict deserves special examination, as it has been of particular concern to both

superpowers and China: nuclear proliferation. India's own nuclear program received its greatest impetus in 1964, with the
detonation of a Chinese test explosion. While the threat from
China has faded over the years, reports of a Pakistani nuclear
program, which first surfaced in the early 1970s, have revived the
Indian debate. Pakistan, of course, was responding to the Indian
nuclear program. (Mrs. Gandhi apparently gave approval for the
1974 Pokhran test during or just before the 1971 war with
Pakistan, at a moment when India was uncertain of its outside
political support.)[12]

Two aspects of South Asian proliferation seem to trouble
outside powers the most. The first is the possibility that a regional
nuclear weapon will be transferred to another region, particularly
the Middle East. An early justification for the Pakistani bomb was
that it would be an "Islamic" device, and it was in fact partially
funded with Libyan and then Saudi funds, according to the best
available public information.[13] Pakistanis themselves deny any
intention of shipping nuclear weapons to the Middle East and
know the opposition they would face if they were to do so, but there
is still room for legitimate concern. More subtly, the superpowers
are concerned about the impact of regional proliferation on their
own security and status. There is less concern about a direct
nuclear attack (although here the Soviets are vulnerable, as are
some American facilities) but more with the prospect that proliferation will dilute the prestige associated with the possession of
nuclear weapons. They are feared as equalizers by the great, which
is part of their attraction for the less great.

While both superpowers are apparently hostile to regional
nuclear proliferation and have committed themselves in the
Non-Proliferation Treaty (and the United States has gone further
in its Nuclear Non-Proliferation Act), the course of regional
proliferation may take one of several directions. Public evidence
indicates that both states are within easy reach of a nuclear device.
However, this may not lead to a test, to a weapons system, to
large-scale deployment. Indeed, one or both states may position
themselves at the edge of—or some distance from—large-scale
weaponization without any public statement, test, or other indication of their plans. In this they would be following the Israeli
pattern. They may even coordinate their nuclear cadence; both
have an interest in keeping up with the other, but neither would
find an outright nuclear arms race particularly useful.

If proliferation does take place, it would lessen the prospect of direct superpower involvement in a regional conflict, especially if both India and Pakistan go nuclear. This seems to be overwhelmingly more likely than only *one* of the two going nuclear, although there may be a tricky period between the time the first and the second state declares itself to be in possession of nuclear weapons. It might, however, lead to greater superpower interaction with India and Pakistan, out of fear and prudence. As in the case of China, there will be some concern that these two states, not tightly linked to either superpower, will be unpredictable. Both superpowers will fear irrational behavior and may even go so far as to prepare ABM or counterforce contingency plans. They might also seek to promote C^3 (command, control, and communications) stability and stay on the friendly side of both states. Optimistically, the development of nuclear weapons by South Asian states will have an overall stabilizing effect and might lead to greater caution by the superpowers in attempting to manipulate regional states for their own ends.

However, the superpowers are not alone in their concern over regional proliferation. There is a strong likelihood that other states will view South Asian proliferation as being important to their own interests. There has been some discussion of a potential Israeli strike against Pakistani nuclear facilities.[14] It seems unlikely that Israel would attempt this unless there was clear evidence of Pakistani nuclear cooperation with an Arab state or the actual movement of nuclear weapons to the Middle East. China also has an interest in regional nuclear developments, and one or more South Asian nuclear systems would have implications for China's own modest deterrent force. One proliferation nightmare would be the evolution of a number of small and medium-sized nuclear forces that could degrade Chinese or even superpower nuclear capabilities and that would make targeting and deterrence too complicated for rational analysis.

Incursions into South Asia

There have also been several conflicts between regional states and outside powers, the two most notable being the 1962 Sino-Indian war and the 1979 invasion of Afghanistan by the Soviet Union.

These are examples of a long history of competition for influence in the limitrophe shatter-zone. The names of the players have changed, but elements of the "great game" remain: It still *does* matter to China, the Soviet Union, India, and Pakistan who controls the marshlands across their borders. States such as Nepal and Afghanistan have survived by maintaining a tenuous balance between their powerful neighbors; recent events in Afghanistan show how tenuous that balance can be and how great is the price of miscalculation.

There have also been incursions from the sea, although none has yet resulted in conflict. The United States deployed the nuclear carrier *Enterprise* in both 1962 and 1971 in an attempt to influence events on land (in the first instance, to deter a Chinese attack on India; in the second, to threaten India during its invasion of Pakistan). With the expansion of Soviet seapower, there is now a heightened prospect of direct superpower competition in the Indian Ocean region and subsequent demands for support, facilities, or even basing from littoral South Asian states. We will consider this separately in the context of our discussion of India-Sri Lanka relations. Historically more important, and potentially of greater regional significance, is the continuing presence of China in territory claimed by India along India's northern borders.

China in South Asia

China and India fought a war in 1962 that was regarded at the time as a conflict between titans, an ideological struggle between communism and democracy, upon which the future of the world rested. Such emotions have since been drained from the conflict, but the substantive disagreement over the proper demarcation of borders remains and involves several tens of thousands of square miles. Because the Sino-Indian conflict so closely parallels that between China and the Soviet Union (based on treaties concluded during czarist and imperial Chinese years), there is some reluctance on India's part to compromise lest the Soviets be alienated, and some reluctance on China's part to yield lest the Soviets claim that as a precedent.

This diplomatic stalemate will be broken when India's dependence upon the Soviets declines, when India calculates that closer relations with China will weaken that state's links to Pakistan, or when China concludes that it is better to try to embarrass the Soviets by giving generous terms to India rather than to continue to treat the Indians as Soviet puppets. Until that day comes, the dispute can itself be used by any of the involved powers to make a diplomatic or military point. It is unlikely that the substantive dispute will *itself* be grounds for a new conflict between India and China, as both countries have learned to live with the present arrangement—just as India and Pakistan have learned to live with the cease-fire line in Kashmir.

ETHNIC DISCONTENT AND GREAT POWER INTERESTS

India, Pakistan, and Sri Lanka are multiethnic states. India, with a larger population than Europe, is more linguistically, culturally, and religiously diverse. Pakistan has four major ethnic/linguistic groups, and a fifth, the Bengalis, successfully broke up the old Pakistan in 1971. Sri Lanka is divided sharply into several groups that have varying racial, linguistic, religious, and cultural identities.

In each of the three countries there are ethnic groups that forcibly resist political or cultural association. Fearing absorption or seeking autonomy, they have in some cases fought the center for decades. Such groups include the Baluchi and Pathans in Pakistan and the Nagas and Mizos in India. There are also major linguistic groups in India, Pakistan, and Sri Lanka that seek greater autonomy from central dominance. Separatist movements have occurred among the Sindhis and Bengalis in Pakistan, the Sikhs, Nagas, and Tamils in India, and the Tamils in Sri Lanka. Most of these center-periphery conflicts are exacerbated by the fact that many ethnic groups in South Asia have close ties to kinsmen across a national boundary. Regionalism, or regional separatism, is thus easily internationalized.

There is also at least the *temptation* for outsiders to meddle in these countries, and there are numerous examples of this occurring. To discuss all such cases is beyond the scope of this chapter, since they are very numerous. Most, however, do not threaten the integrity of the state (this is especially so with India) or are not of interest to any great power (although they may be of interest to a

South Asian neighbor). They share certain common features with the Sikh/Khalistan problem and Tamil/Sinhalese conflict: They arise out of conflicting ethnic perceptions of vulnerability, a breakdown of agreement on shared goals and nonviolent means of achieving such goals, and the corrosion of traditional social and religious systems. However, they create larger problems only when central authority is weakened or when an outside power is able to aid a dissident regional or ethnic group. Thus, rather than devote attention to the Assamese, Naga, Mizo, Baluch, Sind, or Kashmiri "liberation" or terrorist movements, this chapter will focus on the two ethnic-linguistic separatist movements that have the greatest potential for disruption and external involvement: the Sikh/Khalistan movement in the Indian Punjab and the Tamil separatist movement in Sri Lanka. The Baluch, Sind, and Pathan separatist movements of Pakistan are not included in this group because (1) they are at present relatively dormant; (2) the central government of Pakistan has so far been able to contain these movements; and (3) no foreign power has yet tried to use them to destabilize or destroy the Pakistan government. They are movements of potential significance and could flare up quickly, but outside involvement is unlikely unless broader strategic circumstances were to change.

From Punjab to Khalistan?

In one sense, there is no more purely domestic conflict in South Asia than that between the Indian government and the alienated Sikh community. The Sikhs are highly visible and concentrated. Through very hard work they have rebuilt the Punjab into India's most prosperous state. They are also one of the most martial of Indian communities, having dominated the Indian army for many years.

However, they barely form a majority in Punjab. Many Sikhs live outside the state in such cities as Delhi, Bombay, and Calcutta. There are also large foreign Sikh communities in the United States, Canada, and Great Britain. Sikh politics have always been tumultuous and closely linked to the *Gurdwaras* (Sikh temples). Sikhs are members of both the Congress party and other parties, especially the Akali Dal, a purely Sikh party.

When the Akalis began to demand more autonomy for the Punjab and certain symbolic, religious, and political concessions (a capital of their own, access to All-India radio, a ban on smoking in certain cities), Indira Gandhi's response was to pursue a strategy of divide and rule, supporting extremist Sikhs so that the relative moderates would be outflanked and discredited.[15] The strategy got out of hand as the Sikh extremists took over the Golden Temple and launched terrorist attacks against moderate Sikhs and Hindus in the Punjab. These extremists were crushed on June 6, 1984, when the Indian army occupied the Golden Temple. Subsequently, several thousand Sikh soldiers mutinied; a few officers were killed and many terrorists, innocent young men, and mutineers fled to Pakistan for safe haven.

Until this event, there had been no support for a fringe group that advocated "Khalistan," an independent homeland for the Sikh nation. Khalistanis were based in the United Kingdom, Canada, and the United States, with no significant following in India itself. This began to change after the invasion of the Golden Temple and the anti-Sikh riots that followed Mrs. Gandhi's assassination by one of her Sikh bodyguards on October 30, 1984. Figures are impossible to come by, but an educated guess is that no more than 10 percent of Indian Sikhs seriously advocate Khalistan.

What make the Punjab crisis the most serious yet faced by independent India are its strategic ramifications. The Sikhs are a vital component of the Indian armed forces: 18 percent of the officers in the Indian army and Indian air force are Sikhs and about 12 percent of other ranks are Sikhs. There are between 400,000 and 500,000 Sikh ex-servicemen living in the Punjab. The Punjab itself is strategically vital to the Indian armed forces because major road and rail routes to Kashmir run through the area. Simultaneous crises in Kashmir and Punjab would find the army at a severe disadvantage. These factors add up to the makings of a grave national crisis should the Sikhs remain alienated and should there be a new war with Pakistan.

This prospect has led to speculation by Sikhs and others about the breakup of India and the creation of Khalistan. Such a state would presumably encompass the present Indian Punjab and perhaps parts of neighboring Indian states.[16] Some Khalistani supporters press their case by arguing that Khalistan would become an anticommunist ally of the United States. They liken it to Israel and argue that a tier of religiously oriented states, stretching from Israel to Khalistan (and including Pakistan, Afghanistan, and Iran), would be an effective barrier to Soviet communism. If Khalistan were created soon, they promise, it would support the United States in fighting communism in Afghanistan. Khalistan would be able to do this since (1) it would have a martial and well-disciplined population, already militarily well trained; (2) it would control vital resources such as water and foodgrains and thus be able to play a balancing role between India and Pakistan; and (3) it would develop close ties with the United States.

This line of argument is unrealistic. It ignores likely Pakistani hostility to a strong and powerful Khalistan, it glosses over traditional Sikh schisms and internal conflicts, and it fails to consider Khalistan's landlocked location. However, there have been signs of powerful foreign support for Khalistanis. Should the Indian government be unable to achieve a settlement with moderate Sikh opinion, or should another assassination trigger a new round of reprisals against the Sikhs, the whole process would inch further toward calamity. At that point, outside powers, near and distant, may recalculate their own involvement (as in the case of Bangladesh).

Tamil Eelam and Oceanic Politics

In the nineteenth century the British imported thousands of Indian Tamil laborers into what was Ceylon (now Sri Lanka) to work in the tea plantations located in the northern part of the island. These laborers came from the Madras Presidency of India, a mere twenty miles from Ceylon. Earlier Tamil emigrants had already settled on Ceylon; Indian and Sri Lankan Tamils now constitute about 20 percent of the total population of Sri Lanka. In 1964 an agreement was worked out between India and Sri Lanka for the repatriation of some Tamils of recent origin.[17]

However, elements of the Tamil population felt aggrieved. Their working conditions and wages remained poor, and they were often looked down upon by the Sinhalese; religious, racial, and linguistic differences also existed between the Tamil Hindu minority and the Buddhist Sinhalese majority. What had become a difficult situation gave way to low-level terrorism and guerrilla war, and a massive anti-Tamil riot in 1983 killed a large number of Tamils and reached a state of near insurrection in parts of the island.

There is very strong evidence that some Tamil terrorists are based in and receive support from the Indian state of Tamil Nadu.[18] The guerrillas are divided into several groups, some with PLO links, and the Tamil cause is openly supported by the state government of Tamil Nadu. Until recently, the Indian government has been reluctant to clamp down on terrorist camps and has claimed that no such raids are taking place from Indian soil. In turn, they have accused the Sri Lankan government of unnecessarily inviting in foreign military missions (apparently advisory groups from Israel and the British SAS) and of harassing Indian fishermen.

This dispute has its roots in local conditions and local problems. However, because of Sri Lanka's excellent naval facilities, its desire to remain independent from Indian influence, the conservative nature of the present government, and the difficulty it has experienced in containing the Tamil terrorists, there are important potential international and power implications in the crisis.

Soviet interests in the Indian Ocean are threefold. First, free access to the Indian Ocean allows the Soviets to use it to ship bulky items from one part of the Soviet Union to the other, and thus take some of the load off the Trans-Siberian Railway. Second, the Soviets have a growing political presence in many littoral states along with access to ports at Aden and Camrahn Bay and a semi-permanent anchorage in the Indian Ocean. Their small Indian Ocean fleet and their ships transiting the Indian Ocean can play a supporting role in Soviet diplomacy in littoral states. Finally, the Soviet navy shadows the American fleet in the Indian Ocean region. Right now most of these vessels are surface combatants, but trial patrols of SSBNs indicate the potential use of the Indian Ocean as a station for such boats. A Soviet ASW capacity might then be important.

American naval interests are implied in the above. The Rapid Deployment Force, now organized under CENTCOM, requires surface vessels for any serious operation in the Persian Gulf or other areas in the littoral. The Indian Ocean is a vital route for tankers coming out from the Persian Gulf and going to Europe and (especially) Japan; it may be a useful place to deploy SSBNs, presenting any future Soviet ABM system with a southern threat.

Sri Lanka figures in the above calculations because of its strained relations with India and its potential role as a Western ally. Even now Trincomalee is used for U.S. fleet replenishment and recreation; it has the capacity to be upgraded into a first-class naval facility. The only other significant American naval facility in the region is at Diego Garcia; that facility cannot be expanded, although there are discussions about having a facility at Christmas Island (controlled by Australia). The Soviets have no major facilities in the Indian Ocean itself, although they did assist the Indians in building a major port, drydock, and other facilities at Visakhapatnam on India's east coast.

Should Sri Lanka's conflict with India increase (and the conditionality of that statement must be stressed), there might be a closer tie and even a naval agreement between the United States and Sri Lanka. Such an arrangement is unlikely to lead to greater Soviet access to Indian port facilities. However, it will further strain Indo-Sri Lankan relations and might be resisted by a large segment of the Sri Lankan population. Parenthetically, there would also be strong domestic opposition to any foreign base that might be established in Bangladesh or Pakistan, unless either state were under direct external threat and there was a credible offer of foreign assistance in exchange for such facilities.

CONCLUSIONS

These concluding remarks will be divided into three parts: some observations about conflict in South Asia, some remarks about external involvement in the region, and speculation about possible future involvement.

Regional Conflict

Our brief survey seems to support two general conclusions about regional conflict: The first is of a comparative nature, the second concerns the quality of such conflict.

South Asia has witnessed persistent interstate conflict of varying types and persistent internal violence in three of its major states. In this respect, it resembles the Middle East or Southeast Asia more than Latin America, although it has escaped the burden of heavy arms spending that characterizes the Middle East. Further, the sources of such conflict have not declined, and there is the possibility of a nuclear breakout.

Second, to a great degree regional levels of conflict are not only additive but interactive. At the superpower-national levels, the nonalignment of India retarded the formation of regional groupings based on superpower alignments. This has been less true in recent years, during which time some saw an emerging India-Vietnam-Soviet-Ethiopia pattern balanced against an emerging U.S.-Pakistan-China-ASEAN-Somalia grouping. My view is that this may be more apparent than real. However, the national-regional linkage is well established and pernicious. Internal separatist and autonomist movements have regularly drawn encouragement—and at times, direct support—from outside states that challenge the country they oppose. India's Naga rebels received support from China, as the Khampa tribals of Tibet were once supported from India. Sindhis and Baluch in Pakistan may receive support from India, Kashmiris in India may receive support from Pakistan, and so forth. The most recent case—still alleged, but of greatest potential—is Pakistani support for the Sikh Khalistan movement.

The interactive pattern repeats itself at a higher level as individual South Asian states have regularly sought superpower or Chinese support against a regional neighbor. Pakistan led the way, with close ties to the United States from 1953 to 1965 (followed by China); right now, Nepal, Sri Lanka, and Bangladesh also have close ties with the United States and China, in large part to balance their dominant Indian neighbor. India, of course, has an entangling military relationship with the Soviet Union that provides some protection against China and considerable weaponry for use against Pakistan. The informal system of Soviet-India and Pakistan-China resonates at regional and global levels.

Lessons from Past External Intervention

There is a large body of literature as to whether outside powers tend to force themselves upon regions or whether they are drawn in by regional states. Posing the problem this way suggests the obvious answer: there may be a little bit of both, and the mix of internal pull versus external push will vary from region to region, issue to issue, and time to time. Even then, some generalizations concerning South Asia's particular situation can be offered.

1. Neither the superpowers nor China appears to regard South Asia as of vital geographic, economic, or political importance. No past outside intervention has been based on those factors, with the limited exceptions of the Soviet exploitation of natural gas from Afghanistan and the distant prospect of obtaining a port facility on the Indian Ocean (which was probably not a motive for the Afghanistan invasion). The past physical involvement of the superpowers and China in the region has (with one exception) largely been transitory and has stemmed from strategic or extra-regional considerations. Thus, the U.S. "base" in Peshawar was closed down when satellite observation of Soviet missile developments made it unnecessary; American nuclear intelligence and air defense operations in India, directed against China, were similarly terminated after becoming obsolete; the Soviets apparently were briefly given landing rights for aircraft enroute to Vietnam with military supplies; and the Soviet navy's extended presence in and near Chittagong port, ostensibly for mine-clearing, was eventually wound up. This is not to say that all or part of South Asia may not be of *great* and even *increasing* importance to one or more superpowers and to China, but only to point out that their survival and that of their closest allies (Western Europe and Japan in the case of the United States) is not at issue in their regional South Asian involvement. The only permanent presence of an outside power of any military significance is Chinese control over Aksai Chin. With the notable exception of Afghanistan, the superpowers have come and gone at the invitation of local powers but have not stayed on.

2. In South Asia, India (as the dominant power) has been least interested in having outside powers establish themselves locally on a permanent basis, whether in the form of a physical presence or an alliance relationship. India needs outside support to provide the marginal military increment against Pakistan, but more as a balance against the (largely faded)

Chinese threat. Pakistan's style has been somewhat different. Pakistan has continually sought permanent outside allies and in the past has granted them local intelligence and other facilities; Pakistan requires an outside supporter to help it in the regional balance. Thus, Pakistan has sequentially had close ties with the United States, China, France, and now the United States again. India has had limited ties with the United States, Britain, and the Soviet Union. The latter fulfills two functions: a weapons source and a tacit provider of an umbrella against a prospective Chinese nuclear threat. Whereas Pakistan has sought entangling deep ties with outside states to further ensure that in time of crisis they would continue to support an "ally and a friend," India has tried to keep such outside powers at a distance and has deeply resented the limits placed upon aid received in the past. In recent years, however, Pakistan has begun to follow the Indian path, and its new relationship with the United States is quite circumscribed.

3.   The smallest South Asian states—Nepal, Bangladesh, and Sri Lanka—have no chance of playing any significant military role or of deterring India. They have, however, sought long-term outside political ties and limited amounts of military assistance to help offset their self-evident weaknesses. A startling recent example of this was Sri Lanka's request for the permanent stationing of British troops to protect Sri Lankan democracy.[19]

Perhaps of greatest long-range importance, the smallest regional states have been at the forefront of advocating a regional association, first proposed by Bangladesh's Zia ur-Rahman in 1980. This group, the South Asian Association for Regional Cooperation (SAARC), has formally avoided strategic and security issues. However, it has considerable potential as a device by which the smaller regional states can join together in dealing with the largest—India—and may lessen their incentive to bring in outside powers.

4.   Both India and Pakistan have been regularly shaken by their external ties. Pakistanis often cite the three (actually four) cutoffs of American military aid; they were also infuriated when the United States supplied aid to India from 1962 to 1965, apparently without consultation. India was angry with the U.S cutoff of weapons in 1965 and very disturbed

(although not publicly so) with Soviet "neutrality" in the 1965 war, believing that Pakistan should have been condemned for initiating the conflict. This history has made both India and Pakistan wary of outsiders and has even given rise to the suggestion that the two begin to purchase weapons from each other.

Future Involvement

Technology and strategy combine to suggest a number of ways in which the superpowers will again become directly involved in subcontinental affairs other than through the provision of military equipment.

1. Each superpower may seek or even be offered access to regional ports. This is likely only if their utilization of the Indian Ocean increases significantly (especially if SSBNs are based there) and if India, Pakistan, Bangladesh, or Sri Lanka faces an internal emergency that requires the support of a superpower. Neither superpower is likely to request or be granted such facilities if the prospective host country faces an *external* threat from a neighbor. Even then, it is unlikely that such facilities will be granted.

2. Also unlikely, but worth noting, would be regional cooperation with a superpower in an adjacent theater, especially the Persian Gulf or in Afghanistan. The former has been discussed a number of times. Pakistan already has a small military presence in Saudi Arabia and other Gulf countries; if American and Pakistani interests run parallel in supporting a particular regime or state in the Gulf, they may cooperate. More likely would be superpower logistics support for such an operation.

3. Future technologies may enhance the relevance of South Asia states to the superpowers, especially the United States. The Strategic Defense Initiative has components that might be used to provide allied states with limited protection against external threat. Some regional states might also make useful sites for radar and other facilities in connection with such an SDI

system. Conversely, South Asia may be used to monitor the superpowers' arms race. India has offered its territory for seismic stations as part of a six-nation arms control initiative.

4. More likely than the above, outside intervention in South Asia may be stimulated by the proliferation of nuclear weapons. There is no consensus as to whether a line should be drawn concerning the next nuclear power or where such a line should be drawn. Many concede India's nuclear status. Should Pakistan be actively *prevented* from going nuclear if diplomatic and aid instruments fail? Should the United States assist Israel or India, or carry out an attack on Pakistani facilities itself? Or, if Pakistan and India were to go nuclear, should the United States provide technical, intelligence, and other assistance to ensure that their systems were as stable as possible? Should a line then be drawn at the export of nuclear weapons outside of the region? If so, who will enforce it? Given the past ambivalent attitude of China toward proliferation and the strong concerns of the Soviet Union, it is clear that any U.S. policy on these matters will have to take into account the views of these two states, although there is something to be said for unilateral action.

5. Finally, the two truly revolutionary agents of our time, the transistor and the wide-bodied jet, have combined to alter permanently the relationship between the elites and the leading economies of South Asian states on the one hand and the United States on the other. The American electronics culture has penetrated deeply into the region at the consumer level; it is now advancing to the production level, and India in particular will emerge as an intermediate transmitter of high technology to its neighbors and other regions. Meanwhile, the United States has become the country of choice for the education of South Asia's elite families. These American-educated generations are a new and unpredictable factor: They do not subscribe to the British anti-Americanism of the 1950s, and they understand America better. However, their very contact with the United States makes them more sensitive to American slights and can breed its own resentments.

America's paradox is that it still regards the South Asia region as essentially peripheral to its own vital security interests; in the meantime, it has established cultural and economic outposts in each South Asian state. One suspects that the true historic significance of this development will not be fully assimilated until an essentially military definition of "security" is supplanted by one more in keeping with America's ideological and economic, as well as military and strategic, interests.

NOTES

1. For the historic origins of the South Asian region, see Joseph E. Schwartzberg, ed., *A Historical Atlas of South Asia* (Chicago, Ill.: University of Chicago Press, 1978).
2. For the evolution of the term *Third World*, see Leslie Wolf-Phillips, "Why Third World?" *Third World Quarterly* 1, no. 1 (1977): 105–15.
3. From reply to debate on foreign affairs in the Indian Lok Sabha, 17 December 1957.
4. For a survey of such imperial defense plans, see Bisheshwar Prasad, *Official History of the Indian Armed Forces in the Second World War, 1939–45; Defense of India: Policy and Plans* (New Delhi: Longmans, 1963).
5. For the best study of this problem, see Sisir Gupta, *Kashmir: A Study in Indo-Pakistan Relations* (Bombay: Asia Publishing House, 1966).
6. Department of State, *Foreign Relations of the United States* III (1947) (Washington, D.C.: Department of State, Historical Office, Bureau of Public Affairs, 1972), pp. 148.
7. Department of State, *Foreign Relations of the United States* VI (1949) (Washington, D.C.: Department of State, Historical Office, Bureau of Public Affairs, 1977), pp. 28 ff.
8. See Stephen P. Cohen, "South Asia After Afghanistan," *Problems of Communism*, January-February 1985, pp. 18–31. One reason Soviet arms are purchased by India is that they do not include research and development costs; India's own Soviet-designed weapons cost about as much to produce as those purchased from the USSR. Both are cheaper than equivalent Western weapons.
9. The most careful account of the *Enterprise* operation is in Shirin Tahir-Kheli, *The United States and Pakistan* (New York: Praeger, 1982), pp. 44 ff.
10. For an analysis of the impact of the American program on Pakistan, see Stephen P. Cohen, *The Pakistan Army* (Berkeley: University of California Press, 1984), pp. 63–75.
11. A former Pakistani official and ex-ambassador to the USSR, Sajjad Haider, has been the most outspoken advocate of this view. See also

M.B. Naqvi (a distinguished Pakistani journalist), "The Peace Option for Pakistan?" in Stephen P. Cohen, ed., *The Security Future of South Asia* (Urbana and Chicago: University of Illinois Press, 1987).

12. For a thoughtful Indian examination, see Bhabani Sen Gupta, *Nuclear Weapons: Policy Options for India* (New Delhi: Sage, 1983), and for the only careful Pakistani study, see Akhtar Ali, *Pakistan's Nuclear Dilemma* (Karachi: Economist Research Unit, 1984).

13. See Leonard S. Spector, *Nuclear Proliferation Today* (New York: Vintage, 1984), pp. 23 ff.

14. See Shai Feldman, *Israeli Nuclear Deterrence: A Strategy for the 1980s* (New York: Columbia University Press, 1982).

15. For a survey of the origin of the Sikh crisis, see Kuldip Nayar and Khushwant Singh, *Tragedy of Punjab: Operation Bluestar and After* (New Delhi: Vision Books, 1984); and Lt. Gen. J.S. Aurora et al., *The Punjab Story* (New Delhi: Roli Books, 1984).

16. Maps of "Khalistan" published in the United States indicate that it would contain large chunks of Harayana, Rajasthan, and Gujarat, thus providing a corridor to the sea; this would, of course, make Sikhs a minority in such a state.

17. For a clear account of a very complicated problem, see "Introduction," in James Manor, ed., *Sri Lanka in Change and Crisis* (London: St. Martin's Press, 1984); and the chapters on Sri Lanka in A. Jeyaratnam Wilson and Dennis Dalton, eds., *The States of South Asia* (Honolulu: University Press of Hawaii, 1982).

18. This badly kept secret was given full publicity in an important article by Shekhar Gupta, "Ominous Presence in Tamil Nadu," *India Today*, 31 March 1984.

19. Request made by Sri Lanka's president, J.R. Jayewardene, on 13 April 1985, at a banquet in Mrs. Thatcher's honor. "J.R. Jayewardene Wants Troops from U.K.," *Times of India*, 14 April 1985, p.1.

8 NORTHEAST ASIA

Edward A. Olsen

Americans have been concerned in varying degrees about Korea since the 1870s, but only since the United States in 1945 inherited responsibility from Imperial Japan for part of Korea has that involvement become important to Americans. Before then, Korea was an object of attention of three far more powerful neighbors: China, czarist Russia, and Imperial Japan. Since Korea came into existence, it has dwelt in the shadows of much larger and stronger Chinese dynasties; international relations for Koreans long meant a subordinate bond with their Chinese mentors. The China connection defined the parameters of Korea's world.

Korea's traditional world ended suddenly in the last third of the nineteenth century. Living in a fool's paradise, the Koreans earnestly trusted in China's greatness even as it was collapsing around them under pressures from Western imperial expansion. Unlike Japan, which quickly recognized and adapted to China's unprecedented decline and the rise of foreign powers at China's expense, Korea stubbornly clung to the traditional external ties that had served it so well for so long.

Japan's reaction to the altered international environment was to catch up with the new agents of change and influence in Asia by emulating their ways. Korea proved unable and unwilling to play the game by the new rules, preferring instead to conform to rules that had become passé. The events swirling around Korea in the subsequent three decades gave rise to the expression that Korea was like a "shrimp among whales."

Western failure to block or seriously condemn Japanese incorporation and ultimate annexation of Korea simultaneously demonstrated foreign perceptions of Korea as expendable in the "great game" and sealed its fate for four decades, making Korea an official nonentity. Although the protests of Korean nationalists struggling to oust an oppressive Japanese colonial regime were heard by Westerners, with occasional echoes of sympathy for the Koreans' cause, no external power had sufficient interest in Korea to attempt the formidable task of wresting it from the powerful Japanese empire. For practical purposes, prewar Korea was a lost cause for all but the most diehard Korean patriots.

Luckily for Korea, Japan lost the war, freeing all non-Japanese within Tokyo's former domains to pursue their own ways. Less luckily for Korea, that pursuit was short-circuited by postwar events. Initially Korea was divided between the United States and USSR as a temporary expedient. That supposedly expedient division became a fixture of the postwar world because of intervening cold war tensions. Just as late nineteenth-century Korea became the victim of colonial ambition, mid-twentieth-century Korea fell victim to the competing camps in the cold war.

THE EMERGENCE OF POSTWAR MAJOR POWER INTERESTS IN KOREA

Of the four external powers that, in the mid-1980s, have the clearest interests in Korea, two—the Soviet Union and Japan—entered the postwar period with the most explicitly defined interests. Japan clearly had had enough of Korea to last a long time and wanted nothing to do with that country if it could be avoided. Consequently, Japan's virtual policy vacuum toward Korea from the U.S. Occupation until Japan-ROK normalization talks in the early 1960s constituted an explicit policy of abstention. Moscow, on the other hand, purposefully occupied northern Korea, eager to extend its influence in Asia as far as it could. Influencing northern Korea would simultaneously adhere to Lenin's doctrine of exporting communism by shaping the Democratic People's Republic of Korea (DPRK), bolster the revolutionary cause of the Chinese civil war, secure in Korea the spoils of war that the United States denied to Moscow in Japan, and pursue long-standing geopolitical goals the Kremlin inherited from the czars. These included a strengthened strategic buffer in Northeast Asia that would protect ports in the Soviet Far East and might someday provide regular Soviet access to compatible nearby port facilities in Korea. Thus Japan and the Soviet Union were at opposite ends of the spectrum of Korean affairs, one wanting a minimalist profile and the other scheming to maximize its gains from being on the winning side of the war.

In sharp contrast to the relatively clear objectives of Moscow and Tokyo, Washington meandered into post–World War II Korean affairs with little thought about what it should do. Korea was a backwater of U.S. policy in Asia. The focus of that policy was what to do about postwar Japan and, subsequently, what to do about the evident Soviet designs for China and northern Korea. U.S. policy toward South Korea was—at best—a corollary of that toward Japan and the Soviet Union. The United States had no long-standing goals concerning Korea politically, economically, or strategically. Moreover, it was slow to develop ad hoc interim goals. America's only motivation was a desire to revitalize Korea so that its people could get on with their lives. Beyond that vague goal, there was no significant U.S. commitment. Virtually no American policymakers approached Korea with the enthusiasm or aspirations that guided their Soviet counterparts.

In that light, it is amazing that the United States accomplished as much as it did to foster and develop the fledgling Republic of Korea (ROK), starting in 1948. Equally amazing was the level of U.S. support generated on behalf of the ROK during the Korean War, for the United States had negligible national interests in Korea. What accounted for this change of direction by Americans? Basically, the United States faced the full range of implications inherent in its acceptance of responsibility for defeated Japan and the possible adverse consequences for newfound U.S. obligations globally, should communist aggression in Asia succeed. Fears of the Munich syndrome caused Americans to view events in distant corners of the world as threats to the United States through its burgeoning network of potentially strong allies in the cold war. Although Secretary of State Dean Acheson's famous statement excluding Korea from vital U.S. defense interests ostensibly precluded that country being where the United States would choose to draw "the line," once hostilities broke out in June 1950, the United States quickly reacted as though the line had been drawn, then violated by the other side.

During the Korean War and in the years since, the United States has been remarkably steadfast in support of its ROK protégé. Though the limited objectives the United States proclaimed in what was termed the Korean "conflict" required the United States to stop short of the Rhee government's reunification goals, America performed extraordinarily well considering its interests in Korea. Since the end of the war, the United States has stood steadfast by South Korea's side, bolstering the political, diplomatic, economic, and military stances of a cavalcade of regimes in Seoul (none of which fit the criteria most U.S. policymakers hoped for). Hence, U.S.-ROK relations have grown stronger over the three decades since the war, and the credibility of Washington's assertion of U.S. national interests in Korea has increased accordingly.

As the United States became heavily engaged in Korea, the attitudes of the other three powers were altered in reaction. Japan's leaders responded with a muffled sigh of relief. Even knowing that it could not influence the course of events in Korea and that the Japanese public would not tolerate a more activist policy toward Korea, Japan's leaders welcomed the U.S. resolve that led to a stalemate. Washington's decisions served well long-standing Japanese geopolitical interests in Korean stability. United States policy became de facto Japanese policy, with virtually no Japanese risk or responsibility. Moreover, Japan's economic recovery was bolstered by business from Korean War-generated requirements for products, repairs, and "R&R" for U.S. troops. In one stroke, Japan saw its regional and national interests protected by the United States while Tokyo kept aloof, its bilateral bonds with the United States strengthened, and saw Washington proclaim discrete U.S. national interests in Korea separate from those in Japan. Except for the war's proximity, this was an ideal resolution of Japan's concerns about its nearest neighbor. Eager to preserve these circumstances, Tokyo has since tried to maintain some distance between Japan and the two Korean states.

For the first decade after the U.S. occupation of Japan, Tokyo's policy toward Seoul and Pyongyang was "a plague on both your houses." Many Japanese continue to feel that way about Koreans. Partly because of the colonial legacy of ill will, a fractious Korean ethnic minority in Japan, and lingering Japanese wariness about major reinvolvement in any contentious international issues, few Japanese have much enthusiasm for playing an active role in Korean affairs. Nevertheless, in pursuit of economic opportunities and reconciliation with the U.S.-backed South Korean buffer state on Japan's flank, Tokyo engaged in arduous negotiations with

Seoul that led to normalization of relations in 1965. Since then, Japan-ROK ties have blossomed to a magnitude undreamed of twenty years ago. Japan is a major economic partner of the ROK and a major influence on the development model used by the ROK technocrats who created South Korea's "economic miracle." However, until 1983–84, when Prime Minister Nakasone and President Chun exchanged precedent-setting visits, public political relations were dicey. To be sure, there were times during the Park years when Japan-ROK political ties appeared reasonably strong, if tainted by rumors of free-flowing cash and favors. The Nakasone-Chun relationship helped put bilateral political ties on a more respectable, firmer footing. By mutual agreement bilateral strategic ties are far less developed.

The U.S. connection played a major role in Japan's very gradual shift toward South Korea. Because of its proximity and economic aspirations, Japan could reinforce economically what the United States did in Korea militarily and politically. In time, the U.S. connection helped smooth the way for improved Japan-ROK political ties. Ironically, Japanese and South Korean apprehensions about the political reliability of the United States over trade and strategic issues also aided their partial reconciliation. Though most U.S., Japanese, and South Korean analysts are opposed to rushing strategic reconciliation, there are strong arguments that the time has come for real movement on that front.[1]

Japan's relations with North Korea developed differently, partly because no third state could play the articulating role between Japan and North Korea that had been performed by the United States between Japan and South Korea. Japan-DPRK ties have languished since Tokyo's 1965 rapprochement with Seoul. Some left-wing elements in Japan tried to foster improved ties with North Korea, but without success. Similarly, there are periodic murmurs from Tokyo about its hopes to maintain proper relations with both Koreas and to refrain from taking sides. Most of the latter seems designed to mollify anxieties in Japan and, perversely, to stimulate some anxiety in Seoul so that the ROK could not take Japanese cooperation for granted. It also helped Tokyo by signaling Washington that there are domestic constraints on how far Tokyo can go vis-à-vis Korea.

Without giving undue credence to North Korean paranoia, a fair indication of where Japan stands between the two Koreas can be gleaned from Pyongyang's pique over what it sees as a pronounced Japanese tilt toward South Korea. North Korea's perceptions become flawed when they try to explain that tilt as a U.S.-ROK-Japan cabal against Pyongyang. Japan does tilt pointedly, if uneasily, toward South Korea for economic and political reasons, and North Korea has been unable to compete for Japan's attention. Should it persist in preparations for renewed war and periodic overt aggression, it might eventually nudge Japan closer to South Korea strategically as well. In these terms, North Korea's dire warnings about a trilateral cabal could well become a self-fulfilling prophecy.

On balance, then, Japan's reaction to the U.S. assertion of a commitment to Korea produced a gradual reorientation of Japan toward a more natural hierarchical relationship with one part of Korea, increased tensions with the other half of the peninsula, and a quiet abandonment of Tokyo's implicitly hands-off policy of the early postwar period. However, Japan has stopped short of a full-fledged hands-on policy, preferring instead to operate in the political and economic shadows of greatly strengthened U.S.-ROK ties.

Initially, the U.S. shift toward more overt support for the ROK during the Korean War drew the PRC and USSR closer together in their support of North Korea. However, as the PRC provided more armed assistance to Korea, the first Korea-oriented stirrings of the eventual Sino-Soviet rupture emerged, largely unnoticed by the free world. Once these tensions became more palpable, North Korea became simultaneously an arena within which the tensions materialized and the object of Beijing and Moscow's attention. By the mid-1960s, the former partners in arms in North Korea's cause became rivals for reasons that were essentially unrelated to Korea but transferred to the North Korean theater nonetheless. Moscow and Beijing were involved in a contest to show North Korea that their respective brands of Marxist ideology, revolutionary development, and security were most appropriate to Pyongyang's needs.

The North Koreans did not think either brand totally satisfactory, particularly since neither Moscow nor Beijing was sufficiently generous materially, nor supportive geopolitically, to meet Pyongyang's criteria. So, instead of tilting toward either side of the Sino-Soviet split, Pyongyang made a virtue of necessity by transforming its fence-sitting into an alleged policy of equidistance. The

Kim Il-sung regime proclaimed its own third way to Kimist-style communism. Though neither Beijing nor Moscow appreciated Kim's version of orthodoxy, neither could afford to drive Kim toward the other by openly offending his regime. The result has been an intermittent boon for Pyongyang, permitting it to play the Chinese and Russians against each other. This has been risky for Kim, and he would have preferred solid support for Pyongyang's aggressive agenda. On balance, however, Kim has successfully maintained that delicate balance by periodically feinting toward one, then the other. Pyongyang also uses the continued U.S. presence in South Korea as leverage in its relations with China and the USSR. As of mid-1987, North Korea's pendulum has again swung toward Moscow, but precedent and hints of improved DPRK-PRC ties suggest it will swing back.

Chinese and Soviet links with North Korea, awkward as they have been, had a generally negative influence on PRC and USSR relations with the United States and Japan. Despite sporadic attempts at U.S.-Soviet detente and great improvement in U.S.-PRC and Japan-PRC relations, Moscow and Beijing's backing for Pyongyang has been and continues to be a significant stumbling block. Even though Washington and Tokyo value the moderating influences Beijing and Moscow exert on Pyongyang, there is considerable frustration with the communist giants' inability to call off the North Koreans. Until North Korea can be induced to change its aggressive ways and disavow its existing agenda, these uncertainties about Chinese and Soviet purposes are likely to remain.

CONTEMPORARY KOREA: CONCERNS OF THE MAJOR POWERS

The concerns of the major powers will be assessed from three perspectives: strategic, political, and economic.

Strategic Affairs

Despite Korea's being a perennial international hot spot, with border confrontations, an escalating arms race, and the uniquely active involvement of most major powers, there is remarkable agreement among the major powers and both Koreas that the stalemated strategic status quo is valuable and should be preserved. For Korea it amounts to "peace."

What does this mean for the powers? First, regardless of profuse rhetoric praising the concept of Korean reunification and, specifically, the unification proposals emanating from Korea, no major power desires a unitary Korean state. That state would be more difficult to manipulate than a divided Korea, and it could be a more volatile actor in regional affairs. The armed potential of a unified Korean state, about one million heavily armed personnel focusing on an external target, would be inherently more destabilizing than the continued current intramural focus. Further, if that state were to tilt toward one external power, the others might well suffer adverse consequences in ways not presently possible. Thus, perpetuating the stalemated division of Korea appeals to the major powers because it assures there can be neither true peace nor disastrous war, either of which would yield winners and losers. The status quo prevents winners and losers, except for the Korean masses on each side, but then such humanitarian concerns are not the stuff of international power politics.

Though all the major powers share interests in preserving the strategic status quo, each one's particular perspective delineates its stake. Least overtly happy with it are the Sino-Soviet antagonists, who harbor forlorn hopes that Pyongyang might tilt permanently in their direction. Such a tilt would assure the successful suitor a more reliable client. However, considering North Korea's reluctance to tilt irrevocably for its own reasons, both Beijing and Moscow accept the benefits of a stable status quo. Foremost is the reduced risk in not playing to its conclusion what might be a zero-sum game within the communist world. Neither Moscow nor Beijing can safely assume its opponent would not react violently to a pronounced and lasting North Korean tilt. Entrenched Chinese strategic access in North Korea could jeopardize the Soviet Pacific fleet's nearby home port. Conversely, decisive Soviet strategic influence in North Korea—which loomed large in 1986–87—would tighten Moscow's encirclement of the PRC, providing Soviet access closer to Chinese centers of population and industry. These fears, in turn, enable North Korea to perch less precariously on its fence but sharply delimit Pyongyang's options.

Confronted with an intramural communist and the North–South Korean stalemates, Moscow and Beijing attempt to minimize the costs of placating North Korean demands. Though there is a choreographed quality to relations between the Chinese, North Koreans, and Russians, there is no single choreographer. However, compared to South Korea's attempts to manipulate the United States and Japan, North Korea's leaders enjoy a choreographic edge. An irony of this North Korean ability to influence its external environment by threatening to become a loose cannon is that it also supplies Moscow and Beijing with considerable leverage over the United States, Japan, and South Korea. The latters' hopes to preserve the status quo rest on the moderating influences of China and the USSR. This strategic leverage translates into tremendous political and economic capital for Moscow and Beijing as they deal broadly with the United States, Japan, and South Korea. China is most explicit and successful in exercising this power. These successes may have led Moscow to increase the strategic ante in ways that caused Pyongyang to tilt once more since 1985. However, this is a risky game because it gives North Korea a chance to use its responses as leverage. Clearly, assessing these tangled efforts to influence and counterinfluence each other is like viewing a mirror in a mirror; one's interpretations can go on in infinite reflections.

The United States is more content with the strategic status quo than is either China or the Soviet Union. In a world where numerous instabilities pose potential dangers to U.S. interests, the Far East is relatively calm. Even so, U.S. officials periodically warn North Korea against rash actions that could precipitate a new round in the Korean War, citing arms buildups in the DPRK and its warlike rhetoric. Such cautionary U.S. activity is part of their calibrated response to North Korea and its backers, signaling that the United States—despite the neo-isolationist Vietnam syndrome and a desire to reduce tensions with North Korea—is unwavering in its support of the ROK, so that North Korea will not be tempted to gamble. In short, U.S.-ROK preparations and rhetoric are integral parts of the calculus of deterrence that preserves the Korean status quo. Despite general U.S. contentment with the status quo, a sense of uneasiness remains regarding prospects for Korean stability. U.S. concerns can be attributed to American perceptions of North Korean leaders as irrational: witness their involvement in the unprovoked DMZ axe murders of UN forces in 1977, the Rangoon terrorist bombing of the ROK leadership in 1983, and fears that North Korea may try to disrupt the 1988 Olympics to be hosted by Seoul. Neither did the Soviet shootdown of the KAL flight 007 in 1983 help reassure the United States about the certainties of the status quo. Though China now seems on a steady course that will not encourage North Korean irrationality, Beijing's past fluctuations do not reassure qualms about China's future role. Thus, some Americans wonder whether U.S. weapons or technology transfers to China might not someday be used by North Koreans against U.S. and ROK forces. Serious as those warning indicators may be, they can be managed with relative ease by maintaining a high level of readiness to deter the other side.

A more troubling concern is the appropriate distribution of responsibility for maintaining that deterrence, namely, how the burden of South Korean defense should be shared. For decades virtually no one questioned the propriety of U.S. forces bearing the major external load for South Korean security. After all, ROK forces could not do it alone, Japan was unable to help, and U.S. interests in the peace and prosperity of both allies warranted its continued support. Most Americans concerned with Northeast Asian security still are willing to leave existing arrangements untouched. Both South Korea and Japan are pleased by such American attitudes. South Korea does not wish to tinker gratuitously with a viable defense system. More to the point, Japan sees the strategic status quo as virtually perfect. Despite the huge economic advances Japan has made in the mid-1980s, enabling it to do much more for its own and the region's defenses than it does, few critics of Japan's "free ride" have dared to broach the issue of seeking Japanese assistance in Korean security. Clearly, such help is possible and may even be desirable. In its absence, the Japanese rely on the United States to protect geopolitical interests in Korea that are more important to Japan than to the United States. The United States in Korea has become a strategic surrogate for Japan, which refuses to meet its responsibilities. Citing domestic political opposition to bearing any such duties in Korea (or elsewhere) and budgetary constraints, Tokyo happily opts out and heartily supports the status quo.

If the United States could tolerate indefinitely the mixture of Japanese parsimony and timidity motivating Tokyo's self-centered strategic policy toward Korea, there would be no reason to question the viability of the Korean status quo. However, mounting American frustrations with both bilateral U.S.-Japan trade and defense frictions, and appropriate levels of burden-sharing, are timely issues that cannot be postponed forever. Every area of U.S.-Japan mutual security concerns should be open for reassessment. Despite the profound reluctance of most Japanese and South Koreans to see Americans debate Korean aspects of this issue, as well as the distinct lack of enthusiasm of many U.S. officials for this controversial subject, the relatively changed potentials of all three allies clearly make equitable burden-sharing far more possible now than a few years ago. Therefore, despite major drawbacks stemming from the legacy of Japan-ROK enmity, a strong case can be made for the desirability of Japan-ROK-U.S. strategic cooperation. More important, if American public opinion—always a fickle variable—supportive of a U.S. commitment to South Korean security (directly and as a buffer for Japan) is to be preserved in an era that is as influenced by the painful lessons of Vietnam as the early post–World War II era was influenced by the lessons of Munich, no serious questioning of those allies' will to stand and fight beside the United States can be condoned. Such questioning in a new Korean War would likely be devastating. Yet, Japan's refusal to cooperate in Korea and the obvious reluctance of South Korea to sanction U.S. efforts toward Japanese cooperation are precisely the stimuli that could provoke enervating questions. Consequently, the strategic status quo, so beloved by many in Japan and the ROK and relied upon by Washington, contains weaknesses that should be resolved.

Structural weaknesses in the alliances that support the ROK strategically are complicated by differences about the role of nuclear weapons in South Korean defenses. The U.S. nuclear umbrella protecting South Korea plays a crucial role. Without it, far greater conventional forces would be required. However, because of the real possibility of an irrational North Korean attack against the South, which might precipitate a theater nuclear response, it is legitimate to ask whether the security of Korea would not be better served by a substantial conventional buildup by the United States, the ROK, and Japan that would preclude the need for a U.S. nuclear response against North Korea.

While a shift away from prospective use of the nuclear umbrella seems advisable, it must not suggest to South Korea any diminution of the nuclear shield it finds so valuable. Were South Korea to feel insecure because of a U.S. reassessment of the utility of the nuclear umbrella, Seoul might reconsider its own nuclear options. That, in turn, could escalate to a dangerous Korean nuclear arms race, a possibility unpalatable to the major powers. In part, the United States maintains the nuclear umbrella over Korea and its forces there to preclude the ROK's nuclear option. Should South Korea be put in a position where it felt compelled to pursue that option, Japan, too, might have to reconsider its even more formidable nuclear option, with tremendous implications for a status quo that extends far beyond Korea. Moscow and Beijing are less open about their reluctance to see Korean nuclear proliferation, but it seems clear that neither would relish the Kim regime's having its finger on a nuclear button. Nor would they welcome the pressures North Korea could exert on them to supply it with whatever was necessary to keep up with a South Korean regime pursuing its nuclear option. Thus, for a variety of reasons, a conventionally armed strategic status quo is vastly preferable, but it should be one that enhances stability and diminishes the risk of escalation to the theater nuclear threshold.

Political Affairs

The status quo within the politics of each Korean state is accepted by the major powers, but with considerably less enthusiasm than they display in their tacit approval of the inter-Korean strategic status quo. The latter constitutes a structural equilibrium in which major powers have some influence over each Korea—direct for each power's Korean partner and indirect for each one's Korean adversary. However, in each instance of Korean internal political stability, the friendly external powers have marginal influence over "their" Korean state's domestic politics, and the foreign adversary powers have virtually no influence over the domestic political affairs of the opposing Korean state. Despite these differences in the major powers' ability to influence domestic politics in each Korea, they value the internal stability that each half of the major power equation is able to induce in its Korea.

There are remarkable functional similarities in the ways each set of major power backers views its Korea, despite the backers' radically different national interests. In North Korea, both Moscow and Beijing reluctantly accepted the excesses of Kim Il-sung's cult of personality, which has verged on his deification. Similarly, the hard-line Stalinist mode of Pyongyang's politics and government is passé in China and the Soviet Union. Pyongyang's political style reminds its backers of a past they are trying to forget. Though Chinese and Soviet policymakers barely conceal their repugnance for the emergence of the "Kim Dynasty" and its un-Marxist naming of Kim Jong-il as the successor-designate, they have no choice except to go along in order to maintain their channels of communication and influence. So far this "grin and bear it" approach seems to work satisfactorily, but how successful are Beijing and Moscow at lining up their supporters in Pyongyang for any power struggle that might occur after the elder Kim's demise?

In South Korea, its backers do not face a situation nearly as bleak. Compared to North Korea, the South is an outpost of freedom in the Korean nation. However, despite the considerable liberty in the ROK, Seoul's leaders have embarrassed their major power friends, especially the United States. Syngman Rhee's autocratic ways were the bane of his U.S. protagonists. After Rhee's ouster, the slim U.S. hopes that a more well-rounded democracy would succeed him were crushed in Park Chung-hee's 1961 coup. Though the Park regime's economic successes, its strategic reliability in Korea and Vietnam, and its slow political liberalization compensated in part for its authoritarian excesses, neither Washington nor the American people were ever comfortable with Park's liabilities. The Chun Du-hwan regime emerged via another coup shortly after Park's assassination. Though valued for the same reasons as its predecessor, the Chun regime also suffers from the same liabilities. Despite differences relating to its more ambitious and successful foreign policy agenda, Chun's tenure is seen as a condensed version of Park's. Political pluralism showed signs of new health in mid-1987, but a mix of authoritarianism and militarism still makes the United States uncomfortable about proclaiming its protégé's political virtues. U.S. support for the ROK tends to mirror some of the ambiguity displayed by China and the USSR toward North Korea.

Compared to the United States, Japan is simultaneously more and less critical of South Korea's political status quo. The Japanese are prone to carp about South Korea's authoritarianism and bemoan Tokyo's tilt toward Seoul. Japanese critics should put that criticism into an objective, comparative context by regularly juxtaposing Seoul's with Pyongyang's political behavior. Similarly, there would be more respect for Japanese criticism of Seoul's politics if the critics had the humility to recognize that not too long ago Japanese political repression was even worse than South Korea's. For these reasons, and in order not to antagonize further South Koreans and their U.S. friends, Tokyo takes a less critical stance than the Japanese masses toward Seoul's politics. Except for outrageous actions by Seoul, such as the attempt to kidnap Kim Dae-jung in Japan in 1973 or the heavy-handed suppression of the Kwangju insurrection in 1980, Tokyo routinely overlooks South Korean authoritarian excesses. This is part of Tokyo's long-standing *seikei bunri* (separate economics and politics) theme in its foreign policy. However, it is difficult for Tokyo to adhere to this policy toward Korea, given the emotional feelings of the Japanese and Japan's Korean minority.

The United States is deeply troubled by the contradictions in its desires both to protect South Korean political, economic, and strategic stability and to foster the political liberty that is a major rationale behind its long-standing commitment to the ROK. The exigencies of U.S. policy toward South Korea at times compel Washington to compromise profound American human rights principles. This compromise often embarrasses Washington and angers a significant segment of U.S. society. An irony of these U.S. concerns is that they are not shared by Japan. Neither the moral questions accruing from its colonial legacy nor the problems associated with its greater tolerance of Seoul's excesses impinge on the conscience of Tokyo's policy. Indeed, one can question whether Tokyo's policy toward Korea has a "conscience" analogous to the one the American people impose on Washington's policy. If Tokyo—not Washington—bore responsibility for providing Korean security and setting the moral tone inherent in overriding legitimate human rights concerns, there would likely be fewer qualms about dilemmas posed by moral compromises deemed necessary to maintain sufficient discipline.

Just as there are functional similarities between the backers' views of "their" Korea, so, too, are there functional similarities in their attitudes toward the Korea they oppose. The United States and Japan are eager to keep North Korea's fear and paranoia within limits. For years this desire went no further than occasional verbal reassurances to Pyongyang that it need not fear U.S.-ROK defensive measures as long as Pyongyang did not threaten the ROK. Similar reassurances have been expressed about U.S.-Japan measures to assure regional peace. Other than their general effectiveness as part of strategic deterrence, there is no evidence that Pyongyang has ever been calmed by such assurances. Critics in Japan and some in the United States have urged that their countries make further discreet overtures to wean North Korea from its rigid hard-line policies. So far, very little progress has been achieved. The Reagan administration edged in that direction with the so-called smile diplomacy displayed in the early 1980s—not being gratuitously uncivil toward any North Korean representatives they happened to meet. By the mid-1980s, following signs of some economic flexibility in North Korea, Washington expressed tentative interest in improved U.S.-DPRK relations, sanctioned by Seoul and Tokyo, that would foster balanced cross-contacts paralleling those Seoul has engaged in with Beijing and Moscow.[2]

As much as Washington, Tokyo, and Seoul would welcome such gradual progress, their real hopes rest on there being no deterioration in Pyongyang's domestic political stability and in the resulting inter-Korean stability. A central concern is that Kim Il-sung's death might provoke a traumatic succession. A post-Kim regime might be more, less, or just as willing to tolerate and use the strategic status quo. The danger is, of course, that a new regime might be less tolerant of existing arrangements and, perhaps to prove its toughness, would launch an assault on the ROK to do what Kim Il-sung was unable to do in his lifetime. Unlike Moscow or Beijing, there is little Washington or Tokyo can do to influence the succession and its impact on North Korea's policy toward South Korea. However, Pyongyang's major adversaries can offer rewards for good behavior even as they brace themselves for the possibility of "bad" behavior.

Neither Moscow nor Beijing seems to fear that South Korea would risk an attack on the North, despite North Korean warnings of such intentions, the legacy of Syngman Rhee's frustrated desires to go north, and ill-concealed American apprehensions that U.S. forces must stay in Korea partly to restrain South Korean hotheads. Neither China nor the USSR has the same concerns about Seoul as Pyongyang's adversaries. Nevertheless, South Korean strategic, political, and economic successes do make Moscow and Beijing apprehensive about the future. It is this concern that the major powers share toward their adversarial Korea. For Moscow and Beijing, Seoul's probable future successes threaten to create an insurmountable gap between it and Pyongyang. Just as that gap may make North Korea more dangerous for the ROK, the United States, and Japan as the unstable element in the six-country Korean equation, so also may North Korea become more difficult for its ostensible backers to control or to influence. Also, the widening gap would aggravate the already significant costs of PRC and USSR assistance to the DPRK. Consequently, it is in the Chinese and Soviet interest to encourage some degree of cross-contact with the ROK to ameliorate the hurt of the widening gap, but they cannot move so fast or far that their actions antagonize Pyongyang. Conversely, and perversely, Moscow and Beijing use Pyongyang's fear of a "South Korea card" in the hands of its backers to get North Korea to moderate its ways. This, too, is a mirror-in-a-mirror analytical conundrum.

Political relations between the major powers and the two Korean states are the least controllable of the three categories. Strategic affairs and economic affairs lend themselves better to a degree of external manipulation. However, political affairs have too many independent variables—mutual hatreds, prejudices, and ignorance—for anyone to be complacent about the future of political relations between the major powers and Korea.

Economic Affairs

There is no stable status quo in Korean economic affairs. South Korea is on an economic fast track while North Korea is comparatively sluggish. North Korea compares well to many Third World states and has surpassed Korea's prewar status. Thus, North Koreans are proud of how far they have come. However, like the Soviet Union compared to the United States, North Korea's economy lags behind South Korea's. Also like the USSR-U.S. balance, North Korea stands out only in its ability to put together an economy that supports a strong defense. By virtually all other indicators, the North trails the South and the gap is widening.

South Korea is important to all the major powers, but for different reasons. The growth of U.S.-ROK economic ties has been phenomenal. From near the bottom of the list, South Korea climbed to the seventh ranking trade partner by 1986. This trade has also become increasingly important to the United States. However, trade is vital for South Korea, while the United States is less dependent upon trade for its existence. On balance, this casts South Korea as dependent on the United States.

In recent years the ROK has enjoyed a favorable balance of trade at U.S. expense. Because of the similarities between South Korea and Japan (it is known as one of Asia's "new Japans"), there is justification for American concern that South Korea will follow Japan in achieving "too much success." South Korean representatives tell all who will listen that the ROK is not another Japan, but Americans are justified in preempting another Japan-like challenge. Seoul's admonitions against treating the ROK like a budding new Japan seem to be like whistling in the dark.

Actually, Seoul's concern about such a U.S. ploy should signal Americans that South Koreans think it would be effective. So, despite the dilemma posed by wanting South Korea economically strong to bolster the ROK's strategic capability, yet fearing future competition from that same prosperous allied economy, the United States ultimately must attend to its own economic interests first. The United States cannot be a strong strategic backstop for South Korea and a host of other allies if its own economic health is jeopardized by economic challenges posed by those same allies. Though difficult, the ultimate choice is clear.

Such tensions were evident during President Chun's visit to Washington in April 1985. Despite Seoul's efforts to put that visit in the best light, it clearly was marred by frictions stemming largely from South Korea's reluctance to liberalize U.S. access to South Korean markets to correspond to the access South Koreans enjoy in the United States. Some temporary economic frictions can be swept under the rug in the interest of bilateral harmony, but those of lasting significance to the U.S. economy must be resolved equitably. As a consequence of America's need to protect its economic well-being by dealing assertively with Japan and the "new Japans," led by South Korea, future U.S.-ROK economic relations may well be rougher than most observers now seem to expect.

Japan, too, is looking at its Asian competition with apprehension. Taiwan is as much of a challenge as South Korea, but Taiwan's problems with the PRC diminish its ability to nibble at Japan's lead. Were South Korea to be unified with the lackluster North Korean economy, the ROK's ability to challenge Japan's lead might be diminished (in contrast to many analyses that expect such a merger to produce complementarity). Because Korean unification is more of a chimera than Chinese unification, Seoul presumably will not face that handicap. Consequently, South Korea is probably the leading candidate to rival Japan.

For fear that such a prospect could become reality and that the United States might use its influence in South Korea to penetrate the ROK economy as an instrument to compete with Japan, and also to induce the ROK to lower its trade barriers in ways Japan has not, Tokyo seems to take the South Korean challenge seriously. Japan is much less enthusiastic about sharing technologies with the South Koreans than it used to be. Complicating this issue, Japan cannot complain openly about ROK competition because any animus Tokyo might arouse toward South Korea would surely fall more heavily on Japan. Just as South Korea fears being included in an anti-Japanese trade backlash by Westerners, Japan cannot afford to complain about South Korea because such carping could stimulate that same broad backlash.

Though the ROK enjoys a favorable balance of trade with the United States, it does not with Japan. This is a key issue for the ROK, which wants Japan to open its markets more widely as urgently as the United States desires such a move. However, Seoul, too, must be discreet about its complaints about Japanese trade practices lest U.S. critics of both Japan and the "new Japans" turn South Korean economic arguments against the ROK in pursuit of greater U.S. access to South Korean markets. Though South Korea and Japan complain about each other's economic policies, both must be cautious to avoid providing ammunition to protectionist and reform-minded elements in the United States.

Chinese and Soviet concerns with South Korea's economy are different from those of Seoul's partners. The PRC views the "new Japans" as models for China's economic reforms. Because of inherent difficulties in postulating the Taiwanese economy as a prime model, South Korea has drawn considerable Chinese attention. It is doubtful whether the PRC can ever catch the "new

Japans," much less Japan proper, but it certainly will try. In the process, trade with these countries is, and probably will remain, desirable. Since North Korea observes these developments from its fence-sitting perch, China cannot safely accelerate its economic and political ties with South Korea. Polite PRC and ROK behavior and ill-concealed South Korean ardor during two attempted defections by a PRC airliner and ship in the early 1980s demonstrated both sides' desire to improve relations.

In conjunction with its guarded experiments with Chinese economic reforms, which are opening the North to trade and investment from the West, the DPRK is edging the fulcrum of its delicate balance closer to China's ideology and away from the Soviet Union. However, in contrast to this economic-led trend are Pyongyang's apparently improved political and military relations with Moscow, exemplified by hearty North Korean welcomes for various senior Soviet visitors to Pyongyang in 1985–87. Kim Il-sung's May 1987 visit to China may signal Pyongyang's desire to hedge its bets. On balance, China's pragmatic responses to both Korean states, along with a Sinocentric inclination by Koreans on both sides, has produced a gradually improved Sino-Korean atmosphere in which Beijing has something to offer both Seoul and Pyongyang: trade and its good offices. Moreover, both Koreas also seem to relish opportunities to trade with China on the basis of parity.

Despite Gorbachev's July 1986 Vladivostok speech calling for improved economic ties with Asia, Soviet options toward South Korea are more constrained than China's. Though the ROK could be a more useful supplier of consumer goods to the Soviet Union, and though South Koreans are drawn to Siberian resource potentials just like the Japanese, the political costs to Moscow of antagonizing North Korea are too great. Unlike China, with its shared heritage, the Soviet Union often has awkward relations with North Korea due to its superpower status, overbearing manner, and anti-Asian racism within its "greater Russian" culture. Consequently, Moscow must move warily. Further, Moscow knows the ROK is part of a budding anti-Soviet coalition. Soviet concerns about a U.S.-PRC-Japan alignment are clear. Similarly, a possible U.S.-Japan-ROK arrangement would make more sense if it were organized around countering the common threat to each posed by the Soviet Union, rather than countering specifically the North

Korean threat to South Korea. Also the Soviet Union recognizes that South Korea's economic successes are strengthening the U.S.-led correlation of forces. Moscow cannot help strengthen a U.S. ally. It is not surprising, then, that the Soviet Union is not as serious about its version of the "South Korean card" as China evidently is. Though this difference may give China more flexibility than the Soviet Union, in a crisis Pyongyang would likely rely more on Moscow than Beijing to provide necessary assistance.

The North Korean economy's lack of appeal to the major powers is evident. Though North Korea clearly is more autarkic than South Korea, it does trade extensively with, and receive substantial economic support from, the Soviet Union and its satellites. Moscow's blunt reminders of its contributions to North Korea's well-being suggest that it has done for North Korea what no other state could or would do. Thus, Moscow simultaneously exposes the weakness of China and the artificiality of Pyongyang's *juche*. Before Deng Xiaoping's pragmatic reform movement, Beijing did not object to Pyongyang's quest for autarky. After all, that policy reduced demands North Korea made on China's strained resources and echoed the societal experiments of Maoism, though in a uniquely Kimist fashion. However, since Deng's economic reforms have born fruit, Beijing has encouraged Pyongyang to follow its example. North Korea did take some measures, but it is doubtful whether Pyongyang's heart is in the effort as much as Beijng's is. Ideologically, Pyongyang seems caught in a Stalinist-Leninist time-warp, intent on proving that Kimism is a legitimate venue to achieving true communism. Moreover, unlike China, which enjoys the realities and appealing mythology of the "Great China Market," North Korea possesses little to attract foreign entrepreneurs. Its trade and debt records are abysmal. Consequently, North Korea finds it difficult to emulate China's economic pragmatism.

Free world investment in North Korea necessarily must come from capital-rich states in Western Europe, North America, and Japan. The experience of those Western Europeans and Japanese who have dabbled in the North Korean economy is unlikely to encourage their countrymen to follow their lead or to attract North Americans, for whom North Korea is an economic zero with a very poor image. North Korea must go the extra mile to make itself more appealing. Neither the United States nor Japan is eager to foster such trade, but both are concerned that the widening Korean economic gap may cause Pyongyang to disregard prevailing logic about the futility of another war, since it might see itself on a path to oblivion. If Pyongyang were to feel cornered by its lagging economic performance, it may strike out in desperation. That reaction would destroy the strategic status quo valued by the major powers. Thus the West does have reason to facilitate North Korea's uncertain attempts to follow China's example. Its success would add significantly to regional stability.

KOREAN REACTIONS TO MAJOR POWER PRESENCE

Both Koreas react to the continued presence of major powers with a mixed sense of resignation and frustration. There is resignation that Korea remains today what it was in 1945: a pawn in the international relations of big powers. Despite the many changes since the late 1940s, Korea is still a shrimp among the whales. Korean frustration arises from the fact that the nation remains divided, against its deep-seated wishes, necessitating that the two rival Korean states devote much manpower and many resources to coping with each other rather than with the problems a united Korea would confront.

Despite these frustrations, both Koreas make the best of their circumstances. Both seem to find consolation in their ability to manipulate their major power backers more than their foreign supporters are prepared to admit. By being politically, strategically, and economically assertive within the confines of major power constraints, neither Korean state is a puppet. Both Koreas seem functionally alike within the international system, in that each is a kind of Pinocchio—a former puppet miraculously going its own way! While the metaphor is a useful one, it must be used with explicit care lest one stretch it to imply that the two Korean Pinocchios also are inveterate liars. Both Korean states capitalize on the major powers' concerns about Korean instability to extract what each wants, namely, weapons, economic concessions, and defense commitments. Leaders in both Korean states use—and abuse—the status quo to sanction the autocratic harshness of domestic politics. Both Koreas persist in cold war–style rhetoric toward each other and emphasize that rhetoric in their relations with major power supporters.

Yet, each Korea simultaneously conducts more pragmatic overall foreign relations than the hard-line rhetoric would suggest. South Korea, a die-hard anti-communist country, proffers routine overtures to China, the Soviet Union, Eastern Europe, and such radical Third World states as Libya. North Korea, the paradigm of an anti-imperialist/anti-capitalist country, is now faintly echoing the ROK's innovative foreign policy by making overtures to its adversaries. Each Korea seems to harbor some vague hope that its current foreign adversaries may someday, as circumstances evolve, provide useful leverage over or—more remotely—an alternative to its current foreign friends. This suggests an insecurity based on xenophobic fears that foreigners are innately unreliable and quixotic, and this insecurity compels Koreans of all political stripes to dwell incessantly on national unification.

There is a paradox in this quest by Koreans for a unitary state. Both Koreas vow they are sincere about unification, each adamantly insists its unification proposals are realistic, and both scorn their foreign backers' skepticism as cynical. Despite the optimism among ever hopeful Koreans that their preliminary talks will lay the foundation for truly serious talks, there is no sign of unification. The unification rhetoric from Seoul and Pyongyang, always laden with a debilitating catch-22 that guarantees failure of a given proposal, is an admission by each regime that such rhetoric is a precondition for maintaining each one's nationalist legitimacy. The zero-sum clause (which precludes real compromise) inserted in all alternatives so far is a de facto guarantee that each regime's reason for being will persist. However, this helps assure the strategic and political status quo on the Korean peninsula, regardless of how much Koreans may blame the division on external systemic forces.

Is it likely that either Korea would initiate a war? There is always some chance, but the odds are heavily against it if Seoul and Pyongyang behave rationally. The assured destruction certain to be inflicted on both Koreas is reason enough to avoid war. Fears about possible North Korean aggression aimed at disrupting the Olympics seem overrated. That is precisely when the ROK defensive guard will be maintained most acutely. Accidental escalation into war remains a serious possibility but amenable to crisis management. The principal exception to this rather sanguine prognosis is the cornered animal hypotheses, which postulates that North Korea might strike in desperation, hoping to set back severely South Korea's insurmountable lead over North Korea, and that Pyongyang's backers would feel compelled to help. That possibility—not sympathy for North Korea—is what should motivate the ROK and its supporters to assure that North Korea does not get left far behind. This effort must be prudent so that it does not strengthen the North's ability to threaten South Korea, but some benign economic and cultural measures should be undertaken to make Pyongyang's corner seem less angular. If something of this sort is done to draw North Korea into a more neighborly demeanor, the prospects for an irrational war could be substantially reduced.

NOTES

1. See Edward A. Olsen, *"Nichi-bei-kan sogo anpo taisei o nozomu," Chuo Koron,* February 1983; "Security in Northeast Asia: A trilateral alternative," *Naval War College Review* 38, no.1, sequence 307 (January-February 1985): 15–24; *U.S.-Japan Strategic Reciprocity* (Stanford, Calif.: Hoover Institution Press, 1985); and " *'Chiipu raidaa' e fuman"* (Criticizing a "Cheap Rider"), *Chuo Koron,* December 1985.
2. A high-level U.S. official first relayed such views through the *Kyungyang Shinmun* (24 April 1985); see *Foreign Broadcast Information Service: Asia* 4 (25 April 1985): E-3. They have been elaborated widely since then.

9 SOUTHEAST ASIA

Michael Leifer

This chapter sets out to identify the nature of the more significant regional conflicts in Southeast Asia, both active and potential, and to assess in particular their relative capacities for engaging major external powers in a direct military role. It should be noted that such external intervention in direct military form on any grand scale and in a protracted manner ceased in Southeast Asia with the end of American bombing in Cambodia (now Kampuchea) in August 1973. Since then, external intervention of a dramatic kind has been occasional and not continuous. Indeed, it is possible to cite only the examples of America's retrieval of the freighter Mayaguez in May 1975, China's seizure of the Paracel Islands in January 1974, and also its punitive intrusion into Vietnam in February-March 1979 in response to Vietnam's invasion of Kampuchea. Moreover, such acts of intervention were designed to change the external behavior of regional states, not their political identities.[1] Subsequently, Chinese spokesmen have threatened a second punishment, but such threats have not been translated into military action. For example, during the first quarter of 1985, Vietnamese forces in Kampuchea overran the base camps of the three Khmer resistance groups situated along the border with Thailand, but without provoking matching Chinese retaliation.

If free from the kind of intervention that distinguished the Second Indochina War, Southeast Asia has not ceased to be free of serious conflict, both international and domestic. With the exception of China's continuing engagement in cross-border skirmishes and artillery exchanges with Vietnam, however, the regional policies of the major external powers have been pursued in part only through an indirect application of military means. It is in an indirect sense only, through military assistance, that external patrons have supported local clients, enabling them to prosecute conflict with both a regional and an external dimension. This chapter will attempt to assess whether or not such indirect engagement might assume direct form, bearing in mind that neither the United States nor the Soviet Union has placed a prime strategic priority on Southeast Asia. China, as both a regional and an external power, possesses a greater direct interest but a limited military capability for major intervention.

ACTIVE CONFLICTS

The main regional centers of active conflict in Southeast Asia are in Indochina and the Philippines.

At issue in the conflict in Indochina, which has been ongoing since Vietnam invaded and occupied Kampuchea in late 1978, are the political identity and the external affiliations of the Khmer state. The conflict has assumed the form of an internationalized civil war. A Vietnamese expeditionary force has been engaged in trying to protect and consolidate the position of a client Khmer administration subject to challenge from a disparate Khmer resistance movement, with military support provided primarily from China via Thailand.

External support for Vietnam's political purpose has come primarily from the Soviet Union, whose material benefaction is estimated to amount to approximately U.S. $3 million a day. But apart from the dispatch of military advisers to all three states of Indochina, the Soviet Union has been engaged directly in the conflict over Kampuchea only to the extent that some of its aid officials have been victims of guerrilla attack. Moreover, although the Soviet Union entered into a treaty commitment to Vietnam in November 1978 that contains a security obligation of a kind, its government has not been faced with any pressing reason for direct military intervention since China's punitive action in February-March 1979, which failed in its prime political purpose.[2]

Moreover, there is no evidence to suggest that Soviet military intervention—as opposed to military display—was requested then or that the Chinese have been prepared since then to assume the risks and costs of provoking it by contemplating a second punishment. Only in the event of a clear and present threat to the political identity of Vietnam—which was not posed in 1979—could the government in Hanoi be expected to seek recourse to direct application of Soviet countervailing military power. In Kampuchea, the balance of military advantage, certainly in the wake of the 1984–85 dry season, has continued to favor the Vietnamese to the extent that they can sustain their position of dominance without direct military support from the Soviet Union. Indeed, the Vietnamese would be loath to encourage any undue external involvement that might interpose between those special relationships that the government in Hanoi has asserted in its dealings with counterparts in Phnom Penh and Vientiane. Accordingly, although the Soviet Union has extensive bilateral relationships with Kampuchea and Laos, political form would seem to enjoy a measure of significance in Indochina. The Soviet Union enjoys treaty relations only with Vietnam, while Vietnam enjoys treaty relations with both Kampuchea and Laos, as well as with the Soviet Union. If only a symbol of self-denying ordinance on the part of the Soviet Union, the absence of treaty relationships with Kampuchea and Laos indicates Vietnam's proprietorial role in Indochina.

If the condition of conflict in Indochina has not required the Soviet Union to consider seriously direct military intervention, the government in Moscow has been the political and military beneficiary of the profound deterioration in Sino-Vietnamese relations, which is at the root of the Kampuchean issue. While the Soviet Union does not necessarily enjoy permanent base rights in Vietnam, expanded use of military facilities at Cam Ranh Bay and Da Nang since March 1979 has extended the peacetime operational reach of the Soviet Pacific Fleet and has permitted regional aerial reconnaissance and electronic surveillance, as well as a potential air-strike capability, within a radius that encompasses all six ASEAN states.[3] If the Soviet military presence in Vietnam constitutes primarily a regional expression of a long-standing sense of global entitlement, it may be said to serve the specific functions of containing China and countering American naval power in the Southwest Pacific. Soviet deployments constitute a military asset, but their utility in other than a peacetime role is open to question unless major measures were undertaken to overcome limitations in logistics, air cover, and strike power. It has been argued elsewhere that the Soviet military presence in Vietnam is not designed for interdicting regional sea-lanes except in worst-case circumstances that would have an impact well beyond Southeast Asia.[4] Direct employment of Soviet military power in the conflict over Kampuchea would seem most unlikely unless a second Chinese act of punishment seemed designed to challenge the authority of the Politburo in Hanoi and, correspondingly, the credibility of Moscow as a reliable ally.

The Soviet Union does hold a key to a political settlement in Indochina, but by reason of the effect of its material disengagement, not of its military intervention. Thus the suspension of military and material assistance to Vietnam, especially in fuel oil, would arrest the momentum of Vietnamese military activity within Kampuchea. There are good reasons for the Soviet government not to adopt such a course. Its military commitment to Vietnam is not only a function of its bilateral relationship with China, now in a condition of working accommodation. It serves also as an expression of its role as global patron of the Socialist Commonwealth, which in turn serves to vindicate a determinist view of history. Undoubtedly, any conspicuous willingness to compromise Vietnamese security interests would be at the cost of political opportunity. Those interests have been compromised in the past but never in the context of a current treaty relationship that confers strategic as well as political advantage.

The Soviet government has been engaged in a continuing dialogue with its Chinese counterpart in an attempt to become better placed to manage its central adversary relationship with the United States. But it would have to be assured of tangible, certain advantage in any revision of relations with China before contemplating seriously any step that might be deemed an act of betrayal by Vietnam. The Soviet government logically wishes to detach the revision of relations with China from the issue of Vietnam's dominant position in Kampuchea. It is difficult to envisage how this might be possible unless China were willing to lend at least tacit recognition to the political fait accompli imposed by Vietnamese force of arms, which China shows no signs of doing. For the time being, however, it would seem that the Soviet Union is moderately satisfied with a condition of conflict in Indochina in which the balance of military advantage rests with Vietnam. That condition does not require direct military intervention in support of Vietnam. It does demand continuing military assistance, which enables continuing access to base facilities but without obstructing a growing measure of practical accommodation with China. If not exactly having its cake and eating it, the Soviet Union comes close. Military intervention would not serve any practical purpose under present circumstances and would certainly alienate the ASEAN states more than necessary.

As indicated above, within Kampuchea Vietnam's occupation and client administration have been challenged up to a point by a disparate Khmer resistance movement. Spearheaded by the surviving and refurbished military arm of the ousted government of so-called Democratic Kampuchea, in coalition form since mid-1982, that movement has enjoyed a mixture of military support from China. Military equipment has been transported to the border with Kampuchea via Thailand, while a measure of military pressure has been applied along the Sino-Vietnamese border. In this undertaking, designed to reverse Vietnam's policy in Kampuchea, China has entered into an informal alliance relationship with Thailand, reflected in the degree of intermilitary consultation. For example, during a visit to Bangkok in March 1985, Chinese President Li Xiannian expressed a willingness to dispatch military advisers to work with Khmer resistance groups. But in light of China's failure to respond decisively to Vietnam's overrunning of the Khmer resistance base camps in the first quarter of 1985, which also involved tactical encroachments on Thai territory, there can be limited expectation of any substantial military intervention in Vietnam to match the scale of the so-called act of punishment in February-March 1979. Military pressure from China has continued to take the form of acts of harassment and not of intervention.

A sense of military limitation linked to economic priorities would seem to be a major factor in the discrepancy between China's declaratory and operational policies. If it would be fair to say that in 1979 China and Vietnam taught each other a lesson, the experience exposed major operational deficiencies in China's military machine and also imposed heavy costs. Moreover, China is certainly confronted by a much greater degree of military difficulty against the Vietnamese than in 1979. The Vietnamese are now better prepared in reinforced defensible positions in hilly terrain and have the advantage of superior military equipment supplied by the Soviet Union. The factor of Soviet retaliation must be taken into greater account, given the extent to which the credibility of the government in Moscow is at greater risk because it did not take direct action in 1979. In January 1985 the secretary-general of Thailand's National Security Council, Squadron Leader Prasong Soonsiri, announced that the Soviet Union had deployed fourteen MiG 23 interceptors to Cam Ranh Bay early in the previous month, coinciding with the dry campaign season then underway in Indochina. Such a deployment signaled to China the likelihood of Soviet intent in defense of Vietnam's northern border.

China's Vietnam policy, involving the application of military pressure, has evidently served to distort strategic priorities by reinforcing the dependent relationship between Vietnam and the Soviet Union. Apart from considerations of constraint arising from a firm commitment to economic modernization, as well as an interest in assuming a greater balance in relations with the Soviet Union and the United States, China confronts a dilemma in challenging the dominance of Vietnam in Indochina. The policy has failed so far to compel Vietnam to change its external behavior. Yet, in applying limited military means within a wider coalition as part of a strategy of attrition designed to impose breaking strain on Vietnam's society and government, this policy has served only to reinforce a relationship that has been at the center of China's public justification for its antagonism toward Vietnam. Under the circumstances, China's most practical course of action to overcome its dilemma without giving up its opposition to Vietnam's dominance in Indochina would be to persist in a policy distinguished by limited cost and risk. The current policy is intended to force Vietnam to overreach itself and drain its resources to the point of virtual collapse, hoping that in the process attendant tensions will overcome the Soviet-Vietnamese relationship.[5] Indeed, Sino-Soviet dialogue is almost certainly intended to generate such tensions. Regardless of the merits or demerits of such a policy, it is likely to involve a second major act of direct military intervention.

From the time of Vietnam's invasion and occupation of Kampuchea, the U.S. government has supported the position of Thailand and its ASEAN partners. The immediate U.S. response was to suspend negotiations over the establishment of diplomatic relations with Hanoi, which has been tied to a Vietnamese withdrawal from Kampuchea as well as substantial progress in accounting for American servicemen missing in action from the Second Indochina War.[6] During a visit to Washington in February 1979 by Prime Minister General Kriangsak Chamanand, President Carter reaffirmed the validity of America's commitment to Thailand under the Manila Pact of 1954. The strength of American diplomatic support was sustained with the Soviet invasion of Afghanistan and the election of Ronald Reagan. But American support for ASEAN's general objective to deny Vietnamese dominance in Indochina has been expressed primarily in terms of diplomatic and economic assistance, with military aid going to Thailand. Direct military intervention in defense of Thailand has not been contemplated and would seem an unlikely prospect unless the Vietnamese took the step of going well beyond acts of hot pursuit across the Kampuchean border to pose an evident threat to the territorial integrity of the Thai state. Even then, an automatic decision to intervene, say by employing offshore carrier-based air power, would be unlikely. A first response, in line with past practice, would almost certainly be to reinforce the Thai armed forces. To this end, the American government has encouraged the establishment of a war reserve stockpile in Thailand.[7]

Vietnam has continuing problems of military pacification within Kampuchea, while the elimination of Khmer resistance base camps along the Thai border in 1985 has made an enlarged war beyond the bounds of Indochina a less immediate prospect. At issue for the United States has been whether or not Washington should provide a token $5 million in annual military assistance in overt form to the non-Communist components of the Khmer resistance movement. Such assistance was first recommended in March 1985 by the Asia-Pacific subcommittee of the Foreign Affairs Committee in the House of Representatives and subsequently endorsed by the corresponding full committees of both houses of Congress. The object of the aid is to strengthen the non-Communist resistance forces, internally as well as in relation to their Khymer Rouge coalition partner, in the wake of the Vietnamese dry season offensive.[8]

Apart from diplomatic support for ASEAN and military assistance to Thailand, the United States has served as a major source of funds for international relief aid for refugees from Kampuchea through United Nations agencies. This aid has provided not only for their basic needs, but has also helped indirectly to sustain the Khmer resistance groups, including the notorious Khmer Rouge. The American government is believed to provide additional economic aid through covert channels but has been visibly hesitant to provide direct military assistance in any form to any part of the Khmer resistance movement. For example, former Assistant Secretary of State Paul Wolfowitz proposed a modest program of economic and educational aid to the non-Communist guerrilla factions but nothing more in response to ASEAN pressure.

In February 1985, at the height of Vietnam's 1984–85 dry season offensive, the foreign ministers of ASEAN met in Bangkok and called on "the international community to increase support and assistance to the Kampuchean people in their political and *military* [italics added] struggle to liberate their homeland from foreign occupation."[9] That statement was directed primarily at the government in Washington but to no great avail, despite reinforcement by congressional initiative. Apart from an evident reluctance to be linked directly to a resistance movement whose dominant military faction has both a Communist and a genocidal identity, Washington showed no enthusiasm to be tied to the movement's non-Communist components, whose military requirements and fighting credibility have remained doubtful. Evident disadvantages in more than one respect could arise from placing a formal impramatur on their cause. A Pentagon source has been quoted as saying, "If we were to start giving [the guerrillas] arms and money, they'd henceforth be known as 'the U.S.-backed rebels.' "[10] The Reagan administration has been willing only to leave open the possibility of giving military assistance to the non-Communist Khmer guerrilla groups. In August 1985 President Reagan signed a two-year foreign aid bill that gave him authority to allocate $5 million annually in military or nonmilitary form to the non-Communist Khmer resistance. Thus far, the undertaking has assumed declaratory rather than operational significance. Congress subsequently reduced the sum allocated to $3.6 million, with no clear provision for military aid. By mid-1986, none of that sum had been dispersed.

There is an obvious official American resistance even to indirect overt military intervention in Indochina that does not apply to the same extent in Nicaragua and Afghanistan. In terms of American interests and priorities, there is no urgency to intervene more directly in a conflict that has not come near a point of decisive military conclusion. The conflict drains both Vietnamese and Soviet resources without being a central tension in American-Soviet relations and serves in part to sustain a working structure of Sino-American relations. Accordingly, there is no good reason to engage American credibility through greater involvement. The continuing conflict in Indochina does serve to entrench a Soviet military presence in Vietnam. But that presence cannot be reduced by overt American military assistance to the Khmer resistance.

The third Indochina war, if complex in its underlying structure of conflict, has been distinguished so far by the absence of the kind of direct external military intervention that characterized its predecessor. This war continues as a military stalemate because the contending internal parties and their external backers continue to see utility in the application of military means to secure political ends. They also appear willing to accept the costs involved in the process. The external backers, if interested in overcoming military stalemate to the advantage of their favored party, would also appear content to live with it.[11] Accordingly, the prospects for direct external military intervention are limited. They would increase should Vietnam decide to invade Thailand with political intent rather than with a tactical military purpose related to control of Kampuchea. Such intervention could escalate also if a Chinese act of retaliation against Vietnam obliged the Soviet Union to undertake a matching response. Against this prospect should be set the fact that the dry season in Indochina in 1984–85 gave rise to the most intensive military confrontation over Kampuchea since Vietnam's invasion in 1978. That confrontation did not arouse any inclination on the part of major external powers with an interest in the outcome of the conflict to become directly engaged in its early resolution.

At issue in the Philippines, despite the political succession to the presidency of Mrs. Corazon Aquino in February 1986, is the prospect of radical political change being effected through the vehicle of Communist insurgency. The prime external interest involved is that of the United States, which possesses important military-base facilities covered initially by a lease agreement for ninety-nine years, concluded initially in 1947, and subsequently revised in 1969 to terminate in 1991. The United States assumed defense obligations to the Philippines under the Mutual Defense Treaty concluded in 1951 and to a lesser extent under the Manila Pact of 1954. The United States has the overriding incentive to uphold the political identity and prevailing external affiliations of the Philippines as well as to ensure continued operational use of its military bases. Given the exclusively internal nature of conflict in the Philippines, the problem of intervention is of a different order for the United States compared with that faced by the three major powers in the case of Indochina.

Over a decade ago, internal rebellion in the Philippines was primarily a Muslim enterprise. It erupted in October 1972 in the southern islands as an expression of political alienation and was supported externally from Libya and through the Malaysian state of Sabah in northern Borneo. That rebellion has been limited geographically by the pattern of settlement of the Muslims in the Philippines, who comprise only 4 percent of the total population, and has never seemed at all likely to attract major power intervention. It is now in a state of arrested momentum reinforced by a measure of dialogue between some rebel factions and the Aquino government. Much more serious has been the sustained momentum of an indigenous insurgency that originated with the rehabilitation of the Communist party of the Philippines in the late 1960s.[12] That party has enjoyed its degree of success from a skillful strategy of geographical decentralization and, without doubt, from the shortcomings of the Marcos administration, which degenerated into a personal despotism.[13] Almost a year before its collapse, Richard Armitage, assistant secretary of defense, had warned of a Communist takeover by the end of the decade.

The striking feature of the Communist insurgency in the Philippines, which spread from an initial northeasterly redoubt on the island of Luzon directly through the archipelago to southerly Mindanao, has been its self-generating quality. There has not been any conclusive evidence of external support of a material kind. Moreover, the early pro-Chinese (Maoist) orientation of the Philippine party has been replaced by a much more independent position; its nationalist credentials have been strengthened by the delinquent performance of the Marcos administration. The Communist party of the Philippines has made no secret of its determination to eliminate America's long-standing military presence from the country. "Unite all anti-imperialist and democratic forces to overthrow the U.S.-Marcos dictatorship" is the opening phrase of the program of the National Democratic Front (NDF) established by the party in April 1973. The removal of the American military bases has continued to be a priority of both the NDF and the party in the wake of Marcos' overthrow.

The American military presence in the Philippines comprises major naval and air force bases that provide the most important operational facilities for forward surface naval deployment and air staging in the southwest Pacific. As a joint set of facilities for the Seventh Fleet and the Thirteenth Air Force, the military bases in the Philippines cannot be duplicated on any one alternative site in the Pacific. Despite some contingency planning in Micronesia, any attempt to provide a range of alternative and necessarily less efficient facilities at different sites to the east would take time to construct, would involve considerable expense, and would present the prospect of delayed reaction in a crisis. Countervailing arguments have been put forward asserting the virtues of military disengagement from the Philippines, both on the grounds of the political costs to be avoided and also because of advances in military technology that make possible alternative basing and staging arrangements.[14] Such arguments are academic, at least for the time being, because the Reagan administration has made it clear that the bases in the Philippines are of prime importance to American global interests. Moreover, the downfall of Marcos has diluted the sense of crisis. The practical question is how to ensure continued "unhampered military operations" that are the crux of the terms of the bases agreement renegotiated as recently as June 1983 (which took effect as of October 1984). That question involves much more than a renegotiation of terms every five years up to and beyond 1991, when the revised agreement formally lapses, although Mrs. Aquino has indicated a willingness to renegotiate the bases agreement at that time. More to the point is whether the politically discordant administration that she has established is capable both of surviving and of meeting the Communist challenge. The problem for the United States has been rendered more tractable, in part because the new leadership of the Philippine armed forces appears committed to reforms that, if undertaken, should strengthen its counterinsurgency role.

Before the fall of President Marcos, and in the absence of a credible and acceptable political alternative, the problem for the

United States was how to promote reform capable of fending off Communist challenge. Under the circumstances, the American government had taken the view that there was no alternative but to work with Marcos to safeguard its interests. This judgment was indicated in a leaked national security directive signed by President Reagan in January 1985.[15] The logic of that directive was that "while President Marcos at this stage is part of the problem, he is also necessarily part of the solution," on the grounds that reforms could be undertaken only with his assistance or acquiescence. The directive also advised that "an overriding consideration should be to avoid getting ourselves caught between the slow erosion of Marcos' authoritarian control and the still fragile revitalization of democratic institutions, being made hostage to Marcos' political fortunes, being saddled with ultimate responsibility for winning the insurgency or being tagged with the success or failure of individuals in the moderate leadership." The United States was able to avoid such dilemmas not through any positive act of influence, but because President Marcos made a fundamental political blunder. Indeed, President Reagan almost failed to recognize the opportunity for orderly political change that had been the consistent priority expressed in relations with the Philippines. American diplomatic intervention played its part in persuading President Marcos of the political utility of calling premature elections, reinforced by Congress's reluctance to provide aid. Moreover, private American encouragement of the reform movement within the Philippine Armed Forces almost certainly gave heart at the moment of crisis when the political future of the country was in the balance. But more blatant intervention, either to arrest the momentum of Communist insurgency or to help topple Marcos, had been out of the question.

Mrs. Aquino's ascension to power has blunted the growing challenge from the Philippine Communist party for the time being. That party made a series of fundamental errors in dissociating itself from the political process that led to the overthrow of Marcos. The nature of his political downfall enabled the coalition around Mrs. Aquino to seize the middle ground and also to attract support from an alienated constituency that the Communists had hoped to dominate. Although indicating a willingness to enter negotiations as a countergovernment, the hard-liners of the Philippine Communist party have not shown any willingness to give up armed struggle. Moreover, to the extent that tensions within the Aquino government, combined with overwhelming economic difficulties, deny promise of material improvement and frustrate heightened popular expectations, the Communists still have a favorable political environment to exploit.

The more immediate task for the United States is to help in the rehabilitation of the Philippine economy and in the reorganization and reequipment of the Philippine Armed Forces. Intervention is not at issue even if the underlying problem remains and may become more acute by 1991 when, in principle, the bases agreements lapse. Operational control of those bases has become tied to America's recurrent commitment to remain a Pacific power—one reaffirmed with vigor by President Reagan. Apart from the practical difficulties involved in establishing alternative military facilities, any enforced relinquishment of the bases—still the aim of the Communist party—would reduce the credibility of such a commitment. It would certainly cause profound anxiety among the regional partners of the Philippines who, like the United States, have watched with concern the development of a Soviet military presence in Vietnam. To that extent, the American bases in the Philippines have come to enjoy a political symbolism, regardless of any arguments for and against their practical utility.

It does not seem likely that a popular government in Manila would call for the termination of America's military presence by 1991. But if such a request occurred, it would be quite impractical to deny. It would not make sense to insist on retaining military facilities in the face of a hostile host government, especially if that government were itself opposed to a Communist takeover. The issue of intervention would become a practical consideration only if the progress of Communist insurgency, established in most provinces, prompted a request from Manila that is not provided for under the Mutual Defense Treaty of 1951. Obviously, much would depend on the mood of Congress and on the prospect of a military engagement that could well feed the finances of an insurgency it was designed to dampen. The experience of Vietnam would surely count in such a hypothetical circumstance, possibly together with earlier experience in counterinsurgency in the Philippines at the turn of the century, which was a savage encounter at considerable cost.

It would seem impractical to hold on to the military bases in the face of a request for their removal from a popular government in Manila. It would seem even less so should the government's failure to cope with economic decline provide a vacuum the Communists were able to fill. In such circumstances the "Guantanamo option" would not be a practical proposition for the worst possible case, not only because the legal position in the Philippines is not comparable. The American military bases are not concentrated in space or isolated in location. Indeed, their locations, primarily at Clark Field and Subic Bay, make their use impossible without free passage through Philippine air space and archipelagic waters. In such circumstances, "unhampered military operations" would not be a realistic prospect. Perhaps the more immediate likelihood of any of the 15,000 American servicemen stationed in the Philippines becoming involved with military operations would be in defense of base areas, should they be subject to attack by Communist insurgents, which so far has not arisen. In principle, however, defense of the bases is a Philippine responsibility made explicit under the terms of the agreement as revised in January 1979. Yet it may be argued that if the Communist insurgency has progressed to such a stage as to warrant attacks on base installations, their operational utility would be called into question while the American servicemen on base would require substantial specialized reinforcement. Of those servicemen, the vast majority are navy and air force personnel; only some 700 are marines.

Speculation about the future aside, the prospects for American military intervention in a counterinsurgency role or in defense of its bases would seem out of the question. The problem is how to take advantage of the political breathing space accorded by the transfer of power to Mrs. Aquino so that the Communist party of the Philippines is unable to seize the initiative and the issue of American military intervention remains hypothetical.

POTENTIAL CONFLICTS

The major potential conflict that might engage external powers competitively in a direct role is in maritime Southeast Asia. The lines of international conflict are drawn in the South China Sea, which is subject to a host of overlapping claims to jurisdiction to island groups and ocean space, including continental shelves. Among the external powers, only China, a coastal state in the South China Sea, is a party to those claims that include the distended

Spratly Islands, which command navigation routes between the Indian and Pacific Oceans.[16] Such claims serve as a basis for related claims to maritime and sea-bed resources and involve Vietnam, the Philippines, and Malaysia among regional states.

Control of islands in the South China Sea is mixed. China exercises jurisdiction over the northerly Paracel Islands, seized completely in January 1974 and contested by Vietnam. Vietnam deploys troops on some seven of the Spratly group it seized in 1975, while claiming them in entirety, as do China and Taiwan; the Philippines holds at least five by alleged right of discovery and occupation. Taiwan continues to occupy the Itu Aba, the principal island in the archipelago, which it has garrisoned with one short interruption since 1946. Although minor naval clashes have been reported and Malaysian forces occupied a coral atoll in June 1983 and have also advanced a claim to the Vietnamese held island of Amboyna Cay, there has not been a major military confrontation over island territories in the South China Sea since China seized the Paracels.

The lines of competing claims to jurisdiction make a complex pattern and cut across regional alignments; for example, they engage regional partners within ASEAN. However, the major contention over jurisdiction is between China and Vietnam, and there is no sign of either side compromising its position. Equally, over the past decade there has not been any expression of naval confrontation beyond occasional clashes and military display. One diminishing source of constraint is a lack of appropriate naval and amphibious capability, as both are being upgraded by China and Vietnam. More constricting has been the structure of conflict in Indochina. Neither China nor Vietnam is in a political position to prosecute forcibly its claim to jurisdiction in the South China Sea, even though this dispute has been at the root of the third Indochina war. Neither state would appear to want to alienate any of the members of ASEAN over matters of jurisdiction in the South China Sea while that war continues. This measure of self-restraint would seem to be more important for China than for Vietnam because the government in Beijing has been successful in engaging its ASEAN counterparts in a coalition whose members share the common objective of denying Vietnamese dominance in Indochina. Any attempt to actively prosecute claims to, say, any of the Spratly Islands would risk reviving perceptions of threat within

Southeast Asia to Vietnamese advantage and would threaten the cohesion of a coalition already subject to internal strains. Moreover, there would be additional risk of provoking a Soviet naval response within striking distance from base facilities in Vietnam.

For the time being, a political settlement in Indochina would seem an unlikely prospect, but should an acceptable settlement be concluded—for example, arising from a continuing improvement in Sino-Soviet relations—it is possible that the locus of regional international conflict could move southward. Such a circumstance could pose problems for the management of both regional relationships and for relationships between major external powers that have assumed regional commitments. In this respect, it is of interest to note that when an agreement was reached between the American and Philippine governments in January 1979 on the revised terms of use of the military bases, the United States reaffirmed its commitment to the Mutual Security Treaty of 1951. Article V of that treaty, which sets out the *casus foederis*, stipulates that an armed attack includes ". . . an armed attack on the metropolitan territory of either of the Parties, or on the island territories under its jurisdiction in the Pacific or on its armed forces, public vessels or aircraft in the Pacific." That provision was given wider significance in a concurrent executive agreement contained in a letter from Secretary of State Cyrus Vance to Foreign Minister Carlos Romulo of 6 January 1979. That letter specified that attacks on "armed vessels, public vessels or aircraft in the Pacific" or on "island territories under its [Philippine] jurisdiction" need not be within lines drawn in accordance with the Treaty of Paris of 1898, which defined metropolitan territory as covered by the treaty.[17]

Executive agreements are, of course, hardly the same as treaties and are not necessarily binding on subsequent administrations. Nonetheless, that between Vance and Romulo constitutes the basis for a claim by a government of the Philippines on its American counterpart should Filipino territorial interests in the South China Sea be challenged directly. Indeed, to the extent that such a challenge were to become manifest while the United States continued to exercise operational control over military bases in the Philippines, the greater would be the likely pressure for an act of intervention on behalf of a long-standing treaty partner.

If such a challenge were to be posed by Vietnam, which is still in a treaty relationship that allows the USSR access to military facilities there, then the skills of crisis management would be required regardless of the disposition to intervene. Of course, should maritime contention and encounters appear likely to disrupt major sea-lanes of communication between the Indian and Pacific Oceans, the stakes involved would be that much higher. Undoubtedly, the potential for intervention exists, and the disposition to intervene on the part of the United States would appear to have been strengthened as a result of the allocation of resources designed to improve the operational efficacy of its navy in the Pacific.[18] The actual prospect for intervention, to the extent that both Soviet and American naval power would become engaged, despite the disparity between the former and the latter, is more doubtful. Despite the contending interests of junior treaty partners, it would require a matter of the highest security priority for either of the two superpowers to contemplate an act of military intervention in the South China Sea that might lead to a direct confrontation between them.

A much less likely prospect for external intervention is Indonesia, which has experienced a revival of domestic conflict. Since March 1966, with the assumption of power by a military establishment, Indonesia has been an informal defense partner of the United States. Although committed officially to an independent and active formula in foreign policy (a positive expression of nonalignment), the balance of its external relationships, both economic and diplomatic, has placed Indonesia within the wider Western alignment. Indonesia is distinctive within ASEAN in not having a formal defense relationship with an external power, but it does engage in informal defense cooperation with the United States—for example, in facilitating the submerged passage of ballistic missile submarines (SSBNs) through the deep internal waters of archipelagic straits en route between Guam and patrol stations in the Indian Ocean. Although Indonesia and the United States have adopted differing positions over the Law of the Sea Convention, there is no evidence to suggest that their degree of tacit defense cooperation has been affected as a consequence. Moreover, any tensions arising from it should be reduced with the increasing deployment of Trident-class submarines, with their much greater range of strike than Poseidon and Polaris subs.

Although a major source of arms supply, the United States does not look to Indonesia's military establishment for direct assistance. For the time being, there is an absence of any sense of immediate external threat from either of the two major Communist powers.[19] There is a general preference, however, for the United States to play a continuing role in managing the regional balance of power, especially in light of the Soviet military presence in Vietnam. Accordingly, there has been tacit welcome given to America's interest in retaining access to military bases in the Philippines as a positive contribution to a balanced involvement of external powers. Correspondingly, a sense of relief greeted Mrs. Aquino's accession to power in Manila.

Over the past twenty years, Indonesia has enjoyed a considerable measure of political stability, which has contributed to a favorable climate for external investment. To this end, the dominant role of the military has been entrenched within the political system with civilian participation in little more than a technocratic function. Civilian politics has been subject to a policy of demobilization, justified in the interests of economic development. Such development in Indonesia has produced a mixed blessing in political terms. Social tensions arising from population growth, urbanization, and unemployment have been aggravated by conspicuous inequalities of income and corruption. In addition, an underlying problem of national identity, exposed from before the proclamation of independence in August 1945, has persisted. That problem arises from the absence within the distended archipelago of a single great cultural tradition and from the abiding sense of political entitlement of devout Muslims, who do not constitute a numerical majority.

The impact of modernization has had a disturbing expression with an Islamic dimension. Indeed, the politicization of the demobilized civilian sector has been stimulated by the determination of President Suharto to entrench *Pancasila*, the state philosophy enunciated by the late President Sukarno in June 1945, as the sole basis for national identity. This philosophy pivots on the paradoxical formula that all Indonesians have an obligation to believe in a single deity but that every Indonesian is entitled to believe in his own particular god. This formula constitutes an attempt to reconcile the major streams within the cultural diversity characteristic of Indonesian society. For devout Muslims in a country represented as 90 percent Islamic, this symbol of religious tolerance has been regarded as subversive of faith and political entitlement. Criticism of the Suharto government for its treatment of Islam, as well as for its favoring of local Chinese in economic prerogatives, has increased in the form of clandestine circulation of pamphlets and audio cassettes as Indonesia has begun to face economic austerity arising from a dramatic reduction in the price of oil.

Islamic protest received open and violent expression soon after the incipient congress in August 1984 of the United Development Party (a government-enforced coalition of Islamic political parties) had endorsed *Pancasila* as its sole principle. Such endorsement was construed by many Muslims as an enforced renunciation of Islamic identity. In mid-September a riotous confrontation took place between local residents and security forces in the Jakarta port district of Tanjung Priok in which at least thirty people were killed and many more injured. The riot had its origins in rumors of the entry into a local mosque by an army sergeant and his subordinate who did not take off their shoes and who used sewage water to blot out wall posters inside the mosque that were highly critical of the government. Subsequently, a series of acts of terror and protest served to disturb the political composure of the Republic. Bombs exploded in the capital's commercial district and at the internationally celebrated temple of Borobudur in central Java. Unexplained fires broke out in hotels and department stores in and around Jakarta. One such fire destroyed the old royal palace in Solo; others gutted the national radio and television station in the capital. In addition, three ammunition dumps on Java exploded in October 1984 and in January and March 1985 with loss of life.

This sequence of events, which ended by mid-1985, did not necessarily come about entirely by single design, nor was it the responsibility of any one subversive organization. Discounting accidents and insurance-inspired fires, it would seem that a unique pattern of opposition had emerged, with its source in a fused popular discontent and Islamic resurgence. It would be misleading to explain the sequence of events since September 1984 in terms of Islamic fundamentalism. Nonetheless, Islam would appear to have developed a growing attraction to discontented elements who have been unable to find legitimate vehicles for political expression within a system that has been subject to systemic demobilization. Indeed, Islam has begun to fill a spiritual void for younger, educated urban dwellers frustrated in their search for the fruits of development.

The response of government to the riot and to the apparently retaliatory bombings was to arrest suspects and to bring them to trial, pointing out the absence of any political and religious features in cases represented as purely criminal. But the government indicated its sense of concern by having senior military commanders make extensive tours out of the capital to meet with Islamic scholars and to provide assurance that it was not against Islam as a religious faith. Indeed, to make its point, the government banned the Baha'i religion on the grounds that it was contrary to the true teachings of Islam and a threat to Muslim harmony. Such a decision must be considered extraordinary in light of President Suharto's commitment to the *Pancasila* formula.

Although an underlying alienation has been reinforced by a rigid application of the *Pancasila* formula, it is not intended to convey the impression that the government of Indonesia has begun to lose control. There has not been a recurrence of urban rioting. The sequence of bombings was not sustained through 1985, although sporadic fires did occur. Moreover, political unrest has not expressed itself in regional separatist form beyond the rumbling insurgencies that continue in special circumstances in Irian Jaya and East Timor. The key to political stability is still the sense of corporate identity and solidarity of the armed forces, which comprises the only real nationwide institution. Such solidarity could be affected by economically inspired civilian political ferment forming an infectious junction with socially conscious officers. For the time being, however, the measure of challenge within the politically disenfranchised civilian sector has not moved near the crisis point.

In the medium term, Indonesia will be obliged to confront the problem of orderly political succession, and this will be a unique test given the remarkable length of Suharto's tenure and the circumstances of Sukarno's fall from political grace. In such a test, much will depend on the unity of the armed forces, but it is not anticipated that the integrity of the state will be at risk as it was during the mid-1950s. Worst-case scenarios can be readily devised, but the prospect for direct external intervention in local conflict in Indonesia would seem unlikely. The operational reach of China would make it impossible, while that of the Soviet Union in the region is subject to considerable limitation, especially in significant amphibious capability. Both states would be most likely to act diplomatically after the event, rather than during the course of political change. The United States, for its part, has every reason to support the political status quo and, given its prior unhappy experience of engagement in regional rebellion in Indonesia, could be expected to employ nonmilitary means to serve that end.

CONCLUSION

Over ten years after the end of the Second Indochina War, Southeast Asia is still beset by international and domestic conflicts, both active and potential. The degree of major external power engagement in these conflicts has been limited and governed by factors of experience and of regional interest, and by the criterion of managing principal adversary relationships whose prime loci are elsewhere. To make such a judgment is not to diminish the significance of a region in which political polarization has been reinforced by the roles of external powers. Southeast Asia is important globally in terms of its economic resources and its record of economic growth. The region also possesses a strategic value because of the abutting presence of China and the factor of maritime, commercial, and military transit. But it is not an arena of acute East-West competition or tension. Competition is expressed by external patrons' indirect military support of regional clients and by naval deployment but, thus far, not in an intense form. Accordingly, regional conflicts, both active and potential, have displayed only a limited prospect of embroiling major external powers in any direct military role.

NOTES

1. Note the definition of intervention by Neil MacFarlane in his introduction to *Intervention and Regional Security*, Adelphi Paper no. 196 (London: International Institute for Strategic Studies (IISS), 1985).
2. Article Six of the treaty states, "If either party is attacked or threatened with attack, the high contracting parties to the Treaty shall immediately consult each other for the purpose of eliminating that threat and shall take appropriate and effective measures to

safeguard peace and the security of the two countries." British Broadcasting Corporation (BBC) *Summary of World Broadcasts*, Soviet Union/5961/A3/3 (Caversham, England: Monitoring Service of the BBC).

3. See the assessment in *Soviet Military Power 1985* (Washington, D.C.: U.S. Government Printing Office, 1985), pp. 130–31.

4. Michael Leifer, "The Security of Sea-lanes in South-east Asia," *Survival* 25, no. 1 (January-February 1983): 16–24. For a sober assessment of Soviet intentions, see F.A. Mediansky and Dianne Court, *The Soviet Union in Southeast Asia*, Canberra Papers on Strategy and Defence no. 29 (Canberra: Australian National University, 1984).

5. See the discussion in Michael Leifer, *Conflict and Regional Order in South-East Asia*, Adelphi Paper no. 162 (London: IISS, 1980), pp. 13–16.

6. See *Cambodia: The Search for Peace*, Current Policy no. 613 (Washington, D.C.: U.S. Department of State, 11 September 1984), an address by Paul Wolfowitz, assistant secretary for East Asia and Pacific Affairs, to the Conference on the Cambodia Crisis, Washington, D.C., 11 September 1984. In June 1985 President Reagan reversed that order of priorities in stating that Washington would not normalize relations with Hanoi until the Vietnamese accounted for all American servicemen and ended their occupation of Kampuchea. *New York Times*, 7 June 1985.

7. See John McBeth, "Arms for Peace," *Far Eastern Economic Review* 131, no. 12 (20 March 1986) and "Open Arms Cache" vol. 132, no. 17 (24 April 1986).

8. See Donald Emmerson, "The Stable War: Cambodia and the Great Powers," *Indochina Issues* 62 (December 1985): 3.

9. ASEAN Foreign Ministers Joint Statement, Bangkok, 11 February 1985, BBC, *Summary of World Broadcasts* FE/7874/A3/2.

10. "Return to the Killing Fields," *Newsweek*, 8 April 1985, pp. 24–46.

11. Michael Leifer, "Obstacles to a Political Settlement in Indochina," *Pacific Affairs* 58, no. 4 (Vancouver: University of British Columbia, Winter 1985–86): 626–36.

12. For a succinct account of the rise of the Communist party and the nature of its challenge, see David A. Rosenberg, "Communism in the Philippines," *Problems of Communism* 33 (September-October 1984): 24–46.

13. See Francisco Nemenzo, "Rectification Process in the Philippines Communist Movement," in Lim Joo-Jock and Vani S., eds., *Armed Communist Movements in Southeast Asia* (Hampshire, England: Gower, 1984), pp. 71–101.

14. For a full discussion of the utility of the bases to the United States, see Robert Pringle, *Indonesia and the Philippines: American Interests in Island Southeast Asia* (New York: Columbia University Press, 1980), ch. 3.

15. For summaries of the State Department's National Security Study Directive of November 1984, on which the national security directive was based, see Nayan Chanda, "Power to the Palace," *Far Eastern Economic Review* 127, no. 11 (21 March 1985) and Don Oberdorfer, "Report Says U.S. To Employ Leverage to Encourage Change In Philippines," *International Herald Tribune*, 13 March 1985, p. 1.

16. A full discussion of these claims, with an emphasis on China, is to be found in Marwyn S. Samuels, *Contest for the South China Sea* (New York: Methuen, 1982). A brief but useful account is to be found also in Lee Lai-to, "The PRC and the South China Sea," *Current Scene* 15, no. 2 (February 1977): 1–12.

17. This information is drawn from Pringle, *Indonesia and the Philippines*, pp. 78–80.

18. See Richard Nations, "Chores of Deterrence," in *Far Eastern Economic Review* 128, no. 14 (11 April 1985): 36–38.

19. For a representative Indonesian view of the nature of threat, see J. Soedjati Djiwandono, "The Soviet Presence in the Asia-Pacific Region: An Indonesian Perspective," *The Indonesian Quarterly* (October 1984).

10 SOUTHERN AFRICA

David F. Gordon

In the past eleven years, a series of events has profoundly transformed the political landscape of Southern Africa, increasing the significance of the region in international politics. At the same time, powerful external actors are playing a more important role within the region. While not as strategically central to the East-West conflict as the Middle East, Southwest Asia, or the Korean peninsula, Southern Africa has a symbolic significance in world politics that goes beyond its location astride one of the world's most important sea-lanes and its plentiful storehouse of strategic raw materials. The conflicts in Southern Africa mark the final act in the drama of decolonization and have at their heart the question of race, still the most daunting and emotional issue of the twentieth century.

Though Southern Africa is unlikely to become a flash point in East-West relations, events in the region do have a bearing on great-power interactions. More importantly, the interests and actions of the great powers influence events in the region so that understanding the East-West dimension in Southern African regional issues is important. It is equally important, however, to recognize that the sources of conflict and instability in the region are fundamentally internal. Thus, any reduction of Southern African issues to only their East-West component will hinder, rather than facilitate, understanding. While external actors are significant, and are likely to become more so, their importance is felt predominantly through their interaction with various actors within the region. Therefore, any analysis of regional issues and the role of the great powers must start with Southern Africa itself.

Before 1974 Southern Africa was marked by a colonialist-racialist stability that, while running counter to many of the themes of the postwar international system, appeared to have successfully turned back the southward thrust of decolonization in Africa.[1] At the core of the highly integrated regional system was the economically and politically powerful Republic of South Africa, ruled by a white population that comprised less than 20 percent of its citizenry. Most of the other territories in Southern Africa remained under colonial and/or white minority rule. Before 1974 only the sparsely populated former British High Commission Territories of Botswana, Lesotho, and Swaziland were under majority rule. In the northern border area separating Southern Africa from the majority-ruled states of black Africa were several countries that, despite their distaste for the colonialist-racialist status quo in the South, were in no position to challenge it effectively.

Extra-continental actors—with the exception of Portugal, which ruled Angola and Mozambique—played only a limited role in Southern Africa in the decade prior to 1974. While Britain, the other major colonial power, continued to have substantial economic interests in the region, its political influence had become negligible. Other Western countries, including the United States, had growing economic and commercial ties with the region, but these did not translate into either direct influence or political involvement. While the Soviets provided financial and political support to several of the liberation movements in the region, their main interest appeared to be embarrassing the West within the increasingly important Third World political bloc, as well as competing with China for influence among the externally based liberation movements. While both superpowers might have wished for a larger role in Southern Africa, the apparent stability of the regional system and the strength of South Africa within it, along with the distance of Southern Africa from the main arenas of East-West conflict, made the region low priority on the foreign policy agendas of both the United States and the Soviet Union.[2]

THE 1974 PORTUGUESE COUP AND ITS AFTERMATH

In April 1974, military officers in Portugal overthrew the Caetano dictatorship. The Portuguese coup ushered in a series of changes in Southern Africa that abruptly undermined the stability of the old regional system, led to the increased involvement of both the United States and the Soviet Union, and created the conditions for the ongoing tensions that now exist.

By the early 1980s, major regime changes had occurred in three countries in Southern Africa—Mozambique, Angola, and Zimbabwe (formerly Rhodesia). In all three countries radical political movements professing Marxist ideologies came to power in the aftermath of long and bitter struggles against colonial or white-minority governments. All three of these new states were committed to restructuring the regional order in Southern Africa and, ultimately, to undermining the apartheid system of white domination within South Africa itself.

For South Africa, the changes in the region after 1974 were a major motivation behind the government's search for a new domestic order that, while maintaining substantial white privilege, might gain some legitimacy among South Africa's black majority population and with the international community. This policy change was, in turn, the major cause of the subsequent split within the ruling National Party when conservative elements, led by former cabinet minister and Transvaal Province Party boss Andries Treurnicht, formed a right-wing opposition to challenge the nationalists.[3]

The rise of radical regimes in Southern Africa deeply affected black politics in South Africa. The rapid changes in Mozambique and Angola in the mid-1970s gave an added spur to the black consciousness movement and served to embolden the black urban youth in the 1976 uprisings in Soweto and other urban townships. In the longer run, the rise of radical regimes in Mozambique and Angola gave support to the reemergence, in the latter 1970s, of the African National Congress (ANC) as the most important black political group in South Africa.[4] The ANC, the oldest black nationalist movement in Africa, had been banned and its leaders imprisoned by the South African government in the early 1960s.

In the aftermath of the Portuguese coup, interstate relations in Southern Africa have grown more conflictual. More than any other part of Africa, Southern Africa evolved historically as a regional economic system. Trade relations are extensive, especially between South Africa and various other countries in the region. In addition, a network of transportation and communications, as well as an extensive system of labor migration, served to integrate the countries of the region.[5] The dramatic regime changes, particularly in Mozambique and Angola, destroyed what had been a congruence between the regional economic system and political relations in the region. Since the mid-1970s the majority-ruled states, both individually and collectively, have attempted to promote further political changes within the region as well as to strengthen themselves economically while reducing their dependence on South Africa.

These efforts have had limited results. The most successful initiative was that of the Front-Line States (FLS)—an informal grouping of the leaders of those majority-ruled countries bordering on or significantly involved with Zimbabwe—in the resolution of the civil war in Rhodesia/Zimbabwe and the subsequent transition to majority rule in 1980. In the final years of the Zimbabwe conflict, the FLS played a crucial role in facilitating Western conflict-resolution efforts through their unique position of influence with the West, the Communist bloc, the liberation movements, and other African states. These efforts culminated in the 1980 elections that brought Robert Mugabe and the Zimbabwe African National Union (ZANU) to power.[6]

Growing out of their successful cooperation in the Zimbabwe conflict, the majority-ruled states of Southern Africa have attempted to go beyond political cooperation to economic coordination. They have formed the Southern African Development Coordination Conference (SADCC) to promote economic growth and cooperation among member states and to minimize their dependence on South Africa. These efforts, while still in their very early stages, have not been particularly successful. Economic trends of the past decade do not signal a lessening of dependence on South Africa by the black states in the region, nor do they show any real "catching up" economically on the part of those states. Instead, the inherited pattern of highly asymmetrical dependence still remains intact.[7]

Given this continuing dependence in the region—the structural continuity of South Africa's position as core state in a highly integrated regional system—Pretoria is able to wield a powerful economic stick and also proffer substantial economic carrots in its relations with its black neighbors. The South African government has long recognized this fact. As Henry Bienen writes, "Economic cooperation and economic punishment are in the service of South Africa's foreign policy goals and domestic security concerns."[8]

In the late 1970s, however, regional relations in South Africa exhibited an interesting paradox. Despite this asymmetrical dependence and overwhelming economic and technological superiority, and despite the willingness of the South African government to utilize foreign economic ties for explicitly political purposes, South Africa was unable to control, or even substantially dominate, the course of events in the region. The paradox of Southern Africa after 1974 was that by any traditional measure of "national strength," South Africa remained the dominant power in the region; yet Pretoria was consistently incapable of translating its economic, military, and technological strength into political influence and a capacity to control the evolution of the region.

The extent of South African failure was substantial. Not only was Pretoria unable to prohibit independence in Mozambique, Angola, and Zimbabwe, but it could not ensure the emergence of even mildly friendly governments in those neighboring states. In the case of Angola, the outcome of decolonization came close to fulfilling what in the minds of Pretoria's strategic planners must have been the worst-case scenario: a Marxist regime, fully dependent on the Eastern bloc and unswervingly hostile to South Africa, kept in power by thousands of apparently permanently stationed foreign communist troops.

INTERNATIONALIZATION—THE ANGOLAN CIVIL WAR

The key event in the internationalization of the conflicts in Southern Africa was the Angolan Civil War of 1974–76. Much has been written on the Angolan conflict and the Soviet and Cuban intervention that tipped the scales in favor of their local allies—the Popular Movement for the Liberation of Angola (MPLA).[9] There is no doubt that the massive projection of Soviet military power and political influence in Southern Africa marked important turning points both in the region and in broader East-West relations.[10] Moreover, the Angolan Civil War was also important in shaping subsequent American policy in the region and in influencing the various regional actors' perceptions of, and attitudes toward, the United States.

In Angola, at the time of the Portuguese coup, the nationalist movement was split into three competing groups: the FNLA, based among the Bakongo people of northern Angola and closely tied to Zaire, and through Zaire, supported by the United States; the MPLA, based among the urban population in the Angolan capital of Luanda and the Mbundu people of the surrounding area, long supported by the Soviets; and the UNITA, based among the Ovimbundu people of southern Angola and supported by the Chinese. In the period immediately following the coup, two divergent trends emerged. On the one hand, each faction succeeded in increasing military support from its foreign patron, thereby escalating the fighting. On the other hand, the Organization of African Unity (OAU) intensified its efforts to mediate the dispute. Two agreements were actually signed in which the competing factions committed themselves to participate in a coalition government.

The external backers of the competing factions—the United States, the USSR, and China—took an ambivalent stand toward the OAU-sponsored negotiations. Similar to the nationalist factions themselves, the outside powers all followed a two-track policy of publicly supporting negotiations while simultaneously expanding military supplies to their local allies. Both the Soviet Union and the United States had mixed motives in escalating their involvement. The mid-1970s was the high point of Sino-Soviet competition for influence among African liberation movements. It is quite likely that, at least throughout the first half of 1975, Sino-Soviet competition was as much behind Soviet behavior as was East-West competition.[11] For the United States, expanded support for the FNLA was as much a show of support for their patron, President Mobutu of Zaire, as an explicit counter to Soviet activities.[12]

Throughout the first six months of 1975 the fighting escalated. In June the pace of internationalization quickened, and the MPLA, threatened by a powerful FNLA force from the north, requested and received increased Cuban support, including several hundred military advisers. Shortly thereafter, South Africa, in cooperation with UNITA troops, sent an armored column into southern Angola to engage the MPLA forces. At the same time, the United States stepped up covert support for both FNLA and UNITA. In October South African operations escalated.

At this point the Chinese ceased their military assistance to UNITA and, belatedly, put their weight behind negotiations. In the United States, a sharp debate broke out over how to respond to events in Angola. As South African operations escalated, the Soviet Union began an air-and-sea lift of Cuban troops to support the MPLA.[13] Secretary of State Henry Kissinger, in the aftermath of the traumatic U.S. withdrawal from Southeast Asia, wished to demonstrate resolve against Soviet expansionism and saw Angola as the place to do this. Congressional critics, however, feared having the United States getting bogged down in another overseas adventure and felt that military intervention in cooperation with South Africa was an inappropriate method for demonstrating anti-Soviet resolve. The passage of the Clark amendment in December 1975 prevented further U.S. military involvement, leaving the path open for the military victory of the Soviet-backed MPLA.

The South African invasion of Angola in support of UNITA facilitated Soviet intervention in 1975 and 1976. Before the South African military thrust, many African states—both individually and collectively through the OAU—had preferred a negotiated settlement and a coalition government. But for crucial states such as Tanzania and Nigeria, the South African intervention in favor of UNITA and FNLA legitimized MPLA's claim to be the sole authority in Angola, and also the Soviet/Cuban military involvement. At the emergency OAU summit in February 1976, Nigerian President Murtala Muhammed praised "the heroic role which the Soviet Union" played in the Angolan conflict.[14]

AFTER ANGOLA

The Angolan Civil War marked the first active involvement of the two superpowers in the conflict of Southern Africa. Both learned important lessons from the episode. For the Soviets, the lesson of Angola was that Soviet goals can best be served when the United States and South Africa are, or are perceived to be, in an alliance. The main theme of Soviet propaganda concerning Southern Africa is the purported alliance between "imperialist" America and "racist" South Africa. Strategically, the Soviets have sought to influence events in such a way as to make reality match their propaganda as much as possible.[15] For the United States, the lesson of Angola was that its interests could best be promoted through involvement in peaceful efforts to resolve the remaining colonial issues in the region, while at the same time more actively promoting change within South Africa itself.[16]

If the Soviets were the clear "winner" in the Angolan Civil War, they have neither been able to repeat the dramatic success of their intervention nor to consolidate and solidify their position in the aftermath of the war. The assumption, broadly shared, that the MPLA victory in Angola would enable them to consolidate control over the entire country has proved incorrect. The UNITA guerrillas, with a wide popular base in southern Angola and support from South Africa, and more recently from the United States, have shown themselves to be resourceful and tenacious foes. The civil war has never really ended. Despite the continual presence of 15,000 to 25,000 Cuban troops and a wide range of Eastern bloc support personnel, the Soviet position in Angola remains tenuous. While the MPLA is dependent on this support to maintain their control over the major centers and the formal instruments of sovereignty, the continued instability and the narrow base of the MPLA regime have made Angola a poor candidate as a center from which to spread Soviet influence. Elsewhere in the region, the remaining colonial conflicts have not followed the Angolan model of extensive internationalization concluding in Soviet-backed military victories.

Part of the reason for this lies in the shift in U.S. policy in the aftermath of Angola. The United States was totally unprepared in 1974 for major involvement in Southern Africa. American policy was marked by incoherence and conflict, as well as by a gross misreading of regional political realities. After Angola, two challenges faced American policy in the region: first, generating a domestic political consensus that could meld the anti-communist goals of conservatives with liberals' support for decolonization and change; and second, designing policies to reflect the global strategic concerns of the United States while remaining attuned to the complex political realities of the Southern African region.

Beginning in 1976, a rough domestic consensus and a blending of global and regional concerns did occur. This "centrist consensus" was tenuous and was continually attacked from both right and left.[17] As we shall see, in the mid-1980s, for both domestic and international reasons, this consensus has been increasingly difficult to sustain. But in the late 1970s, it allowed the United States to reclaim the international initiative in Southern Africa. The key theme behind American policy was that U.S. goals of limiting Soviet influence could be melded with African aspirations for decolonization and with the potential interest of all regional actors in lessened tensions if arms and military conflict could be made less relevant to regional politics.

Beginning in 1976, the United States became heavily involved in negotiations for conflict resolution in Zimbabwe and Namibia. The principles behind this involvement have been to bring into the negotiation process all relevant regional actors, including the black states, collectively represented through the FLS, and South Africa; to limit armed conflict and external involvement while working toward cease-fire arrangements; to mediate negotiations on independence constitutions that ensure majority rule and protect minority rights; and to establish internationally recognized and domestically legitimate independent regimes through the mechanism of internationally supervised elections.[18]

For its ultimate success, this approach depended upon diplomatic skill and a peculiar configuration of both forces and perceptions among the key regional actors. But even in the absence of successful negotiations, the policy took the initiative in the region away from the Soviet Union and its allies. The Soviets did not become irrelevant; but for the liberation movements and their African backers in the FLS, Soviet military assistance came to be seen as the means by which liberation movements could gain the clout needed to bring their adversaries to the negotiating table, and the threat of increased military support, as the mechanism for sustaining the influence of the liberation movements throughout the negotiating process.

The denouement of the Zimbabwe conflict was the most striking example of this. From a great power perspective, the final stages in Zimbabwe appear as a mirror image of what occurred in Angola. In Angola, as the military conflict escalated, U.S. policy became paralyzed, with the result that Soviet intervention was able to determine the short-term outcome. In 1979 and 1980, as the negotiating process on Zimbabwe gained momentum under Commonwealth imprimatur and British auspices, Soviet policy became paralyzed. Robert Legvold writes about "how docilely the Soviets let the FLS control the state of play, how unopportunistic (or inept) they were in exploiting politics within the Patriotic Front, how feebly they resisted the Lancaster House Settlement."[19]

Despite the failure of the United States to repeat the successful settlement of the Zimbabwe conflict in the Namibia negotiations, Soviet behavior in Namibia has much more in common with the experience of Zimbabwe than it does with Angola. While the Soviets are using the lack of a Namibian agreement as a propaganda stick with which to hit the United States, they have not attempted to retake the initiative through a dramatic increase in military assistance to the SWAPO guerrillas fighting against South African forces in Namibia. Reluctant to engage South African forces, the Soviets and their Cuban allies are unlikely to view SWAPO as an effective ally.

SOUTH AFRICA FIGHTS BACK

The internationalization of the conflicts in Southern Africa, while having mixed results for the two superpowers, was decidedly negative for South Africa and has been detrimental to their efforts to exert influence and control in the region. Given the power disparities within the region, even external intervention that seeks to be as evenhanded as U.S. involvement has been will tend to redress the power imbalance on the ground. Indeed, the FLS strategy of seeking Western involvement in conflict resolution in the region was based on this calculation. The greatest effect African states have had in Southern Africa has been indirect, through their ability to influence Western interventions in a manner that, in sum, reduced South Africa's regional domination.[20]

The erosion of South African influence in the late 1970s led to a re-evaluation of strategy and policies by Pretoria. For many policymakers, especially among the top brass in the South African Defense Forces, the events of the previous years had several lessons:

1. Diplomacy and economic strength, by themselves, are no longer capable of ensuring regional outcomes favorable to the security of the Republic.

2. The West, especially the United States, cannot and should not be trusted.

3. South Africa should not, and need not, acquiesce to other regional actors, especially if those actors engage in activities potentially dangerous to South African security.

This analysis implied South Africa should take a far more active and aggressive regional stance. Thus, the Israelis became the new role models for many South African policymakers.

In January 1981 South Africa launched its "destabilization" counteroffensive with a commando raid against the ANC headquarters in Matola, just outside the capital of Mozambique. Later that year, South African forces again crossed into southern Angola in what was to be a sustained operation involving the practical occupation of large segments of southern Angola by South Africa. Throughout the next two years, South Africa engaged in aggressive and/or threatening acts against Zimbabwe, Lesotho, and Botswana as well as Mozambique and Angola.

Yet there was less coherence and consistency in Pretoria's policy than some observers perceived.[21] For each of the three lessons of the 1970s, there were conflicting interpretations among Pretoria's ruling group between what Peter Vale, for want of a better phrase, has labeled "hawks" and "doves."[22] The hawks, most powerfully represented by several generals on South Africa's influential State Security Council, viewed destabilization as an end in itself. South Africa should not attempt to curry favor through diplomacy, either in the region or internationally. Hawks feel that South African and American interests basically diverge. As for the black states in the region, they cannot be trusted and need to be either permanently weakened or overthrown.

For the doves, destabilization was more of a means. In the dove perspective, articulated by the Foreign Ministry and supported by the economic elites in South Africa, South African diplomacy and the influence of economic strength would be reinvigorated by the exertion of military force and economic sticks. While doves are wary of the United States, they feel U.S. involvement may, especially under a conservative administration, be beneficial to South Africa. Finally, while support by neighboring countries for anti–South African guerrillas of the ANC and SWAPO is intolerable, doves are optimistic that good relations might be possible even with countries of a radical ideological bent.[23]

In 1981 the need to halt the erosion of South African power led to a rough consensus between hawks and doves behind the destabilization offensive. This was reinforced by the domestic political needs of South African leader P.W. Botha, who saw an aggressive external policy as both buying time to push ahead with domestic reforms and dulling the attack from the newly formed right-wing opposition Conservative party. South Africa's aggressive regional stance was couched in strongly anti-communist garb as a necessary response to a communist-inspired "total onslaught" on the Republic. The shift to conservative leadership in the United States facilitated the emergence of a consensus in Pretoria around destabilization.

DESTABILIZATION AND CONSTRUCTIVE ENGAGEMENT

While never approving or condoning South Africa's aggressive behavior toward its neighbors, Washington recognized that, in the aftermath of Angola, the South African Defense Force provided the only real counter to Soviet military strength in the region. In vetoing a 1981 UN resolution condemning South African incursions into Angola, the United States stressed the link between the South African raid and the presence of Cuban troops and Soviet-bloc personnel and equipment in Angola.[24]

But if the Reagan administration was willing to acquiesce in the South African offensive against Soviet military power in the region, it was, at the same time, stymied in its own regional goals by the aggressive stance taken by Pretoria. The South African destabilization initiatives of 1981 and 1982 produced an immediate challenge for Washington. Reagan administration goals were similar to the post-Angolan Southern Africa aims of the Ford and Carter administrations. The top priority was forging a Namibian settlement that would bring genuine majority rule to that country, thus countering left-wing charges, both domestic and international, that "constructive engagement" was "soft on apartheid"; it would also assure the removal of Cuban troops from Angola, thus quieting right-wing critics and furthering the broader anti-communist themes of the Reagan administration's foreign policy.[25] Yet these general goals of the administration, as well as its specific aims in Namibia, were threatened by South Africa's aggressive policy in the region. The key issue for U.S. policymakers became how to change Pretoria's mind about destabilization.

Recognizing South Africa's negative experiences in the period following the Portuguese coup, Reagan administration policymakers believed South African cooperation in U.S.-led international diplomacy in the region could not be garnered—and thus could not succeed—without more serious explicit consideration given to the security concerns of the South African government. This was more than a tactical shift based on realpolitik, for U.S. policymakers also believed that South African politics were now dominated by a pragmatic, moderate coalition that, though hesitant, was committed to long-term basic reform in South Africa and thus deserved American support.[26] Based on these two premises, "constructive engagement" tried to entice South Africa into cooperation with the United States.

Because of the assumed need to win South African confidence as a precondition for diplomatic success, the option of utilizing pressure tactics, especially economic pressures, as a means of changing South African policy was explicitly taken off the U.S. agenda. American officials sought rather to increase their credibility within South Africa's ruling group by assisting South Africa doves in their internal conflicts with the hawks.[27] These efforts achieved only limited success, demonstrating the degree to which American policy became hostage to the initiatives of, and conflicts within, the South African government.

THE NKOMATI AND LUSAKA ACCORDS

In late 1983, just as the full impact of South Africa's destabilization was becoming more apparent, trends in the region again shifted direction. South African and Mozambican officials, encouraged and facilitated by the United States, held a series of meetings that culminated in the Nkomati Accords of March 1984. Essentially, Nkomati is a nonaggression treaty committing both states to the principles of good neighborliness and peaceful coexistence. The immediate goals of Nkomati were to end Mozambican support for ANC guerrilla operations and to stop South African support for the anti-Frelimo Mozambique National Resistance (MNR).

At the same time, an agreement between South Africa and Angola was reached at Lusaka. The Lusaka Agreement included a cease-fire in southern Angola, the removal of South African forces from that territory, and the creation of a joint monitoring commission that would supervise these agreements. Both the Angolans and the South Africans also made significant concessions in their positions concerning the removal of Cuban forces from Angola and South African implementation of UN plans for Namibia independence. These concessions appeared to increase substantially the possibility of settling the Namibian conflict. Elsewhere in Southern Africa, the tensions were also diminishing.

What were the sources behind these new developments? Did they mark a major turnabout in regional relations or merely a blip on a continuing trend line of increasing conflict? To understand these changes we must examine regional factors, domestic forces in both South Africa and the black states, and broader international influences. In the region, South Africa's destabilization offensive had been a substantial success. What had appeared only a few years before as an almost inevitable erosion of South African power had been decisively blunted. This had been accomplished, moreover, without rupturing relations with the major Western powers, especially the United States.

Yet while destabilization was a substantial success, by late 1983 it was becoming evident that significant costs and limits to the approach existed. South Africa's economy was descending into what was to become its deepest crisis since the Great Depression of the 1920s. The financial burdens of an aggressive and ambitious regional policy were already high and threatened to increase further. Maintaining military control over Namibia and bankrolling the territory's administration by itself cost $1.3 billion, 8 percent of South Africa's total budget.[28] If dissidents supported by South Africa succeeded in toppling governments in other neighboring states, another burden would be coded to the already financially strapped budget. Especially for South African doves, the time appeared right for a new round of diplomacy.

International pressures reinforced the economic and financial constraints on destabilization. By late 1983 American patience was wearing thin. The Reagan administration's policy of constructive engagement, having little to show, was under attack both domestically and internationally. The United States began to diversify its regional initiatives. In 1983 the United States slowly and quietly began to improve relations with Mozambique. President Machel, threatened by a South African-supported insurgency, beset by ever-worsening economic woes, and unable to gain entry to the Soviet-bloc economic association CMEA, attempted to improve relations with the West while simultaneously trying to negotiate seriously with South Africa.[29] The Mozambican-South African negotiations became the cement for the de facto alliance between U.S. officials and South African doves, leading the latter away from destabilization.

Despite misgivings, the Soviets also played a role in the events leading up to the Lusaka Accord. In December 1983 the South African military embarked upon its most ambitious—and disastrous—offensive in Angola, Operation Askari. Askari had as its goals the capture of several major Angolan towns and the positioning of South African forces for a possible assault on Luanda. But South African forces faced heavy and effective opposition from the Angolan army, making the outdated South African air force vulnerable to the Soviet surface-to-air missiles operated by the Angolans.[30] In addition, the Soviets informed South Africa that any effort to topple the MPLA regime would not be tolerated. While some South African military officials were eager to test Soviet resolve, in sum, the Soviet demarche served to strengthen the case of those South African policymakers who were ready to shift to a more diplomatic approach. Thus ensued the negotiations culminating in the Lusaka Accord.[31]

The agreements of 1984 were particularly encouraging for the United States. American mediation had been crucial in the Mozambican-South African and significant in the Angolan-South African negotiations. The Nkomati Accords were particularly important to Washington because they might, if successfully consolidated, weaken both South African and Angolan hesitations regarding a Namibia agreement based on Cuban troop withdrawal. If South Africa could live cooperatively with the Marxists in Mozambique, the commitment and cost of denying SWAPO power in Namibia would no longer make sense. For the Angolans, Nkomati would demonstrate both the willingness and ability of the United States to act as an honest mediator and the trustworthiness of South Africa.

The United States also had longer-term hopes for the impact of Nkomati on domestic change in South Africa. If Nkomati could be consolidated, South African fears that their neighbors were part of a "total onslaught" conspiracy led by the Soviet Union might be proven groundless. If so, American officials hoped the influence of South African hard-liners in both domestic and regional policy might be reduced.[32]

The accords of early 1984 generated unrealistic and mutually inconsistent expectations for the regional actors. South Africans expected the Nkomati Accords, as well as their nation's successful intimidation of other neighboring states, to provide domestic breathing space necessary to reform the apartheid system while still retaining white domination. South African leaders also hoped lessened tensions in the region would enable them to significantly improve relations with the West.

Mozambique expected the Nkomati Accords to allow it to gain military superiority over the dissident MNR. In addition, President Machel saw Nkomati as a way to increase access to South African and Western economic resources such as trade, investment, and tourists. This access would be instrumental for Mozambique to reverse the downward spiral of economic disintegation as well as to regain popular support, especially in rural areas.[33]

Angola's expectations following the Lusaka Agreement were more difficult to discern. The MPLA expected the agreement to lead to the removal of South African troops from southern Angola and probably hoped that South African support for UNITA would diminish. Whether they saw the Lusaka Agreement as leading to a Namibia settlement is less clear. While Angola desires a resolution of the Namibia dispute and has been willing to negotiate on the reciprocal issue of the removal of Cuban troops from its land, it has been wary of any settlement that might increase its vulnerability to the UNITA opposition. The Nkomati and Lusaka Accords were not viewed favorably by all the relevant actors. Disquiet came from two very disparate sources. First, the anti-communist guerrilla movements in Mozambique and Angola (MNR and UNITA), as well as their supporters in South Africa and the West (including some elements of the far right in the United States), were upset at being left out of the emerging regional framework. Second, the ANC and its supporters, particularly in African countries outside of Southern Africa, feared the emerging regional stability might become the stability of apartheid itself.[34] Finally, there is no doubt the Soviets viewed the two agreements as short-term setbacks. The Soviet response was basically one of waiting, in the expectation (rather different than the ANC's) that, in the longer run, events would again shift in their favor and against the United States.[35]

SOUTHERN AFRICA TODAY: REGIONAL TENSIONS REEMERGE

The Nkomati and Lusaka Accords did not generate a sustained momentum toward easing regional tensions. Unfulfilled expectations have led to increased frustration and distrust. The rise of sustained urban unrest in South Africa and its impact on both the South African government and U.S.-South African relations have dramatically demonstrated the evanescent nature of any regional security initiative while domestic tensions in South Africa are so strong. It is in this sense that apartheid is the ultimate source of instability in the entire region.

Symptomatic of the renewed tensions in the region is the demise of the Nkomati Accords. Simply put, the benefits from the accords accrued overwhelmingly to South Africa. While Mozambique acted to restrain the ANC's ability to use Mozambique as a take-off point for incursions into South Africa, South Africa played a more ambiguous game. The MNR threat to Mozambique increased, rather than diminished, in the year following the signing of Nkomati. This was due to a number of factors. First, South African arms, with or without top government approval, moved across the border to MNR in large numbers just prior to Nkomati. Second, elements within the SADF—probably in military intelligence—saw the continuation of MNR pressure on the Mozambique government as a means of both maximizing Mozambique's dependence on South Africa and maintaining the credibility of South Africa to the various South African-supported dissident groups elsewhere in the region, especially UNITA. Third, South Africa turned a blind eye on activities by Portuguese South Africans, many of whom had fled Mozambique, who were ferrying supplies to MNR.[36]

By early 1987 South Africa had ceased to pay anything but lip service to the accords. South Africa stepped up support to the MNR as it became an increasing threat to the Mozambican government. In October 1986 President Samora Machel of Mozambique was killed in a plane that crashed while flying over South African territory. It is still not known whether or not the South Africans or the MNR played any role in the incident, but tensions had heightened in the weeks preceeding the crash. But South Africa and the MNR are by no means the sole cause of Mozambique's current difficulties.

Just as South Africa overstates the importance of outside threats—what was previously called "total onslaught"—Mozambique is loath to admit that its own policies and actions, especially toward the rural areas, allowed its enemies to flourish.

The demise of the Nkomati Accords are important to the United States for several reasons. Mozambique's efforts to improve relations with the West, culminating in Nkomati, were based on the view that Western, rather than Soviet, links would be more effective for its security and development goals. While Joaquim Chissano, the new Mozambican president, is unlikely to invite back substantial numbers of Eastern-bloc military personnel, a political swing back toward the Soviets is possible.[37]

More importantly, given the difficulty in achieving a breakthrough on the Namibia issue and the antagonism of African nations toward the U.S. tactic of linking Namibian independence to a withdrawal of Cuban forces from Angola, the American-brokered Nkomati Accords became a symbol of U.S. policy and a test of U.S. credibility in the region. For the African states, Nkomati tested whether the United States could cooperate with a nonaligned country with which it had a large ideological gap and whether the United States has the will (rightly or wrongly, African states feel the United States does have the means) to leverage South Africa into a policy of regional restraint.

Just as Nkomati did not achieve its desired results, the Lusaka Agreements between South Africa and Angola failed to generate a resolution of the Namibian issue. South African forces did not fully withdraw from southern Angola, nor did their support for UNITA decrease. In May 1985 South African commandoes preparing to sabotage a Gulf Oil Company facility, Angola's most important economic asset, were caught by Angolan forces. This episode further diminished the small chance of reaching an agreement between South Africa and Angola for an internationally recognized settlement in Namibia.

The United States had seen the Lusaka Agreement as a step toward a broader U.S.-brokered package to include Namibian independence. It is evident, however, that South Africa had something quite different in mind. For several months after Lusaka, South Africa, independent of the United States, attempted to broker its own Namibia agreement by offering the Angolans the "carrot" of dropping linkage in return for allowing SWAPO to share power in Namibia with other forces friendly to South Africa.[38] This effort failed and in June 1985 the South Africans installed a new internal administration made up of anti-SWAPO groups in Namibia.

With the outbreak of severe and sustained domestic unrest in South Africa in late 1984, any chance of South Africa's moving ahead on any Namibia settlement within the U.N. framework disappeared. Not only would President P.W. Botha face hostility from his right-wing opposition, but the message such a move would send to the regime's black domestic opponents would be exactly the opposite of what the government's strategy requires.

Angolan cooperation in American diplomatic efforts has also been limited. The Angola government watched the evolution of Nkomati as a measure of South African willingness and capacity to break with the dissident movements it had utilized in its destabilization efforts. Given the continuing strength of the MNR in Mozambique, the demise of Nkomati told Angola to be extremely cautious on the issue of reducing Cuban forces in their country. When, in early 1986, the United States began military support for the UNITA guerrilla movement fighting the Angolan government, Luanda responded by effectively withdrawing from the American-led negotiating effort. Thus, for a number of reasons, the diplomatic resolution of the Namibia issue appears to be highly unlikely in the near future.

THE CRISIS IN SOUTH AFRICA

It is impossible to understand regional security issues in Southern Africa without examining domestic events in the core state of the region—the Republic of South Africa. The actual and latent instability of South Africa greatly complicates both the search for regional security and the analysis of regional security issues. Seldom has the connection between events in South Africa and regional security been stronger than in late 1984 and 1985 when sustained black unrest in South Africa played a major role in the reemergence of sharpened tensions in the region.

Domestic events in South Africa failed to live up to either the hopes of the South African government or the fears of the ANC and some African states in the aftermath of Nkomati. The status quo in South Africa did not become more viable (the fear of the ANC, but never a real possibility) nor was the government's ability to control the process of change (a real, if limited, possibility) enhanced. Rather, South Africa entered its most profound crisis— both economic and political—since the Great Depression. This by no means suggests fundamental change lies around the corner in South Africa nor that the South African government faces an immediate challenge to its continued rule. Yet there is no question that contemporary South Africa is in great flux, and judging events today by the yardsticks of the past is likely to be misleading.

Five themes highlight this new conjuncture:

The practical breakdown of apartheid.   Quite simply, apartheid as a system of racial separation never did work, and increasingly and more visibly does not work. The apartheid laws are increasingly enforced in an ad hoc manner, while some are openly violated. Even the most conservative elements in the white community admit that apartheid in the traditional sense can no longer be sustained. The breakdown of the existing system has generated a broad debate among white South Africans over possible "new dispensation," and has reinforced the militancy of the black opposition.

The incoherence of government policy.   In the early 1980s, the South African government began to move away from its "Grand Apartheid" vision to a "neo-apartheid" plan that included labor and educational reforms, provision for colored and Asian parliamentary representation, and increased rights for those blacks already permanently resident and employed in South African cities.

But neo-apartheid has failed to become a coherent vision giving clear direction to government policy initiatives in a range of different spheres. The massive bureaucratic and repressive apparatus created to enforce apartheid still exists. In the absence of the guidance once provided by the ideology of "Grand Apartheid," the bureaucracy has become increasingly difficult to direct and control. This problem is exacerbated by economic and political crisis, which makes a long-term approach to policymaking virtually impossible. Battered by an unusually wide range of pressures, the South African government has been reduced to an ad hoc respondent rather than becoming a shaper of events.

The unprecedented rise of black anti-government mobilization.   Ironically, the heart of the neo-apartheid package, the 1983 constitution, set into motion the most extensive and sustained anti-government mobilization in South African history. The extensiveness and effectiveness of this mobilization, manifested in a wide range of organizational forms ranging from trade unions, civic organizations, and church groups to umbrella organizations such as the United Democratic Front (UDF) and the National Forum (NF), indicate the important changes in South African society that are gradually but inexorably raising the bargaining power of the black majority population.[39]

The new activism in the business community.   Despite the business sector's uneasiness over apartheid, until recently the government's ability to deliver on the bottom line—profitability and stability—made the government largely immune to business pressures. In 1985 the deep economic crisis, the continuing mobilization by black protest groups, and the threat of punitive measures by Western governments encouraged the business sector to push the South African government for a variety of reforms. Commercial confidence, both international and domestic, reached a low ebb. Ironically, however, the implementation of sanctions and the pullout of American firms, which escalated dramatically in 1986 and 1987, served to limit business pressure on government. While sanctions were a threat, business sought to pressure government to reform in order to avoid sanctions; once sanctions were implemented, business had to work in conjunction with government to evade them.

The growing importance of the ANC in the public debate in South Africa.　　Taken together, the aforementioned elements of the new South African context lead to the final theme: the emergence of the African National Congress as a central factor in the South African equation. In 1985 and 1986, leading businessmen met with the ANC's exiled leadership, and there were persistent rumors of secret talks between the ANC and the government. The speeches and statements of Nelson Mandela, for years reproduced only in underground newspapers, were seen in the pages of the commercial press. Liberal whites promoted the idea of an immediate dialogue between the government and the ANC, fearing that the longer talks were postponed, the less likely the ANC would be able to control internal militants and remain a coherent opponent in talks.[40]

Where will this new conjuncture lead? The South African government is caught in a terrible dilemma. President Botha realizes the necessity of change yet is committed to retaining the influence and security of whites, especially the Afrikaners. His room for maneuver is severely limited. The government cannot be seen to be acting in response to black political pressure, lest government-led reforms fuel anti-government mobilization. At the same time, Botha fears the right-wing opposition movement, whose platform is centered around maintaining the status quo. Both of these political constraints weaken the impetus for reform within the South African government. In mid-1986 the South African government shifted to the right, leaving behind even the appearance of attempting to respond constructively to the pressures for change being exerted upon it. At least for the short run, the possibility of government-led reform has been taken off the agenda.

At the same time, the black opposition is still a long way from effectively challenging the government for power. The current situation in South Africa, then, is best seen as an interregnum—the old order is dead but the new is not yet born, not even in outline form—that could persist for a very long time. The conflicts in South Africa will center on both the shape of that new order and on the relations of power within it.

THE FUTURE ROLE OF EXTERNAL ACTORS IN SOUTHERN AFRICA

Despite waning direct Soviet influence in Southern Africa in recent years, the Soviet leadership remains optimistic about the future of the region and continues to benefit from using Southern Africa to score points against the West.[41] Given pressing problems elsewhere in the world that demand Soviet attention and resources, the distance of Southern Africa from the main areas of Soviet strategic concern, the relatively cheap benefits of their present policies, and the risks involved in attempting to substantially increase their role, Soviet policy is unlikely to shift much from the pattern established after the Angolan Civil War. The Soviets will attempt to maintain their substantial influence in Angola, using this influence to discourage Angolan participation in either Western- or South African-sponsored agreements in Namibia unless Soviet interests are explicitly taken into account. In addition, the Soviets will try to regain influence in Mozambique and increase it in Zambia and Zimbabwe by proffering military assistance and diplomatic support. While they will continue to arm and support the ANC and SWAPO, the Soviets are unlikely to be drawn into a serious commitment of power.

The Soviets are very concerned about their credibility as a patron and, conversely, about limiting American credibility. Their aim in Southern Africa is the polarization and confrontation of Africans against the West.[42] But the ability of the Soviets to exert influence, except on the MPLA, is not extensive. The central dilemma facing Soviet policymakers in Southern Africa is that the growth or decline of the USSR's influence is highly dependent on the actions of others.

The future Western role in Southern Africa is harder to discern. In recent years, the major Western powers have attempted to avoid, on the one hand, the trade-off between basic support for

South Africa combined with expressions of concern for improvement there and, on the other hand, alignment with the Front-Line States and international organizations in opposition to South Africa and in support of the liberation movements. The policies of the major Western governments, under varying political parties, have all been well between the two stark alternatives.

Given trade and investment ties, as well as the importance of Southern Africa as a source of mineral supplies, all Western governments have an interest in peace and stability in the region. But all have also recognized the inevitability of fundamental change in the medium to long term.[43] The gravest risk facing the West—the worst-case scenario to be avoided—is a generalized war in Southern Africa. The minimum aim of Western policy is avoidance of total polarization. The broader aim is to promote fundamental change while retaining peace and stability. Although the overall goals of the West are fairly straightforward, the policy implications are much less clear.[44]

Are Western interests in stability and change promoted by a supportive relationship with South Africa, or should the West limit its ties to Pretoria and exert pressure through the weapon of economic sanctions? Can economic involvement promote change in South Africa through corporate codes of conduct and other mechanisms? Should the West develop more formal ties with the liberation groups such as the ANC? How much leverage can external actors have in influencing South African outcomes? All of these questions defy easy answers and complicate the search for an effective Western response to the Southern African conundrum.

Economic ties to South Africa have proved to be a particularly sensitive issue for Western governments, especially the United States.[45] Politically embarrassing, these ties have economic benefits and create potential leverage for the Western powers. But how to exert that leverage? The recent conjuncture of South African economic recession, sustained political unrest, and increasing public concern in Western countries has generated heightened pressure for the West to impose economic sanctions on South Africa. The U.S. Congress overrode a presidential veto and banned new investments in South Africa. The European Economic Community limited the access of several categories of South African exports to member countries' markets. Despite these moves, Western governments remain skeptical about the impact of sanctions yet lack credible alternative policies.

Given the uncertainty surrounding the impact of sanctions, the difficulty of enforcing comprehensive sanctions, and the mineral dependence of Western countries and overall economic dependence of the black states in Southern Africa, the likelihood of Western countries enacting mandatory universal sanctions against South Africa in the foreseeable future is slim. Rather, given the likelihood that the international and domestic pressures for sanctions will intensify, the most plausible future scenario is what might be called "creeping sanctions." These would take the form of policies such as restrictions on loans, export guarantees and tax credits, termination of preferential trade arrangements, discouragement of new investments, and embargoes on an ever-expanding range of goods.[46] These sanctions will be more a response to international and domestic political pressures than a serious instrumental effort to generate change in South Africa.

THE IMPACT OF AMERICAN POLICY

By 1985 U.S. policy in Southern Africa had reached an impasse. The "centrist consensus," which developed after the Angolan Civil War and enabled the United States to regain the international initiative in the region, was no longer holding. "Constructive engagement," Assistant Secretary of State Chester Crocker's articulation of this consensus for a conservative administration, came under attack from all sides. In its regional component, constructive engagement was being undermined from the right—by congressional anti-communists opposed to improved U.S. ties to Mozambique and supportive of renewed American assistance to UNITA in Angola. In its approach to South Africa, constructive engagement was assailed from the Left—growing out of frustration over the lack of change and continued repression in South Africa. Both sides viewed existing policy as inadequate at best. In 1986 both the Right and the Left succeeded in altering American policy. U.S. assistance to UNITA, sponsored by congressional conservatives, effectively ended U.S. regional diplomacy, while congressionally mandated sanctions, promoted by liberals, marked the end of constructive engagement with the South African government.

How should American efforts in Southern Africa in the past decade be evaluated? It is difficult to assess the precise results of U.S. actions in the region; outcomes have been due to a multiplicity of factors, of which U.S. policies are generally minor. There is no question, however, that U.S. policy has had some success in its regional goals. The peaceful resolution of the Zimbabwe conflict would have been impossible, for example, if the Carter administration had bent to pressure to recognize the internal settlement regime of Bishop Muzorewa. While the British and the Commonwealth nations took the direct initiative in the talks leading up to the Lancaster House agreements and the 1980 election, it is likely these efforts would have failed without the full and active cooperation of the United States.[47]

Similarly, the commitment of all recent U.S. administrations to a negotiated settlement of the Namibia dispute has played a positive role in keeping the possibility of an internationally recognized resolution alive. While the Reagan administration applied the linkage tactic too stringently, linkage has not been the main reason for the lack of a Namibia settlement. Should South Africa wish to settle in Namibia, linkage may help to resolve the domestic political problem they will face. Although the United States has had some effect in curbing the designs Pretoria's hawks have on destabilizing various neighboring countries, the United States has failed to influence decisively the hawk-versus-dove debate in South African policy circles.

It is more difficult to determine the impact of United States policies on the domestic situation in South Africa. While South Africa never publicly admits responding to external pressure, there is little question that external pressure is an important source of change in the country.[48] Yet it is almost impossible to disentangle external pressure from the major domestic sources of change: the increased bargaining power and political assertiveness of blacks, the growing inconsistency between the status quo and continued economic growth, and changes in the thinking and approaches of the white leadership. It is clear, however, that none of the efforts of various U.S. administrations has had a major impact on the domestic situation in South Africa.

A basic problem in American policy has been a tendency to overestimate the leverage of the United States on the South African government.[49] Under the Carter administration, this was expressed by overstating the similarities between South Africa and the American South just prior to the civil rights revolution.[50] Under the Reagan administration, this problem has been manifested by putting far too much faith in the *verligtes*, the so-called enlightened, more liberal whites, and their assumed commitment to undertake fundamental change in South Africa.[51] In 1986, as the South African government gave up even the pretext of reform while the U.S. Congress imposed a program of mild economic sanctions, relations between Washington and Pretoria reached an all-time low.

The South African government was bitter at the Reagan administration for not taking a more forceful stance in opposition to sanctions. Washington was furious at the reemergence of South African aggression in the region and the continued repression of urban protesters. This severe deterioration of relations resulted in part from unrealistic expectations, on both sides, about forging a new, cooperative relationship. Both failed to recognize the limited overlap between American and South African interests.

Paradoxically, the weakened bonds between Washington and Pretoria may increase the capacity of the United States to exert influence in South Africa. Support for anti-apartheid legislation might, ironically, give constructive engagement a bite it previously lacked. There is no question that the threat of economic sanctions plays a positive role in the calculus of change in South Africa.

Unfortunately, it is less clear whether the actual implementation of large-scale sanctions would enhance the longer-term leverage of the United States or even increase the prospects for effective change in South Africa. The experiences of previous attempts at economic coercion emphasize the difficulties involved in riding the tiger of sanctions to one's desired destination.[52] The political rationales for sanctions are more convincing than arguments focusing on their effective instrumentality.

There are several fallacies in the American domestic debate concerning economic pressures on South Africa. Opponents of economic sanctions often emphasize the belief that capitalism, by creating a need for skilled black labor and increasing the role of the black consumer, is by itself tearing down the system of apartheid.[53] While business has become an important pressure for fundamental change in South Africa, this in itself is a result of pressures from black unions and the international community, including the threat of sanctions. American officials have stated that any measures that weaken the South African economy will be counterproductive to efforts to undermine apartheid.[54] Yet it is impossible to make such definitive statements on this question. If a weak South African economy lessens the pressure for change, how can one explain the current conjuncture of economic weakness and intense pressure for change?

On the other side, many supporters of sanctions tend to see them as a panacea for the problems of South Africa. Yet outside pressure can be only a relatively minor factor in affecting events in South Africa and will be effective only if brought to bear in conjunction with internal pressures. Supporters of sanctions are also often too quick to slough off the question of who will bear the brunt of sanctions.[55] The South African government will be positioned to determine who pays those costs, both within South Africa and in the neighboring countries. Because there are more than 500,000 foreign workers employed in South Africa, the South African government, if it so chooses, can substantially pass on the costs of economic sanctions through limits on foreign employment.

While the debate over sanctions dominates the domestic politics of U.S. policy in Southern Africa, the deteriorating regional situation presents an equally daunting challenge to American policy. The reassertion of hawk tendencies in South Africa, continued U.S. military support to UNITA, and the conflict between the administration and Congress over constructive engagement have paralyzed U.S. efforts in the region. Both Democrats and Republicans, for partisan reasons, have understated the degree to which granting U.S. support and assistance to UNITA marks a break from the approach followed by all administrations since the Angolan Civil War. From the perspective of any of the regional actors, a U.S. policy that simultaneously puts economic pressure on the South African government while giving assistance to UNITA appears utterly inconsistent and confused and is hardly the basis for generating long-term American credibility and influence.

NOTES

1. This was the assumption of the U.S. government as expressed in National Security Study Memorandum no. 39 of 1969. See Mohamed A. El-Khawas and Barry Cohen, *The Kissinger Study of Southern Africa* (Westport, Conn.: Lawrence Hill, 1976). For a discussion of regional relations before the Portuguese coup, see L. Bowman, "The Subordinate State System in Southern Africa," in Timothy M. Shaw and Kenneth A. Heard, eds., *Cooperation and Conflict in Southern Africa* (Washington, D.C.: University Press of America, 1976).

2. See David E. Albright, "The USSR and Africa: Soviet Policy," *Problems of Communism* 27, no. 1 (1978): 20–37.

3. James Barber, "Afrikanerdom in Disarray," *World Today* (July/August 1982): 288–96.

4. For the most recent detailed survey of ANC actions and policies, see Tom Lodge, *Black Politics in South Africa Since 1945* (London: Longman, 1983).

5. A recent survey of interstate economic relations in Southern Africa is found in Thomas M. Callaghy, ed., *South Africa in Southern Africa* (New York: Praeger, 1983).

6. For a detailed account of the role of the Front-Line States, see Robert Jaster, *A Regional Security Role for Africa's Front-Line States: Experiences and Prospects*, Adelphi Paper no. 180 (London: International Institute for Strategic Studies, 1983).

7. Arne Tostensen, *Dependence and Collective Self-Reliance in Southern Africa* (Uppsala: Scandinavian Institute of African Studies, 1982).

8. Henry Bienen, "Economic Interests and Security Issues in Southern Africa," *International Affairs Bulletin* 8, no. 1 (1984): 56.

9. See John A. Marcum, "Lessons of Angola," *Foreign Affairs* 54, no. 3 (Spring 1976): 407–24; Jiri Valenta, "Soviet Decision-Making on the Intervention in Angola," in David E. Albright, *Communism in Africa* (Bloomington: Indiana University Press, 1980); and E. Gonzalez, "Cuban Policy Towards Africa: Activities, Motivations and Outcomes," in David E. Albright and Jiri Valenta, *The Communist States and Africa* (Bloomington: Indiana University Press, 1983).

10. Henry Kissinger stated in April 1976, "The principal element in the deterioration of relations with the Soviet Union is Soviet actions in Angola."

11. Colin Legum, "The Soviet Union, China, and the West in Southern Africa," *Foreign Affairs* 54, no. 4 (Summer 1976): 745–62.

12. Stephen R. Weissman, "The CIA and U.S. Policy in Zaire and

Angola," in Rene Lemarchand, *American Policy in Southern Africa* (Washington, D.C.: University Press of America, 1981), pp. 430–41.

13. Valenta, "Soviet Decision-Making."

14. Quoted in Keith Somerville, "The USSR and Southern Africa Since 1976," *Journal of Modern African Studies* 22, no. 1 (1984): 77.

15. See Seth Singleton, "The Natural Ally: Soviet Policy in Southern Africa," in Michael Clough, ed., *Changing Realities in Southern Africa* (Berkeley: University of California, 1982), p. 194.

16. Robert Price, "U.S. Policy Towards Southern Africa: Interests, Choices, Constants," in Gwendolen M. Carter and Patrick O'Meara, eds., *International Politics in Southern Africa* (Bloomington: Indiana University Press, 1982), pp. 49–54.

17. For a discussion of the centrist consensus, see Helen A. Kitchen and Michael Clough, "The United States and South Africa: Realities and Red Herrings," *CSIS Significant Issues Series* (Washington, D.C., 1984).

18. Jeffrey Davidow, one of the U.S. diplomats involved in the Zimbabwe transition, outlines U.S. actions in *Dealing with International Crises: Lessons from Zimbabwe*, Stanley Foundation Occasional Paper no. 34 (Muscatine, Iowa, 1983).

19. Robert Legvold, "The Soviet Threat to Southern Africa," *International Affairs Bulletin* 8, no. 1 (1983): 13.

20. See A. Mazrui and D. Gordon, "Black African States and the Struggle for Southern Africa," in James Seiler, *Southern Africa Since the Portuguese Coup* (Boulder, Colo.: Westview Press, 1980).

21. Robert Price, for example, overstates the coherence of South African policy in his otherwise useful article, "Pretoria's Southern Africa Strategy," *African Affairs* 83, no. 330 (1984).

22. Peter Vale, "Hawks, Doves and Regional Strategy," *The Johannesburg Star*, 3 August 1982.

23. Deon Geldenjuys, *The Destabilization Controversy: An Analysis of a High-Risk Foreign Policy Option for South Africa*, Conflict Studies Paper no. 148 (London, 1983), pp. 22–25.

24. "African Update: Angola," *Africa Report* (November/December 1981), p. 36.

25. Kitchen and Clough, "The United States and South Africa," pp. 3–7.

26. Chester Crocker et al., "A U.S. Policy for the 1980s," *Africa Report* (January/February 1981), pp. 12–17.

27. Simon Jenkins, "America and South Africa: Anti-Apartheid Without Tears," *The Economist* 294, no. 7387 (30 March 1985): 17–34.

28. A. DuPisani, "Namibia: The Political Economy of Transition," *South Africa International* 15, no. 3 (1985): 154.

29. For a discussion of the beginning of Mozambique's move to the West, see Allen F. Isaacman and Barbara Isaacman, "In Pursuit of Non-Alignment," *Africa Report* (May/June 1983), pp. 47–54.

30. John A. Marcum, "Angola: A Quarter Century of War," *CSIS Africa Notes* no. 37 (December 1984): 4.

31. Jenkins, "America and South Africa," pp. 20–22.

32. Discussions with officials in the State Department's Bureau of African Affairs, January and February 1985.

33. Gillian Gunn, "Post-Nkomati Mozambique," *CSIS Africa Notes* no. 38 (January 1985): 6–7.

34. See, for example, National Forum Committee, "Let's Fight the Organ-Grinder: An Azanian Perspective on the Nkomati Accords," *Race and Class* 26, no. 3 (1985): 47–62.

35. For a discussion of Soviet views concerning Nkomati, see J. Gus Liebenow, *Southern African Hegemony: The Impact of the Nkomati Accords*, Universities Field Staff International Report no. 25 (Hanover, N.H.: 1984), pp. 3–5.

36. This paragraph is drawn from conversations I had with individuals in numerous countries in Southern Africa in March 1985.

37. This might take the form of Soviet military support for substantial assistance by Zimbabwean and Tanzanian forces for Frelimo's anti-MNR efforts. Mozambique, in turn, would renounce the Nkomati Accords. While not probable, this option was being discussed by various governments in mid-1985.

38. M. Spicer, "Namibia: The Long Road to Independence," *South Africa International* 15, no. 3 (1985): 137–39.

39. For a recent sample of the views of the black opposition, see Stephen R. Weissman, "Dateline South Africa: The Opposition Speaks," *Foreign Policy* 58 (Spring 1985): 151–70.

40. See text of speech by Tony Bloom, one of South Africa's leading industrialists, in *South African Foundation News* 10, no. 12 (December 1984).

41. Singleton, "The Natural Ally," pp. 192–95.

42. Unlike the Middle East, where the Soviets partially share with the West an interest in limiting conflict, in Southern Africa they have no interest in regional accommodation.

43. For the Reagan administration, the first explicit statement of this recognition was Under Secretary of State Lawrence Eagleburger's speech in June 1983 to the National Conference of Editorial Writers

in San Francisco. On the significance of this speech, see Helen
Kitchen, "The Eagleburger Contribution," *CSIS Africa Notes* no. 17
(July 1983).

44. For a good discussion of Western options, see James P. Barber,
Christopher R. Hill, and Jesmond Blumenfeld, *The West and South
Africa* (London: Routledge and Kegan Paul, Ltd., 1982).

45. For a balanced discussion of the U.S. corporate presence in South
Africa, see Desaix Myers et al., *U.S. Businesses in South Africa:
Economic, Political and Moral Issues* (Bloomington: Indiana University
Press, 1980).

46. See David F. Gordon, "The Politics of International Sanctions: A
Case Study of South Africa," in Miroslav Nincic, ed., *Dilemmas of
Economic Coercion* (New York: Praeger, 1983).

47. Davidow, "Dealing with International Crises."

48. See Robert M. Price, "Apartheid and White Supremacy: The
Meaning of Government-Led Reform in the South African Setting,"
in Robert M. Price and Carl G. Rosberg, eds., *The Apartheid Regime*
(Berkeley: University of California, 1980).

49. See the concluding remarks by John de St. Jorre in his article,
"Africa: Crisis of Confidence," *Foreign Affairs: America and the World
1982* 61, no. 3, p. 691.

50. As a result of his experiences in the American civil rights movement,
Ambassador Andrew Young was particularly prone to this view.

51. For the most articulate expression of this perspective, see Chester
Crocker, "South Africa: A Strategy for Change," *Foreign Affairs* 58,
no. 2 (Winter 1980–81): 323–51.

52. For a recent effort to systematically analyze the experiences of
economic sanctions, see Gary Hufbauer and Jeffrey Schott, *Economic
Sanctions Reconsidered: History and Current Policy* (Washington, D.C.:
Institute for International Economics, 1985).

53. The most influential statement of this view was written by Herman
Nickel, later to become U.S. ambassador to South Africa, in "The
Case for Doing Business in South Africa," *Fortune* 97, no. 12 (19
June 1978): 60–63.

54. See, for example, Ambassador Nickel's introduction to Senator
Edward Kennedy's speech, "U.S. Involvement in South Africa," to
South African business groups in *South Africa International* 15, no. 4
(1985): 210–12.

55. For an excellent analysis of the interplay between sanctions and
employment, see Stephen Gelb, "Unemployment and the Disin-
vestment Debate," *South African Labour Bulletin* 10, no. 6 (1985):
54–66.

11 CENTRAL AMERICA

Richard L. Millet

For well over a century and a half, the political panorama in Central America has been characterized by internal instability and external intervention. This has contributed to a political atmosphere dominated by violence and a constant search for foreign support in efforts to gain or maintain domestic power. This atmosphere, of course, has often produced a disturbing and frustrating effect on the policies of the dominant power in the hemisphere, the United States. Promoting domestic stability in Central America and preventing or at least minimizing external intervention in the region have been constant, though not always compatible, themes of U.S. policy in the twentieth century. As the current situation clearly indicates, the net result of these policies has been considerably less than satisfactory.

The root causes of Central America's instability and of its vulnerability to external interventions are numerous and interrelated. Its location on the rim of the Caribbean basin placed it in a zone of international conflict as early as the sixteenth century. Rivalry between the Spanish, the British, the French, and the Dutch in the Caribbean had frequent repercussions in Central America. While European conflicts in the region declined after the seventeenth century, the emergence of the United States as a regional and, ultimately, a world power kept Central America in the arena of international conflict. Efforts to control traffic across the isthmus and projects for a trans-isthmian canal played a special role in focusing attention on the area.

The isolation of Central America's Caribbean coast from the population centers in the highlands and along the Pacific contributed to instability and foreign interventions. It facilitated the

British incursion into Belize and their efforts to establish virtual protectorates along the Caribbean coasts of both Nicaragua and Honduras. It contributed to the virtual autonomy of the U.S. banana companies when they developed their operations in the early twentieth century. In the case of Nicaragua, the Caribbean coast became a favored launching pad for efforts to topple national governments, a trend reflected in the current struggle between the *contras* and the Sandinistas.

Ethnic divisions have also contributed to Central America's chronic instability. These are most obvious in Guatemala, where even today half the population are Indians who speak a variety of languages and who resent and distrust the ruling Europeanized elites who have consistently oppressed and exploited them. Along the Caribbean coasts the population consists largley of a mixture of blacks and indigenous groups, many of whom speak more English than Spanish. Having little in common with national ruling elites, they have a continuing potential for separatist movements.

Ever since the sixteenth-century Spanish conquest, Central America's economic systems have produced instability, class conflict, and external dependence. Land concentration, domination of the economy by a few export crops, cycles of boom and bust, and a justification of ruthless exploitation of workers on the grounds of economic necessity have all characterized the region's economic life for centuries. In recent years, the increase in population, especially in urban areas, the growth of government, the tremendous increase in debt, and the extreme fluctuations of prices for both basic exports and such vital imports as petroleum have played a key role in increasing internal instability and conflict. The success of earlier efforts to promote regional economic integration has, if anything, exacerbated this situation, making the entire region much more vulnerable to political and economic upheavals in any single country and giving even greater weight to disputes over trade and debts among the five republics.[1]

Central America's political systems both reflect and contribute to instability. During the century following independence, politics were dominated by traditional liberal and conservative parties. Except in Nicaragua and Honduras, these parties have generally ceased to exist, but the system they helped foster is very much alive. One aspect is the extent to which politics is a matter of traditional family or regional loyalties rather than a competition among alternative ideologies.[2] The ideological differences that exist were often imported, with European models often serving as the basis for Central American politics. This was true for nineteenth-century Liberals and Conservatives; it is also true for modern-day Christian Democrats and Social Democrats. While many contemporary leaders show a greatly increased willingness and ability to adapt the formulas of external ideologies to the realities of domestic conditions, the dependence on foreign political models remains a resistant characteristic of the region.

Other aspects of Central America's political tradition are at least equally persistent and even more destructive. With the exception of Costa Rica, violence rather than voting has been the consistent arbiter of political disputes.[3] Political compromise has been a rare phenomenon, while political murder, especially in recent years, has been almost a daily event. At times this has meant that the primary arena of political competition has been for the loyalty and support of the officer corps, not the allegiance of the mass of voters. With violence so central both to gaining and to maintaining power, politics produces bitter personal and family feuds. In many cases, Central American political leaders have preferred foreign intervention to defeat at the hands of their domestic opponents. Even that model of Central American anti-interventionism, Nicaragua's General Augusto Cesar Sandino, at one point seemed ready to accept a U.S. military government as an alternative to the continuation of the rival Conservative party in power.[4]

International as well as domestic factors have contributed to the high levels of violence in Central America's history. During the colonial period, the Spanish devoted only limited attention to delineating the borders between their administrative units, a problem exacerbated by the fact that such boundaries frequently ran through the most rugged, least populated areas. As a result, border conflicts have plagued these nations. Memories of old disputes linger in relations between Nicaragua and both Honduras and Costa Rica and also between Guatemala and Mexico. Current conflicts include those between Guatemala and Belize, between El Salvador and Honduras, and, over claims to territory in the Caribbean, between Nicaragua and Colombia. Central America was originally a single independent nation, and the desire to recreate that union has been an important factor in its history.[5] On the positive side, this desire has provided stimulus toward regional cooperation and integration. But it has also contributed to numerous wars in the region; to rivalries among Guatemala, El Salvador, and Nicaragua for regional dominance; and to the tendency of Central American governments to view the presence of a differing ideology in a neighboring state as a threat to their own survival. All told, the five Central American nations have fought over twice as many wars among themselves as have the ten nations of South America. Efforts to dominate Honduras, which has the misfortune of being both the least developed state in the region and also the only one that borders on each of the three claimants to regional dominance, have been a constant theme in these conflicts. Another result of both the ties and the rivalries between these nations has been their long tradition of harboring supporting, and even arming each other's exiles. In this regard, Sandinista support for El Salvador's guerrillas and Honduran and Costa Rican aid to—or at least tolerance of—the *contras* continue a long-established Central American tradition.

A major factor in Central America's instability continues to be the relative weakness and high degree of external dependence characteristic of most of its institutional structure. In recent decades, the dominant institution has been the military. This, however, reflects the weakness of competing institutions and the centrality of violence to the political process rather than the strength of the military institution. Officers frequently give their loyalties more to the institution, to their graduating class from the military academy, to their current commander, or to family ties than to the nation as a whole. Their prime motivation is to preserve the privileges and autonomy of the military, an attitude that often leads them to view civilian politicians as their natural enemies. In El Salvador, Guatemala, and prerevolutionary Nicaragua, the primary mission of the military was to protect the government from its domestic opponents rather than to protect the nation from external threats. Tendencies toward corruption, brutality, and political manipulation have been strengthened by the close links between the armed forces and the police and other internal security units.[6]

Compared to the military, most other Central American institutions were relatively underdeveloped. Labor unions were generally weak and divided, and political parties were all too frequently dominated by individuals or families and lacked nationwide organizations and producers. Chambers of commerce and industry developed slowly and concentrated their energies on defending narrow economic interests. The Roman Catholic church had some influence but suffered from an acute shortage of national priests throughout Central America. By the 1970s, over 80 percent of the priests in most Central American nations were foreign missionaries, and even with this influx of missionaries, the ratio of priests to population was extremely low. In addition, the church suffered lasting effects from nineteenth-century church-state conflicts, found it difficult to shed its traditional image as a steadfast supporter of the status quo, and faced growing challenges from evangelical groups. Revolutionary violence and the rise of liberation theology have produced deep divisions and tensions within national churches and between the more radical elements of the clergy and Rome.[7]

THE U.S. RESPONSE TO INSTABILITY

Extra-regional intervention in Central America was both a product and a contributing cause of the region's chronic instability. Outside powers sought to determine the outcome of internal conflicts, and local forces sought to involve such powers in these conflicts. The Spanish-American War and the subsequent U.S. decision to construct the Panama Canal made the United States the area's dominant power and led to a greatly increased U.S. role in domestic events. Throughout the twentieth century, stability has been a prime goal of U.S. policy in Central America. At its most extreme, this policy led to armed U.S. intervention and virtual occupation, most notably in Nicaragua in 1912 and again from 1926 until 1933. In the eyes of many Central Americans, U.S. policy seemed aptly summed up by Tom Lehrer's satiric song, "When in Doubt, Send the Marines." Hoping to avoid direct military intervention, the United States used at least twelve other approaches in its efforts to promote stability in Central America.

One favored approach, beginning in the second decade of this century and continuing today, was to train, equip, and attempt to reorient national military and police forces. Dana G. Munro, the State Department's leading Central American specialist in the 1920s, observed, "The old armies were or seemed to be one of the principal causes of disorder and financial disorganization. . . . We thought that a disciplined force, trained by Americans, would do away with the petty local oppression that was responsible for much of the disorder. . . . "[8] This attitude persists in the current confident declarations that U.S. training and assistance will help reform the military structures in El Salvador, Honduras, and Guatemala, making possible the establishment of functioning democratic systems.

Another tactic was to promote and even supervise elections, offer advice on rewriting electoral codes, and pressure existing governments to allow broader and fairer electoral participation. In Nicaragua, the United States took total responsibility for supervising the 1928 and 1932 elections; in more recent times, the elections in El Salvador provide the best example of the continuity of this tactic.

Supervising finances was another part of U.S. efforts to promote stability in Central America in the early twentieth century. At times this led to the establishment of customs receivership and the gaining of a virtual veto power over the national budget. Today, such pressures are more likely to be exerted throught the International Monetary Fund or some other multilateral agency, but on occasion, as in Costa Rica in 1984, the United States is still quite willing to make financial reforms a prerequisite for continued U.S. aid.

As early as the presidency of William Howard Taft, the United States was advocating economic development as a means of promoting stability. At that time this meant largely direct U.S. investments and loans from U.S. banks, a policy, it was claimed, that would enable the United States to substitute "dollars for bullets" as an instrument of policy.[9] In the 1960s it was development assistance, administered under the "Alliance for Progress," that was supposed to serve as a barrier to leftist subversion. The Reagan administration seems to be attempting to combine elements of both approaches, providing increased direct aid while pushing for an increased role for private investments.

The United States has also frequently supported regional integration and cooperation. Early in the century this was exemplified by the American role in pushing for the establishment of a Central American court to deal with regional disputes. In the 1960s Washington gave considerable support and encouragement to the development of the Central American Common Market and the formation of a Central American Defense Council (CONDECA). The Reagan administration has shown some interest in a revival of CONDECA and in 1982 attempted to sponsor the short-lived Central American Democratic Community, which excluded both Nicaragua and Guatemala. Efforts have also been made to limit the size of armies and regulate the type and quantity of arms coming into Central America. In 1923 the United States sponsored a conference of Central American states that had as its objective promoting such limitations.[10] Today the concern seems largely confined to efforts to limit the amount and the size of the arms acquired by Nicaragua's armed forces.

Another objective of the 1923 conference was to neutralize Honduras, curbing the constant efforts of neighboring states to install sympathetic governments. Currently the policy seems reversed, with the Reagan administration striving to involve Honduras in the internal affairs of neighboring states.

During the 1950s the United States signed a series of bilateral defense and military assistance pacts with Central American states. Together with the more general provisions of the Rio Treaty, these were supposed to promote regional security and stability. Today such commitments are often cited as evidence of American commitment to the defense of friendly nations in Central America.

When conflict threatened or seemed actually about to break out, the United States frequently stepped in to mediate or even to impose a settlement. At times, parties to civil conflicts would be summoned on board a U.S. warship and virtually ordered to resolve their problems or face armed intervention. U.S. mediation helped settle Costa Rica's boundary dispute with Panama and imposed a partial settlement on Nicaragua's 1926 civil conflict. In 1969 strong U.S. pressures, largely mediated through the Organization of American States (OAS), helped end the fighting between El Salvador and Honduras. Renewed pressure from Washington in the early 1980s contributed to the restoration of diplomatic relations. Other recent efforts, notably those of the Carter administration to mediate Nicaragua's 1978–79 civil conflict and the ongoing attempts to resolve Guatemala's dispute with Belize, however, have not met with success.

For decades, using military units, especially naval forces, to "show the flag" has been a part of Washington's efforts to defend

American interests and promote Central American stability. In the 1920s and 1930s, a naval squadron was regularly based in Panama for just this purpose.[11] The positioning of major naval units off the Central American coasts and the ongoing maneuvers in Honduras continue this practice today.

The United States has also tried to minimize or eliminate the activities of other nations in Central America. Frequently citing the Monroe Doctrine as justification for such a policy, the State Department has endeavored to negotiate treaty arrangements with Central American nations and with extra-regional powers that would enhance the dominant position of the United States in the region. The Clayton-Bulwer Treaty of 1850, the Hay-Pauncefote Treaty of 1900, and the Bryon-Chamorro Treaty of 1913 are all examples of such efforts. Using the 1954 Caracas Conference of the OAS to obtain a declaration, aimed at Guatemala, that communism was incompatible with the security of the Americas and that the communist political control over any nation could justify intervention represented a multilateral application of this principle.[12]

On several occasions the United States has assisted or even created rebel forces, justifying its efforts to overthrow existing governments on the grounds that the regimes in question were disrupting regional stability and subverting neighboring states. This was the case in Nicaragua in 1910 and in Guatemala in 1954, and is so in Nicaragua today. Similar arguments have been advanced to support numerous military coups, notably in Panama in 1940 and in El Salvador in 1961.

THE CURRENT SITUATION

Unstable political structures, violent civil conflict, and staggering economies are all characteristics of contemporary Central America. In the past any one of these factors could have provoked some external intervention; the combination of all three would have made such action virtually inevitable. The current situation is most dangerous in Nicaragua. The most obvious, but by no means the only, element in this situation is the ongoing struggle between the Sandinistas and their armed opponents, the *contras*. Partially the product of external involvement in Central American affairs, this conflict raises the constant prospect of escalating that involvement on both sides. Related to this is the extensive presence of Cuban, Soviet, East European, and other foreign advisers to the Sandinistas, a situation that significantly contributes to U.S. hostility.

Divisions within the Sadinista leadership and between various groups of their opponents also contribute to instability and increase the tendency of competing factions to seek external involvement on their behalf. The disastrous economic situation further contributes to the situation, providing ammunition for critics of the Sandinistas and leading the government to make more open efforts to secure direct assistance from the Soviet bloc in both military and economic areas.[13]

Regional conflicts further complicate matters. The Nicaraguan government continues to provide support to the guerrillas in El Salvador, although the exact extent of this support is disputed. The *contras* operate from bases in Costa Rica and Honduras, which strains relations and leads to frequent border incidents and charges of territorial violations by both sides. Thus, there is a constant danger of regional war.

While Costa Rica also suffers severe economic problems and shows signs of internal political polarization, its situation is much less likely to provoke external intervention than the one in Nicaragua. Violence along Costa Rica's border with Nicaragua is a serious, ongoing problem, but the level of conflict has, if anything, declined recently. There has also been a slow improvement in the capacity of Costa Rica's Civil Guard to police its own territory. Tensions with Nicaragua remain high, and Costa Rican public opinion is overwhelmingly anti-Sandinista. But Costa Ricans also strongly oppose creating a professional army and having direct U.S. military intervention in the region.[14]

The nation continues to be plagued by severe economic problems. These, in turn, have led to deteriorating public services, rising levels of poverty and unemployment, and a growing dependence on external economic assistance, largely from the United States. Costa Rica's large middle class has been hard hit by the economic crisis, but the net effect has evidently been to drive it more to the Right than to the Left. In the recent national electoral campaign, the major opposition to the government of then

President Luis Alberto charged that his administration has not been tough enough in dealing with the Nicaraguans and urged even closer ties with the United States.

While Honduras has received only limited public attention, the potential for a major crisis in that nation is quite high. Two major upheavals in the military command structure during 1986, the presence of a weak government, and the ongoing crisis over the presence of the *contras* on Honduran soil are all symptoms of a political system in turmoil. The political situation is further exacerbated by the depressed economy. This has been temporarily alleviated by high coffee prices, low petroleum prices, and substantial U.S. subsidies, but none of these factors is likely to endure long.[15]

The international situation of Honduras is no better than its domestic situation. Tensions continue with El Salvador over unresolved border issues dating from the 1969 war. The presence of tens of thousands of Salvadoran and Nicaraguan refugees adds to existing political and economic strains. Responding to the activities of the *contras*, the Nicaraguan military launched two major and numerous minor incursions into Honduras during 1986, embarrassing the Honduran government and raising the risk of a major armed clash between the two nations. The Honduran military and the bulk of the politically aware population have little faith in the abilities of the *contras*; harbor distrust and fear of the Sandinistas; and, particularly in 1986, show increasing concern about the reliability of the United States as an ally. In an effort to ensure continued U.S. support, Honduras has been reluctant to oppose the Reagan administration's use of its territory as a launching pad for anti-Sandinista operations, but this has badly damaged its international image and has not produced the anticipated benefits from the United States. Combined with the nation's massive domestic difficulties, these international problems could easily produce a political explosion.

While conditions have been deteriorating in Honduras, there have been some signs of improvement in El Salvador. The recent victory of the Christian Democrats in the legislative elections has produced the possibility of a more effective government that can negotiate with the insurgents from a position of relative strength. Death squad killings have been reduced, the military's performance against the guerrillas has improved, and even the economy may finally have ended its steady decline of the last seven years.

There are, however, still major negative aspects of the Salvadoran scene. The extreme Right remains strong and determined to defend its privileges. To date, its adherents, along with all members of the military's officer corps, continue to have a virtual immunity from effective prosecution for any crimes they may commit against political opponents. The recent electoral defeats may encourage some elements of the far Right to return to terrorist tactics in an effort to recoup their position. The successes of the Christian Democrats and the military situation are extremely fragile and could be quickly reversed. An assassination of President Duarte, for example, would throw the entire situation into chaos. El Salvador has improved, but the situation is still a long way from being stabilized.

Geography, history, and internal political dynamics have combined to remove Guatemala from the heart of Central America's conflicts. That nation has more than enough problems of its own, including a continuing major insurgency. The economy is crippled, the dispute with Belize goes on unresolved, and the political process is undergoing severe strains as the military seeks to restore some type of civilian rule. As in El Salvador, assassination has been the traditional means of resolving political conflicts, and the military remains the final arbiter among rival claimants to power. At the heart of the nation's political problems lies the still unresolved question of the status of the Indian majority.

Like El Salvador, Guatemala has made progress in recent months. Relatively honest elections installed a moderate civilian government, but it is not clear if this government will be allowed to exercise any effective power. The situation remains extremely tense, and the potential for instability and increased violence is still quite high.

SCENARIOS OF EXTERNAL INTERVENTION

Throughout this century, internal instability in Central America has produced external intervention. At the moment, extra-regional powers are deeply involved in the region's affairs, with the real possibility that both the nature and the extent of this involvement may increase significantly in coming months. A wide variety of developments and decisions could contribute to such an increase.

Any direct military attack by one Central American nation on another would certainly generate an immediate increase in the level of external involvement in the region, up to and quite possibly including the introduction of military forces into the conflict. The most commonly presented scenario of this type involves a Nicaraguan attack on its neighbors, most probably against Honduras.[16] Other possibilities would include more limited, cross-border incursions by the Sandinistas against guerrilla camps in Honduras and Costa Rica, a Honduran military attack on Nicaragua, or naval clashes among Central American forces in the Gulf of Fonseca or along the Caribbean coast. Remote possibilities would include a Guatemalan attack on Belize or a resumption of fighting between El Salvador and Honduras.

An all-out Nicaraguan attack on Honduras or a Guatemalan effort to resolve its claims against Belize by force would almost certainly trigger a prompt and decisive armed response by the United States or, in the case of Belize, by the British. This alone makes such developments highly unlikely. Military clashes, short of all-out attacks, along borderlands or water areas, however, are a much more real possibility. Nicaragua could use the examples of Israel and South Africa as precedents for such operations, but political ideology and alignments would make them reluctant to raise such examples. On the other hand, Honduras and Costa Rica would have a difficult time responding to such attacks as long as they continue to assert that anti-Sandinista forces do not have bases in their territories. If such operations were conducted quickly and on a limited scale, they would also reduce the chances of international involvement.[17] Such conflicts on water inevitably raise conflicting claims over locations, violations of territorial waters, and responsibility for initiating such clashes. While such clashes can provide a pretext for the introduction of extra-regional military forces, they are rarely the actual cause of such actions.

Prolonged cross-border operations by Nicaragua, more extensive than those that took place in March and December of 1986, could produce a military reaction from outside the region as well as draw Honduran or Costa Rican forces into the conflict. The use of U.S. helicopters to ferry Honduran troops to the frontier in both March and December was a very low level example of this sort of involvement. In both cases, Nicaraguan forces quickly withdrew, defusing the situation. A more prolonged or extensive Nicaraguan incursion could elicit a request for U.S. military support from Honduras, on the grounds of existing treaty obligations. The *contras'* deteriorating military and political situation increases the possibility that they will try to provoke a situation that would lead to direct clashes between Nicaraguan and Honduran forces, but their reduced credibility, combined with the weakened foreign policy position of the Reagan administration, reduces the chances that conflicts along the frontier will ultimately lead to U.S. intervention.

A dramatic change in the military situation in either Nicaragua or El Salvador, or the development of a major insurgency in Honduras or Costa Rica, could produce a significant increase in external intervention. Such developments are most likely in Nicaragua. Should the *contras* experience increased success, especially if they were able to seize territory and install a provisional government, it could accelerate involvement by both allies and opponents of the Sandinistas. Under such circumstances, the Sandinistas would press for accelerated, more modern arms, for additional "advisers," and perhaps even for Cuban combat units. They are unlikely to get the latter, but might get arms and advisers, which, in turn, could generate a strong U.S. reaction. In any case, the United States, and possibly some Central American nations, might recognize any provisional government installed on Nicaraguan soil and move rapidly to provide it with arms, supplies, and perhaps advisers. Even the provision of direct air support under these circumstances is not inconceivable, although it is unlikely to happen immediately.

The critical factor in such a situation is its instability. The insurgents cannot simply sit and await developments in a town with a provisional regime, and the Sandinistas cannot allow the insurgents to maintain such a presence. The campaign must either advance or collapse. The Reagan administration would find it very difficult to allow such an opportunity to collapse, while Cuba and the Soviet Union would be under great pressure to help keep it from succeeding. Again, deteriorating prospects for the *contras* would encourage them to try to force such a situation, hoping to provoke more direct U.S. involvement. Events in 1986 have significantly reduced the chances of success in such an effort, but the possibility still remains.

The situation in El Salvador offers similar possibilities, although the role of external actors is somewhat reversed. The most likely development here, other than the continuation of an indefinite, indecisive struggle, is a gradual expansion of areas under government control and a decline in guerrilla strength. If such a trend continued, Cuba, Nicaragua, and other supporters of the Farabundo Marti National Liberation Front (FMLN) would be under strong pressure to take at least some action to restore the military balance. The most obvious would be the introduction of SAMs to the insurgents to nullify the advantage of the Salvadoran air force.[18] Such a development, in turn, would place great pressure on the United States to undertake direct action to restore the previous government advantage. A process of escalation could begin, the ultimate outcome of which would be impossible to predict. A similar scenario is possible in Nicaragua if the *contras* obtain 5A7s or their equivalent to use against the Sandinistas' Mi-24 helicopter gunships although, again, the role of external actors would be reversed.

The inauguration of new insurgencies in Honduras or Costa Rica is less likely than a change in the existing military situation in either El Salvador or Nicaragua, but it is possible. Such a development, especially if there were clear evidence of Cuban or Nicaraguan support for the insurgents, could produce a major increase in United States involvement. This might not only increase assistance to the nations threatened but could also encompass direct military action against Nicaragua.

There are numerous possible scenarios involving neither Nicaraguan attacks on their neighbors nor victories by the *contras* but that could still produce increased external involvement in Nicaragua. As evidenced by the trade embargo decision, the Reagan administration seems determined to get the Sandinistas to "say uncle," either by abandoning their ties to Cuba and the Soviet Union and agreeing to a share of power by the opposition or by being overthrown. Few observers think that either the trade embargo or the current level of *contra* activities is likely to produce that result. This means that further steps up the ladder of escalating pressures are likely. Restricting travel to Nicaragua by

U.S. citizens, freezing Nicaraguan assets, and even breaking diplomatic relations are all possible steps but are hardly likely to be decisive. Direct invasion, at least under existing circumstances, is also unlikely. What is possible is some sort of effort at a blockade. This would necessarily be accompanied by great pressure on Honduras and Costa Rica to close their borders to Nicaragua. But a blockade is an act of war and would produce major domestic and international opposition. Furthermore, to have any hope of being effective, it would have to be maintained over a prolonged period, which would give the oppostion increased time to mobilize. To be totally effective, it would have to interdict air, as well as land and sea, traffic with Nicaragua, and this could necessitate attacks on commercial aircraft, an extremely controversial step. But the most dangerous aspect is that it could place the United States in direct confrontation with other nations, most notably the Soviet Union but possibly also allies and neutral nations.

Setting up a blockade would also force major decisions on the Soviets and Cubans. They would protest and denounce such action, and it is quite probable that the United Nations would pass a resolution condemning the action. Condemnation, however, would not be the major issue; the real question would be Soviet-Cuban testing of the blockade. Any such action could produce a direct confrontation between the superpowers that might serve well the aims and interests of some sectors among the Sandinistas but would not be in the interests of the superpowers or of the prospects for world peace. Under such circumstances the temptation to escalate to a formal blockade, while possible, is likely to remain an unexercised option.

There are actions by the Soviets or their allies that could greatly increase the possibility of external intervention and superpower confrontation in the region. The MiG crisis of November 1984 is an indication of such action. Providing high-performance combat aircraft to Nicaragua, using Nicaraguan ports for calls, provisioning or stationing Soviet or Cuban naval units, introducing combat units into Nicaragua from nations hostile to the United States, or a host of similar events could provoke an immediate crisis. Barring any major escalation of U.S. military activity in the region or a marked deterioration of bilateral relations, such actions by the Soviet bloc seem unlikely.[19]

The United States, the Soviet Union, and Cuba (and, in the

special case of Belize, the United Kingdom) are not the only nations with the potential to increase their military involvement in Central America. During Nicaragua's 1978–79 civil war, Venezuela came close to direct military intervention. Combat aircraft were dispatched to Costa Rica to provide protection for that nation, and Venezuela became a major supplier of arms to the Sandinistas. A few years later, the Venezuelans were on the other side of an insurgent conflict, providing training to Salvadoran army units. At the moment, Venezuelan participation in the Contadora process makes any resumption of such roles improbable, and even if Contadora should collapse, lack of public support and high political costs would result from such actions. Mexico is even less likely to become directly involved militarily except along its border with Guatemala. There, the possibility of limited military clashes, especially if Guatemalan troops cross the border looking for guerrillas, is always present. Mexico is also unlikely to stand idly by if Guatemala attacked Belize. But under existing circumstances, direct intervention by either Venezuela or Mexico is highly unlikely.

Israel, South Korea, Saudi Arabia, and even Taiwan have been mentioned as possible substitutes or surrogates for the United States in military involvement in Central America. Israel has supplied important training and technical assistance to Guatemala, has sold arms to most nations in the region, and has been rumored to be involved in providing arms and funds for the *contras*. Defense Minister Ariel Sharon's December 1982 visit to Honduras was concrete evidence of Israel's strong interest in the region. Since Israel's last elections, however, its level of activity in Central America appears to have declined. Political controversy surrounding its Central American policies and preoccupation with internal affairs have played a role in this.[20] While not about to withdraw from the area, Israel will probably play a limited role, barring some dramatic escalation of the Palestine Liberation Organization (PLO) presence in Nicaragua or elsewhere in the region.

South Korea, Saudi Arabia, Taiwan, or other nations sympathetic to more conservative forces in Central America may be sources of limited funds, arms sales, and perhaps even training, but these countries are not at all likely to increase significantly their involvement under any foreseeable circumstances. The same is true for the major nations of South America. Under the previous military government, Argentina played an active role in training *contras*, but that role has been ended by President Raul Alfonsin, and there seems no chance it will be resumed in the next few years.

The Sandinistas and other forces on the Left also have their supporters among the world's most controversial nations. Libya, Iran, the PLO, and even North Korea have been cited as sources of military and economic aid for Central America's Left. But, like their counterparts on the Right, they lack the capacity and interest required to increase significantly such commitments. Their presence can be an irritant, providing further ammunition for those interested in raising the level of U.S. involvement, but it is unlikely to affect significantly the outcome of the region's basic conflicts.

Before the Nicaraguan revolution, the level of Western European involvement in Central American political and security concerns was very low and seemed destined to stay at that level. But in September 1984, most Western European foreign ministers were willing to travel to Central America to meet with regional leaders. Developments in the region and the U.S. policy response had become significant political issues in Europe, and Central American leaders were making regular trips to Western Europe for meetings at the highest levels.[21]

While concern over U.S. policy helps motivate Western European involvement, the importance of the region in American policy also serves as a limiting factor on the scope of Europe's presence in Central America. The members of the Atlantic Alliance do not want to let their Central American policies become an issue within the alliance or between themselves and the United States. France's decision to sell arms to Nicaragua nearly precipitated such a situation and is unlikely to be repeated. At the same time, domestic political considerations as well as European assessments of Central American realities make it most improbable that NATO members will become directly involved in support of the *contras*.

An important part of Western European activities in Central America involve party-to-party rather than government-to-government ties. Christian Democrats, Social Democrats, and Liberals all seek to reinforce their ideological counterparts in the region. They also work to promote negotiated settlements to regional disputes. While increasingly important, such ties do not lend themselves to direct intervention in regional conflicts, especially on the military level. Indeed, much of the emphasis on peaceful solutions and the Contadora process represents Europe's desire to limit, not expand, its regional involvement.

The exact extent of Soviet, East European, and Cuban involvement in Central America is a subject of continuing controversy. What is clear is that in the event of an American intervention in Nicaragua, the Soviets and Cubans will not come to Nicaragua's aid with military forces. As in Grenada, those Cubans stationed in Nicaragua at the time of an attack would resist but could expect no additional help. The Cubans have been even more careful to avoid direct introduction of their personnel into the guerrilla conflicts in El Salvador and Guatemala. Training, supplies, and political support for these insurgents is likely to continue and may even increase, but there seems no prospect that Cuban or Soviet military forces will enter the conflict directly even to prevent a total defeat of their allies.

While most scenarios of external intervention in Central America involve a further deterioration of existing conditions, there is one that grows out of a regional peace settlement such as that currently being sought through the Contadora process. It is possible that, should Contadora ultimately succeed, a part of the verification process will necessitate the introduction into the region of a force of "International Inspectors" functioning in many ways as peacekeepers.[22] It is even conceivable that a larger, more traditional peacekeeping force may ultimately be required.

The composition, size, and exact functions of any such international presence in Central America are difficult to predict. It does not seem likely that either the United Nations or the OAS will organize and operate those involved, but rather that the four Contadora Group nations—Colombia, Mexico, Panama, and Venezuela—or some other ad hoc arrangement will be used.[23] The size is likely to be relatively small and the personnel unarmed. Some of those involved could come from the Contadora nations themselves, although Mexico traditionally has avoided participating in such peacekeeping forces. Canada has indicated some interest in assisting. Other possible candidates would include Yugoslavia, Brazil, India, and Sweden. While not constituting external intervention in any traditional sense, the creation and insertion of any such body into Central America would certainly represent a major new development in international participation in Central American affairs and would produce a substantial alteration in the existing patterns of instability and conflict.

CONCLUSIONS

Internal instability and external interventions are basic factors in contemporary Central America and will likely continue to be so for some time to come. While most Central American actors give ritual assent to the principles of nonintervention and self-determination, the reality is that extra-regional support for their positions is not only welcomed but actively sought and cultivated. In many cases, both past and present, it appears that parties to Central American conflicts would prefer major external military interventions to defeat at the hands of their domestic opponents. In today's Nicaragua, many Sandinistas would prefer confronting American military power directly rather than sharing any power with the *contras* or taking other actions, such as severing ties with Cuba and the Soviet Union, that they would view as abandoning the revolution.

External involvement in Central America is frequently justified as contributing to restoring or enhancing regional stability, but under existing circumstances, it is more likely to be destabilizing. It perpetuates the historical pattern of Central Americans seeking to resolve internal conflicts by seeking outside support rather than by negotiating with domestic rivals; it raises the level of conflict without resolving the issues; and it increases pressures on external supporters of other factions to expand their own participation in the region. For Central Americans, the results of higher levels of outside intervention are likely to be disastrous. Polarization within the region will be accelerated, the level of conflict and destruction is likely to rise, and prospects for any viable peace settlement will recede even further.

Regional stability is clearly in the interests of the United States, Western Europe, and much of the rest of the international community. Instability and the consequent Western preoccupation with Central America has certain clear advantages for the Soviet Union and Cuba. But it is not in the Soviet Union's interest to allow events to deteriorate to the point of direct superpower confrontation in the region, and it is not in Cuba's interest to see the

Sandinistas overthrown. What is most disturbing in this panorama is that the continuation of current levels of conflict, while not the desired outcome for any of the major external actors, is something they all can live with. Political rhetoric from both Left and Right has tended to define possible Central American outcomes in terms of ideological and geopolitical victories or defeats for world capitalism and communism. Under these circumstances, preventing defeat becomes more important and certainly less risky than achieving victory, a position that can promote protracted conflict in the region.

The Contadora process seemed to offer at least a partial escape from this vicious cycle of instability, violence, and external intervention, but it can succeed only if the major external actors as well as their regional allies want it to succeed. At the moment it is not at all clear that such is the case. In any event, Contadora's capacity to deal with civil conflicts is much less than its capacity to mediate interstate disputes.[24] And any regional settlement not accompanied by major progress toward resolving existing civil conflicts is not likely to endure long. It may reduce the levels of external intervention in the short run, but if insurgent struggles continue, the temptation for Central Americans once again to seek to resolve internal conflicts through external intervention will grow rapidly, and the temptation for outside powers to respond to calls for assistance from their ideological allies in the region will likely prove irresistible.

In the absence of a Contadora agreement or some similar arrangement, the prospects for Central America are grim at best. The level of regional conflict will remain high, and the danger of direct military intervention by outside powers will constantly be present. Such intervention could take the form of naval blockades, air strikes, support for one side in a war among Central American nations, or even a major introduction of foreign combat units on the ground. Military actions could be confined to a few specific targets or could escalate to a level such as that reached in Grenada, with the virtual occupation of an entire nation. Whatever forms such actions might take, they are not likely to resolve the issues that have produced the current instability, nor will they end the destruction in Central America. In a May 1982 speech in Panama, Costa Rica's president at the time, Luis Alberto Monge, aptly summed up the region's dilemma when he declared that:

The political crisis that afflicts our region has internal roots of old injustices and lost hopes, which are jumbled together with the intervention of foreign interests. There will be no peace in Central America and the Caribbean while the infernal game of hegemonic interest continues in our region. In the cruel conflicts of our people, the Central Americans provide the bodies and others gather the advantages.[25]

NOTES

1. A useful study of the impact of economic development on Central America is Ramon Mayorga Quiros, *El crecimiento desigual en Centroamerica* (Mexico, D.F.: El Colegio de Mexico, 1983).
2. For a description of this see Samuel Stone, *Las Convulsiones del istmo Centroamericano: Raices de un conflicto entre elites* (San Jose, Costa Rica: Estudios del Centro de Investigaciones y Adiestramiento Politico Administrativo, no. 1, 1979).
3. An accurate, if cynical, expression of this reality was Guatemalan President Romeo Lucas Garcia's February 1979 declaration that political violence was "an allergy one must learn to live with."
4. Neill Macanulay, *The Sandino Affair* (Chicago, Ill.: Quadrangle Books, 1967), p. 65.
5. Thomas L. Karnes, *The Failure of Union: Central America, 1824—1960* (Chapel Hill: University of North Carolina Press, 1961).
6. For an expanded description of Central America's armed forces, see Richard Millett, "Praetorians or Patriots? The Central American Military," in Robert S. Leiken, ed., *Central America: Anatomy of Conflict* (New York: Pergamon Press, 1984), pp. 69–94.
7. Most recent studies of the church in Central America are characterized by a high degree of political partisanship. Contrasting views are found in Margaret E. Crahan, "The Central American Church and Regime Transformation," in Wold Grabendorf et al., eds., *Political Change in Central America: Internal and External Dimensions* (Boulder, Colo.: Westview Press, 1984), pp. 139–54; and in Humberto Belli, *Christians Under Fire* (San Jose, Costa Rica: Puebla Institute, 1984).
8. Letter from Dr. Dana G. Munro to Richard Millett, February 14, 1965.
9. For a description of Taft's policies in Central America, see Walter V. Scholes and Marie V. Scholes, *The Foreign Policies of the Taft Administration* (Columbia: University of Missouri Press, 1970), pp. 45–80.

10. Thomas M. Leonard, *United States Policy and Arms Limitation in Central America: The Washington Conference of 1923* (Los Angeles: Center for the Study of Armament and Disarmament, California State University at Los Angeles, 1982).

11. For the activities of this force, see Richard Millett, "The State Department's Navy: A History of the Special Service Squadron, 1920–1940," *American Neptune 35* (April 1975): 118–38.

12. J. Lloyd Mecham, *The United States and Inter-American Security* (Austin: University of Texas Press, 1961), pp. 440–43.

13. President Daniel Ortega's April and May 1985 visit to the Soviet Union and to the nations of Eastern Europe, reportedly in search of at least $200 million in economic assistance, is a vivid example of this.

14. For a description of Costa Rica's position in Central America's conflicts, see Jennie K. Lincoln, "Neutrality Costa Rica Style," *Current History 84* (March 1985): 118–21, 136.

15. For details on the situation in Honduras, see U.S. Congress, House of Representatives, "Nicaraguan Incursion into Honduras," *Hearings before the Subcommittee on Western Hemisphere Affairs of the Committee of Foreign Affairs*, 99th Cong., 2d. sess., 8 April 1986.

16. For a presentation of this case, see John F. Guilmartin, Jr., "Nicaragua Is Armed for Trouble," *Wall Street Journal*, 11 March 1985, p. 29. For a contrasting view, see Edward L. King, *Analysis of the Military Situation in Nicaragua*, April 1985 (Boston, Mass.: Unitarian Universalist Service Committee, 1985). Both authors are retired U.S. military officers.

17. An 8 January 1985 encounter between Costa Rican Civil Guardsmen and what were apparently Nicaraguan Government Troops at Agua Dulce, Costa Rica, illustrates the problems of identifying and responding to limited incursions. See *Rumbo Centroamericano* (San Jose, Costa Rica), 17–23 January 1985, pp. 6–7.

18. A dramatic illustration of the effect of the introduction of SAMs into such a conflict occurred in the October 1981 battle of Guelta Zemmour during the conflict between the Moroccan government and the insurgents of the Polisario Front for control of the former Spanish Western Sahara. Utilizing strong air support, the Moroccans had been enjoying considerable success in the struggle until the insurgents suddenly introduced SA 6 missiles into the conflict at Guelta Zemmour. In just over a day, the Moroccan air force lost four aircraft and a helicopter and virtually retired from the conflict for several months. See Tony Hodges, "The Endless War," *Africa Report* (July/August, 1982): 6.

19. Nicaraguan President Daniel Ortega's 27 February 1985 declaration

that Nicaragua would indefinitely postpone "the purchase of new weapon systems and the interception aircraft required to complete the antiaircraft system in the country" seems to make development of this scenario even more unlikely. The text of President Ortega's remarks can be found in Foreign Broadcast Information Service (FBIS), *Latin America: Daily Report* 6 (28 February 1985): pp. 4–7.

20.   Cindy Arnson, "Israel and Central America," *New Outlook: Middle East Monthly* (Tel Aviv), April 1984, pp. 20–24.

21.   For a discussion of the September 1984 meeting of Western European response to United States policies, see *Central America Report* (Guatemala City: Infopress Centroamericana), 5 October 1984, pp. 305–6.

22.   A possible framework for such an international presence is contained in the draft "Statute on the Verification and Control Mechanism for Security Matters under the Contadora Act on Peace and Cooperation in Central America," presented to the Contadora Group by Costa Rica, El Salvador, and Honduras in April 1985. The text has been distributed by the United Nations as document A/39/889 S/17104, dated 16 April 1985.

23.   The United States would not accept such a direct role for the United Nations in Central American disputes, and the OAS, which is still suffering the effects of the Falklands/Malvinas conflict, would not be acceptable to Cuba and Nicaragua.

24.   For a description of some of the obstacles and prospects of confronting peacemaking efforts in the region, see Jack Child, ed., *Maintenance of Peace and Security in the Caribbean and Central America*, Report no. 18 (New York: International Peace Academy, 1984).

25.   Speech by President Luis Alberto Monge to the Central American Conference on Commerce and Development, Panama, 14 May 1985.

INDEX

ABOUT THE EDITORS

Robert S. Litwak directs the Wilson Center's International Security Studies Program. He was previously a research associate at the International Institute for Strategic Studies in London and a post-doctoral fellow at Harvard University's Center for International Affairs and Russian Research Center. He was educated at Haverford College and the London School of Economics.

Dr. Litwak's publications include *Strategic Defenses and Soviet-American Relations*, edited with Samuel F. Wells (Ballinger Publishing Co., 1987), and *Détente and the Nixon Doctrine*, a study of U.S.-Soviet competition in the Third World during the 1970s.

Samuel F. Wells, Jr., is associate director of the Woodrow Wilson International Center for Scholars in Washington, D.C., and chairman of its European Institute. Previously he taught history and defense studies at the University of North Carolina at Chapel Hill. He had earlier served as an artillery officer in the U.S. Marine Corps, rising to the rank of captain. He has held fellowship appointments at the Hoover Institution, the Woodrow Wilson International Center for Scholars, and the Institut Français des Relations Internationales and was the recipient of a three-year Ford Foundation grant for research in international security.

Dr. Wells was educated at the University of North Carolina at Chapel Hill and at Harvard University with specialties in the history of American foreign relations and European and Russian history. He has written on a wide variety of historical and contemporary subjects with particular attention to the interaction of political and military issues and economic and strategic questions. In addition to having written numerous scholarly articles, he is co-editor of and a contributor to *Economics and World Power: An Assessment of American Diplomacy Since 1789* (Columbia University Press, 1984) and co-editor of *Limiting*

ABOUT THE EDITORS

Nuclear Proliferation (Ballinger, 1985) and *Strategic Defenses and Soviet-American Relations* (Ballinger, 1987).

ABOUT THE CONTRIBUTORS

Shaul Bakhash is the Robinson Professor of History at George Mason University. In 1984–85 he was a fellow with the Wilson Center's International Security Studies Program. He is the author of *The Reign of the Ayatollahs: Iran and the Revolution* and was educated at Harvard and Oxford.

Shahram Chubin is director of research of the Program for Strategic and International Security Studies at the Graduate Institute of International Studies in Geneva. Educated at Oberlin College and Columbia University, he is the author of *Security in the Persian Gulf: The Role of Outside Powers*. In 1984 he was a guest scholar with the Wilson Center's International Security Studies Program.

Stephen P. Cohen is professor of political science at the University of Illinois-Urbana. Educated at the Universities of Chicago and Wisconsin, he has written several books on South Asian security affairs, including *The Indian Army: Its Contribution to the Development of a Nation*. During 1985–87 he served as a member of the State Department's Policy Planning Staff.

Christopher Coker is a lecturer in the department of international relations at the London School of Economics and Political Science. His publications include *NATO, the Warsaw Pact, and Africa*, and he is the editor of a forthcoming volume, *The United States, Europe, and Military Intervention in the Third World*. He was educated at Cambridge and Oxford and is a member of the Council of the Royal United Services Institute.

David F. Gordon is associate professor of international relations at Michigan State University and senior researcher at the Center for Research on Economic Development at the University of Michigan. Educated at Bowdoin College and the University of Michigan, he is the author of *Decolonization and the State in Kenya* and numerous articles on Southern Africa and African development issues.

Michael Leifer is a reader in international relations at the London School of Economics. He was educated at the University of Reading and received his doctorate from the London School of Economics; in 1986–87 he was a visiting professor of political science at the National University of Singapore. His most recent publications include *Indonesia's Foreign Policy*, and he was the editor of *The Balance of Power in East Asia*.

S. Neil MacFarlane is associate professor of government at the University of Virginia. During 1986–87 he was a research associate at the Center for Slavic and East European Studies at the University of California at Berkeley. He is the author of *Superpower Rivalry and Third World Radicalism* and numerous articles on Soviet foreign policy and Third World security, and is currently researching Soviet perspectives on Third World conflict. He was educated at Dartmouth College and Oxford University.

Richard L. Millet is professor of history at Southern Illinois University and a senior advisor for political risk analysis to Frost and Sullivan, Inc. of New York. Educated at Harvard and the University of New Mexico, he has written over fifty books and articles on Latin America and frequently testifies before Congress on Latin American affairs.

Edward A. Olsen is associate professor of national security affairs and Asian studies at the Naval Postgraduate School and is currently director of the Northern California World Affairs Council project on U.S.-Korea relations. He was educated at the University of California at Berkeley and American University and is the author of *Japan: Economic Growth, Resource Scarcity, and Environmental Constraints*. From 1975–80 he was an intelligence analyst for Japanese and Korean affairs in the State Department's Bureau of Intelligence and Research.

Robin Alison Remington is a professor in the chair of political science at the University of Missouri in Columbia. She received her doctorate at Indiana University and in 1981 went to Yugoslavia on a Fulbright Faculty Research Grant. She is the editor of *Winter in Prague: Documents on Czechoslovak Communism in Crisis* and *The International Relations of Eastern Europe: A Guide to Information Sources*.

Charles Tripp is a lecturer in politics at the School of Oriental and African Studies of the University of London. Previously he was the assistant director of the Program for Strategic and International Studies at the Graduate Institute for International Studies in Geneva. Educated at Oxford and the School of Oriental and African Studies, his recent publications include *Egypt, Sudan, and Libya: Domestic Politics and*

Regional Security and an edited volume, *Regional Security in the Middle East*. He is currently completing a book on Iran and Iraq with Shahram Chubin.